Sport and Society

Series Editors

Benjamin G. Rader
Randy Roberts

A list of books in the series appears at the end of this book.

Muhammad Ali, the People's Champ

MUHAMMAD ALI

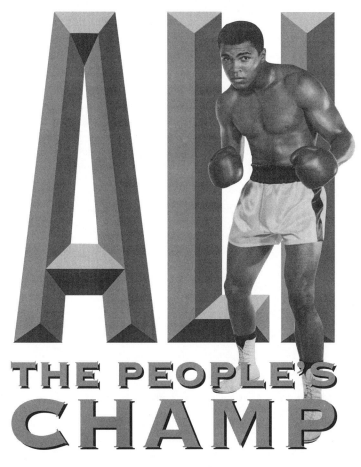

THE PEOPLE'S CHAMP

EDITED BY ELLIOTT J. GORN

A Lawrence J. Malley Book

Published by the

UNIVERSITY OF ILLINOIS PRESS • URBANA AND CHICAGO

This book is printed on acid-free paper.

Library of Congress Cataloging-in-Publication Data

Muhammad Ali, the People's Champ / edited by Elliott J. Gorn.
p.   cm. — (Sport and society)
"A Lawrence J. Malley book."
Includes bibliographical references and index.
ISBN 0-252-02188-6 (cloth : acid-free paper)
1. Ali, Muhammad, 1942–   . 2. Boxers (Sports)—United States—
Biography. I. Gorn, Elliott J., 1951-   . II. Series.
GV1132.A44M85   1995
796.8'3'092—dc20
[B]   95-2358
                                                             CIP

For Muhammad Ali

CONTENTS

INTRODUCTION

Elliott J. Gorn

Mention Muhammad Ali's name and you hear stories. Chance meetings with the Champ, unexpected kindnesses, Ali showing up in unlikely places, Ali doing magic tricks—everyone has an Ali story, including me:

When I was driving Ali and his friend Howard Bingham from the Cincinnati airport to Miami University in Oxford, Ohio, for the conference out of which this book comes, Ali fell asleep and started snoring. Howard told me that the Champ sometimes gets tired when he travels. Ali snored louder and started pounding the side of the van. Howard said this was not good, maybe Ali hadn't taken the medication that helps control his symptoms of Parkinson's syndrome. Ali snored louder, pounded harder. Howard looked worried, said sometimes Ali starts reliving his fights. Once they were in a limousine and Ali dreamed he was back in the ring. He wrestled another passenger to the floor and was fighting him. "He was a young guy, a writer like you," Howard added. Just then—just as I started to sweat—Ali flipped up his shades, looked at me and said, "We had you." They still have me.[1]

We tell stories about Ali to bask in his fame, to borrow a bit of his charisma. Always there is a note of surprise: here is a man so celebrated, yet at the same time so human, so knowable, so approachable. But beyond being famous and successful, Ali has become one of those figures who helps us to make sense of the history, to give it shape and meaning. Our stories about Ali keep our past alive, and they give us a personal connection to the larger chronicle of our days.

When Cassius Clay defeated Sonny Liston to become heavyweight champion on February 24, 1964, I was not quite thirteen years old. For the next decade, he was constantly in the news, and he was never far from my awareness. Like me, most of the essayists in this volume also were born around midcentury, so we all grew into adulthood in the age of Muhammad Ali. During our formative years, Ali was the very embodiment of an American hero, and our individual histories intersected with his.

For over a hundred years now, American men have taken sports heroes as emblems of their lives. Early in this century, for example, the poet Vachel Lindsay memorialized his own coming of age through the image of a prizefighter:

> When I was nine years old, in 1889,
> I sent my love a lacy Valentine.
> Suffering boys were dressed like Fauntleroys,
> While Judge and Puck in giant humor vied.
> The Gibson Girl came shining like a bride
> To spoil the cult of Tennyson's Elaine.
> Louisa Alcott was my gentle guide . . .
> Then . . .
> I heard a battle trumpet sound.
> Nigh New Orleans
> Upon an Emerald plain
> John L. Sullivan
> The strong boy
> of Boston
> Fought seventy-five rounds with Jake Kilrain.[2]

Throughout the twentieth century, sports champions have preoccupied the emotional lives of men. Lindsay wrote in an era when America had passed from a land of farms, modest enterprises, and small towns to an urban, corporate, highly industrialized nation. Such changes meant that the very idea of manhood itself had to be redefined. Becoming an independent producer was no longer even a possibility for most men, but earning a good wage and finding pleasure in the realm of commercialized leisure—especially sports—grew increasingly important as a social ideal. Above all, at the turn of the last century, men felt a need to distance themselves from all that appeared weak or feminine, to reassert their masculinity when the old male ideal of autonomy seemed threatened by a world of mass institutions.

Certainly we are heirs to these changes, and few things are as emotionally compelling as individual heroism in an impersonal world. But our era put its own mark on this old story. For Americans of my generation, coming of age meant passing through what has come to be known simply as "the sixties." The era lasted longer than a mere decade, and the phrase is a rather imprecise evocation of political upheaval and cultural change. Most people would agree that the ethos of the sixties nurtured a sense of limitless possibility that we associate with youth. Perhaps it was illusory, but those who journeyed through adolescence and into adulthood during the sixties experienced extraordinary hopes for personal transcendence and social transformation.

Muhammad Ali was at once an emblem of that era and a shaper of it. It was not only Ali's political and social commitments that mattered, but also his personal style—he was outrageous, yet deadly serious, the prophetic trickster, the sacred clown. who helped define the times. The journalist Jack Newfield believes that Ali was the very embodiment of sixties America:

> Those were rebellious conflict-ridden times, but they were also a period of great hope. . . . Ali, like Robert Kennedy and the Beatles, was full of passion and willing to challenge authority. In a rapidly changing world, he underwent profound personal change and influenced rather than simply reflected his times. And he survived. John Kennedy, Robert Kennedy, John Lennon, Martin Luther King, Malcolm X; all the other great heroes of the sixties are dead. So are the icons like Elvis Presley and Marilyn Monroe. But Ali is alive, and not just in the flesh. He's in the hearts of everyone who experienced those times.[3]

A friend of mine in Los Angeles expressed the point even more concisely. Just as I heard the news bulletin on February 15, 1978, that Ali had lost his title to Leon Spinks, the phone rang: "Does this mean the sixties are over?" my old high-school buddy Gary Ogimachi asked.

What better symbol for the infinite possibilities of life than an African American prizefighter? Blacks in 1960 faced a society that, with few exceptions, condemned them to obscurity, poverty, and rigid stigmatization. But blacks as a group had begun to challenge that old order, and just as the civil-rights movement crested, *this* black American became perhaps the most famous human being in the world. He changed his name and his religion, defied the legal system, became a spokesman in one of the great freedom struggles in human history, and fought his government over an unjust war. He brought warmth and outrageous humor and charm to his crusades. And his bully pulpit was the lowly prize ring.

The last point is important because Ali refused to accept old athletic stereotypes; he insisted by his actions on creating a new kind of sports hero. Few who follow boxing would disagree that he was the greatest heavyweight of all time, and he certainly would not have been a celebrity without his great athletic skills. The prize ring gave Ali visibility, and he seized it to make an impact on the world. The *New York Times* journalist Robert Lipsyte described how, the very day after Ali won the championship, the very day he went public with his conversion to the Nation of Islam, the fighter told reporters at a packed press conference that he would not conform to their stereotypes: "'I don't have to be what you want me to be; I'm free to be me.' And among the things he didn't have to be were Christian, a good soldier of American democracy in the mold of Joe Louis, or the kind of athlete-prince white America wanted."[4]

Muhammad Ali remains very much a presence in the world. He spends roughly half his days on the road. He is a devoted Muslim, and he lends his name and his presence to countless charitable causes. While his body and his speech have been slowed by Parkinson's syndrome, his mind is still fresh; those of us who spent time with him on that spring weekend in Oxford, Ohio, felt the sharpness of his wit but also the warmth of his affection. And there was something more. His biographer, Thomas Hauser, concludes *Muhammad Ali: His Life and Times* with a scene of Ali on an airplane, returning from a triumphant tour of Indonesia, the world's most populous Muslim country: "The cabin was dark, and everyone else was asleep—except Muhammad. His overhead light was on, and he was wide awake, reading the Qur'an. And in that moment, bathed in light, he looked stronger and more at peace with himself than any person I've ever known."[5] Prizefighting ravaged Ali's body, did irreparable harm to his nervous system. Yet he possesses an almost palpable inner strength that comes from a deep sense of peace with himself and the world.

Still, it is the young Ali we remember in these pages, the man who imposed himself on history in a way almost too astonishing to believe. Sometimes, when I try to explain Muhammad Ali to students, I become frustrated and mutter something like "you just had to be there." Robert Lipsyte captured some of the poignancy of trying to explain. Lipsyte noted that during the buildup to the first Liston fight, younger reporters saw young Cassius Clay as the real story, while the older ones spent more time with Sonny Liston, and with Joe Louis, the former title holder who was a fixture in the Liston camp:

> I remember talking with one of the older writers, Barney Nagler— they were all around Louis—and I asked him, "How can you hang around that old mumbling has-been, when here's this young beautiful hope of the future?" and Nagler said to me, "You don't understand; he was so good when he was young." And I didn't understand that until many years later when I was at the Mike Tyson–Larry Holmes fight, and I was one of the old reporters hanging around an aging mumbling ex-fighter once known as Cassius Clay, who'd been so wonderful and given us all so much to treasure when he was young.[6]

Vachel Lindsay and John L. Sullivan, Barney Nagler and Joe Louis, Robert Lipsyte and Cassius Clay—young men of memory grown strangely old.

The essays in this volume try to explain what it meant to be there in the 1960s and 1970s, to explore why Ali looms so large in our collective memory. As with any set of conference papers, some subjects overlap a bit, certain important themes are slighted. For example, I have argued elsewhere that sports are about nothing so much as gender, so it is an irony that this book falters on that very issue. But we hope that these essays are only the beginning of an assessment of Ali's place within the broad contours of American cultural history.

Our contributors come from a range of professions and academic disciplines. Three are American historians, two are specialists in literature, two are professors of sport studies, one is a journalist, and one a poet. Robert Lipsyte's Prologue recalls his days covering the Champ for the *New York Times.* In the first chapter, Michael Oriard discusses Ali in the larger context of American sports heroes, and he pays particular attention to the role of mass media in shaping modern-day icons. In chapter 2, Randy Roberts shows how Ali was a harbinger for a new age of television coverage, not just of sports but of politics and society. Next, Othello Harris places Ali in the context of black activism and the athletic rebellion of the 1960s. Gerald Early explicates Ali's autobiography, *The Greatest,* in chapter 4 and uses that text as a way to capture the Champ's presentation of himself in American culture. In the fifth chapter, David K. Wiggins tells the story of Ali's association with the Nation of Islam, then discusses the wider implications of that organization for American history. Thomas Hietala then discusses Ali and the politics of the Vietnam era. Jeffrey Sammons assesses Ali's place in an era characterized by social ferment and cultural rebellion. Finally, Elizabeth Alexander evokes in verse the legend of Ali.

I have incurred many debts as editor of this work. The Department of History and the American Studies Program at Miami University provided generous funding for the conference, as did the College of Arts and Sciences, the Graduate School, and the provost's office. Thomas Hauser lent important advice and encouragement. Chris Webb helped with a thousand details of planning, and Allan Winkler offered unflagging support. Jeffrey Sammons provided good counsel on countless issues. Howard Bingham gave his time and energy to help make the conference and book successful—he is one of the most thoughtful and generous men I have ever met. Larry Malley has encouraged and nursed and nurtured not only this project but countless others in sports studies in particular and American history in general. He is the perfect editor; more, he is the perfect friend. Carol Betts provided outstanding copyediting, while Richard Wentworth has given this book a fine home at the University of Illinois Press.

Finally, this book is dedicated to Muhammad Ali. When I drove him back to the Cincinnati airport after the conference was over, we discussed his place in boxing history. Ali said he believed that Jack Johnson was the finest fighter of all time. You're entitled to your opinion, Champ, and Johnson was great; but *you* were the greatest— and not just in the ring.

Notes

Royalties from this book will be donated to a charity chosen by Muhammad and Lonnie Ali.

1. I was not the first victim of this ruse. See William Gildea, "For Ali, Greatness Takes Another Form," in *Best American Sports Writing, 1992,* ed. Thomas McGuane (Boston: Houghton Mifflin, 1992), 124.

2. For a discussion of Vachel Lindsay's "John L. Sullivan, The Strong Boy of Boston," and of turn-of-the-century masculinity, see Elliott J.

Gorn, *The Manly Art: Bare-Knuckle Prize Fighting in America* (Ithaca, N.Y.: Cornell University Press, 1986), 247.

3. Newfield, quoted in Thomas Hauser, *Muhammad Ali: His Life and Times* (New York: Simon and Schuster, 1991), 259.

4. Lipsyte, quoted in Hauser, *Muhammad Ali,* 84.

5. Hauser, *Muhammad Ali,* 516.

6. Lipsyte, quoted in Hauser, *Muhammad Ali,* 80.

Muhammad Ali, the People's Champ

"When You're with Me, You Always Got .Something to Write About."

Robert Lipsyte

On February 18, 1964, in a damp, crowded dressing room in the Fifth Street Gym in Miami Beach, Cassius Marcellus Clay, Jr., stretched out on a rubbing table and cast a twinkly eye at the sweaty scribblers hunched around him.

"I'm making money," he said, "the popcorn man making money, and the beer man, and you got something to write about."

I wrote that down.

On April 28, 1975, in that very same room, Muhammad Ali stretched out on a rubbing table and accepted a subpoena from a federal officer, then handed the papers to me.

"See how I take care of you, Bob. When you're with me, you always got something to write about."

I wrote that down, too.

Like Chuck Wepner, Bundini Brown, and Don King, I owe some of my identity to Muhammad Ali. And I didn't even have to step on his foot or scream "Float like a butterfly" at him, or promote his fights. I only had to write down what he said to get my name on the front pages. I followed him around the world and learned a great deal about racial politics, celebrity, decline and fall and resurrection, hope and nostalgia, and the fakelore that fuels our dreams.

He always gave me something to write about, and most of it turned out to be true. This has made me something of an Ali junkie. I will read, screen, listen to almost anything about him.

In August 1992 I went to a one-actor play called *Ali* in New York. I walked out at intermission. The actor was enormously talented and attractive but he simply wasn't The Greatest. Ali's memory, I hope, has not, will never, enter that cheese world of Elvis impersonators.

And so, the academic conference that spawned this book was a gift. Not only would it mean delicious hours of Ali explication and reconstruction, it would be this journalist's dream of finding out what he actually saw with his own eyes. After almost thirty years of covering the man, I am still thrilled when historians fill in the empty nooks and crannies of my notebooks.

Ali, of course, is a sponge, a prism, a mirror of his times. I don't know that he is a truly complex character, although his life was complicated and its threads wove through a complex time and through all our lives.

He appeared in the year of the Beatles, and his declaration, "I don't have to be what you want me to be, I'm free to be who I want," changed sport forever. "I ain't got no quarrel with them Vietcong" became a national anti-battle cry. Coincidentally, I happened to be there for both lines. He always gave me something to write about.

Perhaps coincidentally, I left sportswriting soon after Ali lost to Joe Frazier in 1971.

We only squabbled once. In 1986, as a TV correspondent, I walked into an Atlanta hotel room while he sat with his feet in plastic pans of water containing electrical massagers. He was trying to stimulate a response. So was I when my first on-camera question was about the so-called "divine mission" he had claimed ten years earlier.

"I have nothing to say," snapped Ali. "You are a tricky man, a wise man trying to make me look bad. You were sent by the power structure." He pointed to my producer, an African American. "And you brought a nigger, a dark one, along to help you."

I was angry and embarrassed, but I tried to play cool. I sent my producer and camera crew away, and sat in the corner with my notebook. I would get something out of this, I thought, something to write about. After all, this was the nadir of his career; shilling for a Don King fight in exchange for walking-around money and the chance to distribute Qur'ans.

An hour or so later, two teen-aged women came up to the suite for an autograph. Ali clambered out of the pans and led them into a curtained-off sleeping alcove. He winked over his shoulder at me. "Hey, Bob, just like old times." I wrote that down.

When I told that story to open the conference from which this book sprang, Ali himself stood up, glared fiercely, and cocked his fists at me. His longtime squire and best friend, Howard Bingham, wrapped his arms around Ali and pretended to hold him back, as he had when Cassius Clay pretended to go crazy during the weigh-in for the first Liston fight. They pulled off that trick in Miami Beach, Florida, twenty-eight years earlier, but in 1992, at Miami University in Ohio, we all broke out laughing, especially Ali.

It was a great conference, not only because Ali showed up or because the papers that were presented reconstructed and explicated and enlarged Ali's life in useful and important ways, but because he gave me more to write about.

An old friend, Peter Levine, an historian at Michigan State, attended the conference and asked me to introduce him to The Greatest. As they stood together, I was surprised at how similar they were in size. Had Ali shrunk, had Peter grown, do we create images out of proportion? I suddenly realized that the two of them were waiting for me to speak, and so I smoothly blurted, "Champ, this here's the great white hope."

Ali looked Peter up and down and said, "Looks more to me like the great white dope."

I wrote that down.

1

Muhammad Ali: The Hero in the Age of Mass Media

Michael Oriard

In saluting Michael Jordan as *Sports Illustrated*'s sportsman of the year for 1991, David Halberstam called Jordan "A Hero for the Wired World," declaring that "in the satellite age, Michael Jordan has become the global star of a global show." Halberstam reflected on Jordan's fame as something he had not seen since 1960, when Elvis Presley returned to Memphis from the army and John Kennedy won the presidency. Rock stars such as Mick Jagger, Halberstam suspected, "deal with this [sort of fame] all the time." As for athletes, Halberstam mentioned two possible rivals to Jordan: Joe DiMaggio and Magic Johnson (this was before Johnson tested HIV-positive). But Halberstam noted that DiMaggio's fame "was limited largely by the boundaries of the 48 contiguous states," while Johnson never attained Jordan's status as "both athlete and entertainer." Jordan, Halberstam concluded, "plays in the age of the satellite to an audience vastly larger than was possible in the past and is thus the first great athlete of the wired world."

In considering Johnson and Jordan together, Halberstam also touched on a point that has emerged over the past few years: the NBA's premier stars are the "only two black American athletes" to become "true crossover heroes—that is, they receive more commercial endorsement deals with the predominantly white, middle-class purveyors of public taste than do white athletes." With his black skin and shaved head, Jordan also represented "a new definition of American male beauty," his beauty as well as his artistry contributing importantly to his global popularity. Finally, Halberstam mentioned two other athletes, Pelé and Muhammad Ali, who might earlier have been what Jordan had in fact become, "the first new-age athlete." Halberstam declared, "Had the satellite been pervasive 20 years earlier, Pelé, also playing an international sport—soccer—on a level above even the best players of his day and with a charm that radiated easily across national boundaries, might have been first." As for Ali: "Perhaps Muhammad Ali might have been first, but he was politicized by his conversion to Islam and the Vietnam War. Besides, Ali's considerable charm notwithstanding, boxing was never the ideal sport for the young, with whom all idolatry of this kind must start. Ali, far more graceful than most boxers, conquered his opponents by stylishly punching them senseless; Jordan meets his opponents and conquers by gracefully soaring over them."[1]

In declaring Michael Jordan not just a great athlete but by some measure the greatest ever, Halberstam merely followed a tradition as old as sports journalism. The present is always the best time in the world of sport, but so is the nostalgically remembered past. This contradiction rests easily in the minds of sports fans. But if guided by a formula, Halberstam fleshed it out with several striking assumptions. The idea that basketball, with its premium on grace, has more powerful and universal appeal than boxing, with its premium on violence, strikes me as utopian thinking not easily documented. Halberstam seems on firmer ground in emphasizing the relationship of fame to the dominant medium for any era: the claim that Michael Jordan was not just a more popular hero but a different kind of hero because of the communication satellite. It has been a truism of sports studies that television "created" professional football as a major spectator sport in the 1960s. My own recent research has convinced me that the daily newspaper in New York in the 1880s and 1890s did the same for the original American version of the sport, the college game. We all know that sports have been experienced differently through different media; in print, on radio, on film, or on television, baseball, football, basketball, and boxing come to life in different ways, and come to mean different things to their audiences.

What most strikes me in Halberstam's essay, however, is the way he addresses a cluster of related concepts. He distinguishes athletics from entertainment, as I would surely do, but in doing so he ties fame to entertainment, not to sport. Of the major spectator sports in the United States—baseball, football, basketball, and boxing—basketball is the one in which the boundary between sport and entertainment is rubbed thinnest. In none of the other three sports is *how* the athlete does what he does nearly as important to the audience as *what* he does. Yet if the fame of the star athlete is indeed due to the entertainment he provides rather than to his physical achievement, then the very nature of sport and its cultural function have undergone profound transformation in a very short time. For now, I will leave the question open, but I will return to it later.

While linking fame to entertainment Halberstam also ties it to heroism—suggesting that the stature of the hero is measured by the extent of his fame—and, in a more stunning move, connects both to product endorsements: what makes Michael Jordan and Magic Johnson "true crossover heroes"—*heroes,* not entertainers—is the fact that "they receive more commercial endorsement deals from the predominantly white, middle-class purveyors of public taste than do white athletes." Here is a truly radical proposition, however casual its statement. Heroes have long been said to embody personal qualities that a people most value. If heroes in America are now the products of the products they peddle on television and in magazines—if our heroes are not just used but *created* by Madison Avenue—the implications are stunning. Again, I will leave the question open for now but will return to it. In addition to these most fundamental assumptions, Halberstam's essay makes a few others. Both *artistry* and physical *beauty*—the beauty of a Gary Cooper, a Gregory Peck, a Paul Newman, a Robert Redford—are necessary elements to be heroic and famous. Finally, the hero, the man of global fame, cannot be political: in addition to his sport itself, Muhammad Ali's conversion to Islam and refusal to be inducted into the army prevented his being the "hero" that Michael Jordan has become.

I want to take this cluster of concepts—the hero, fame, sport, entertainment, beauty, artistry, commercialization, and politics—as the starting point for my own reflections on the career of Muhammad Ali. My intention is not to make Ali's case, against Jordan's, as "the first new-age athlete" and hero, although the case could certainly be made. To insist on Jordan's unprecedented international popularity seems oddly amnesiac; could Jordan in the early 1990s possibly be better known in Africa and Asia than Ali was twenty years ago? Ali was not just known but lionized in Germany and England, and not only in Western but in developing countries as well. But I am more interested in the nature of the sports hero in our time, whether a "new age" or a continuation of the old, and in what's at stake when we define him in specific ways. Certainly I concur in distinguishing athletes from entertainers. Our best athletes entertain us, but their achievements also teach us about our human possibilities. Simply to care who wins or loses puts something at stake beyond the pleasure of being entertained. But in equating heroism with fame, and both with entertainment and commercialization, Halberstam's essay raises for me the fundamental question whether it is even possible to have heroes in an age dominated by the electronic media, and if heroism remains possible, what its nature might be. The career of Muhammad Ali seems to me the proper place to seek answers.

I'm not concerned here with Muhammad Ali the man, but with Ali as cultural representation. To find the "real" Ali is a quest for biographers; as a student of American culture, I'm interested in the public images of Ali, and in the power they had in the 1960s and 1970s. Those of us who came of age during the Ali era share certain memories of Ali, however we might have differed, or differ now, in our responses to him. We can all hear Ali's voice, declaiming, "I am the greatest!" We can still hear him predicting the round in which an opponent would fall; we can hear him chant, "Float like a butterfly, sting like a bee"; if we don't remember the precise words, we nonetheless retain impressions of his poetry and his taunts at weigh-ins and even in the ring, and his seemingly hysterical tirades before and after fights. For all their familiarity, however, we should not forget how we first encountered these outpourings from the Louisville Lip, as he was called early on (a less charming later nickname termed him The Mouth). We need to remember that in his first dawning on public awareness, Ali radically changed the self-presentation of the American athlete.

The hero's boast has a long ancestry: from Achilles before the walls of Troy through the latter-day "flyting" of ring-tailed roarers on the American frontier, nearly into the age of modern sport with John L. Sullivan and his fellow bare-knuckle brawlers. But the lineage of our sporting etiquette looks more to the tradition of Castiglione's courtier and his spiritual offspring on public-school playing fields in Britain. America's sportsmen through the first half of the twentieth century were not uniformly "sportsmen" in this honorific sense, but officially they subscribed to the aw-shucks code of Frank Merriwell.

Those born after 1960 or so might accept as commonplace something that perhaps thrilled, perhaps offended, but in all cases startled us when we first heard a maniacally exuberant young Cassius Clay declare, "I am the greatest!"—shattering a century-old image of the sportsman. The Merriwell code still hovered over American sport before Ali's emergence. During televised games, players studiously looked away when they sensed a television camera pointed in their direction. They kept their game faces on and their mouths shut; they left the voting on #1 to pollsters and waited until after the game to say "Hi" to their mothers.

After Ali, we heard Joe Namath outrageously predict that his Jets would beat the Colts in the 1969 Super Bowl. Not quite two years later, the Kansas City Chiefs' Elmo Wright, a rookie wide receiver, introduced the first end-zone dance to the NFL—a simple two-step considerably less artful than the Ali Shuffle. Wright's antics so outraged tradition-minded opponents that a defensive back for the Oakland Raiders broke his nose for him as a little lesson in sporting manners. But the rest, as they say, is history: within a few years, elaborate variations of Elmo Wright's two-step were being rehearsed and choreographed and trademarked and packaged all around the league. Now we routinely see mediocre linebackers, beaten by four touchdowns and mired in yet another losing season, jump up finger-pointing and trash-talking after making a good tackle for the first time all game. And we regularly see such behavior picked up by the children who watch television: nine-year-olds fist-pumping and high-fiving on the basketball floor, after simply standing in the way of some poor kid who dribbled the ball off his foot.

These details of sporting manners reflect a major cultural transformation in post-1950s America. Surely Muhammad Ali is one of the emblems of self-assertion and self-regard in an era whose cultural mainstream has become preoccupied—obsessed—with the self. This is not to say that Muhammad Ali represented the values now associated with "me decade" narcissism and Reagan-era greed, with Yuppie self-indulgence and Donald Trump. When Cassius Clay first declared, "I am the greatest!" this was an original and radical act. It defied the spirit of gray flannel suits and social accommodation; it shattered the mask of humble silence and nonassertion demanded of blacks in America, particularly of blacks in the South. It was also full of risk: proclaiming himself the greatest, Clay/Ali challenged opponents to beat him into a liar. Moreover, at least initially, he risked the outrage of the audience on which his livelihood depended. Anachronistic or not, Merriwellian modesty was the guise that athletes were expected to adopt if they were to be accepted as popular heroes. In this matter of self-presentation Clay/Ali represented something genuinely radical.

But the commercial marketplace in contemporary America has an extraordinary capacity to defuse and absorb cultural radicalism, to transform radical acts into marketable gestures. Today's conventional displays of self-promotion risk nothing and may earn a Brian Bosworth an eleven-million-dollar contract. We've moved from "I am the greatest!" with all its risk, to "I am, too," with none at all. Clay's proclamation was as original and radical as Walt Whitman's "barbaric yawp," when it first clanged in the ears of those accustomed to rhymed couplets and iambic pentameter. It was a far cry (my apologies for the bad pun) from the clichéd sound and fury of today's average athlete, which signifies nothing but a pitch for endorsements and an appearance on a late-night television show.

Ali was not only the greatest, he was also, as he constantly reminded us, the prettiest; in a sport, and in a division, associated with strength and violence, Muhammad Ali made us think about beauty. Ali's sculpted body and "pretty" face, together with his gentleness with children, undoubtedly accounted for much of his appeal to women of all ages, who were not typically drawn to prizefighters. This was most conspicuously the "feminine" aspect of Ali, the physical incarnation of those elements of his boxing style (his dancing, his speed and quickness—as opposed to his power) and of his poetry that American culture defines as feminine. I can think of no one in our time who so successfully embodied cross-gendered wholeness. As a professor of American literature, I am more accustomed to looking at this matter from the other direction: at the dilemma of the American male artist who feels driven to assert his masculinity because art and literature have been culturally defined as feminine. Probably only the heavyweight champion of the world could declare "I am the prettiest" and not diminish his aura of physical prowess. Certainly it hasn't worked the other way: writers such as Hemingway or Mailer, for instance, insisting they are the toughest sonsabitches around, have been considerably less convincing.

Ali was the prettiest and the greatest; he was fighter and dancer, loudmouth and poet, exuberant child and heavyweight champion of the world. In describing Ali as a sum of many parts, I have been circling around one of the principal claims I want to make in this essay. *Our* Muhammad Ali is the one we know through television, radio, newspapers, magazines such as *Sports Illustrated,* and closed-circuit screenings of his fights—the collection of images transmitted through those media. The crucial fact about those images is their extraordinary range. Various images of Muhammad Ali might be assigned to different stages in his career. One might reasonably identify an early brash, youthful, and exuberant Cassius Clay, who changed with the changing of his name after winning the title from Sonny Liston in 1964. This new Muhammad Ali grew increasingly militant as a spokesman for black separatism; then another new Ali, the political martyr, emerged with his defiance of the draft board and his three-and-a-half-year exile from boxing; then yet another Ali appeared with his return to boxing in 1970, an older, more mature figure of physical and mental courage in the Norton, Frazier, and Foreman fights. Finally, Ali became the aging champion who fought too long, who not only lost bouts to Leon Spinks, Larry Holmes, and Trevor Berbick, but who also lost his physical health and verbal agility to the sport he had transformed.

Certainly there is much truth in this account of the changes over the course of Ali's career, but it is also essential to recognize that at every stage of his career there was not a single Ali but many Alis in the public consciousness. The brash Cassius Clay could seem either braggart or free spirit; the dancing Ali could seem an artist or a coward; the Muslim Ali could seem a religious or a political man; the conscientious objector could seem a con man, a pacifist, a traitor, or a martyr. To the late-1960s white counterculture, Ali surely was identified more with the antiwar movement than with black separatism; to blacks during this same period he surely represented chiefly racial pride.

All of us—young and old, black and white, poor and privileged—knew these various Alis through the media. The media did not construct a single Ali but the multiple Alis we have been considering. The anthropologist Clifford Geertz has taught scholars to approach cultural expressions as "texts" in which we can read the larger culture that produces them. In reading the texts of a complex modern culture such as ours, it is essential to acknowledge that no single interpretation is likely to be possible. Students of American culture who attempt to interpret the texts of our past confront an overwhelming challenge to discover how ordinary people interpreted them. Students of sport have this advantage: the sports journalism that has always accompanied organized sport virtually from the beginning offers, not direct access to the minds and hearts of its readers, but at least closer access to them than is usually possible. Sportswriters are themselves individual interpreters of the events they describe; at the same time, they mediate between these events and those who read their accounts. What one finds in the reporting on Ali over the years is, first, an awareness among sportswriters that Ali was a "text" that could be read in competing ways and, second, a record of the ways he was read.

To approach Ali as a "cultural text" I read through the coverage of his career in *Sports Illustrated,* and I discovered, among other things, that journalists understood Muhammad Ali in just this way, without recourse to Clifford Geertz or any other theorist. Ali fascinated some of our most respected journalists—Norman Mailer, George Plimpton, and Wilfred Sheed come most quickly to mind—but I was particularly struck by the writing of *SI's* Mark Kram, a much less famous sportswriter. Ali's own artistry in and out of the ring clearly challenged sportswriters to create a commensurate art of their own. Kram chiefly covered Ali's second career, beginning with his return from exile to fight Jerry Quarry in 1970. In welcoming Ali back to boxing, Kram described him as a "clever dramatist" who "was creating a new theme for his fight with Quarry." Kram identified Ali's scripts for his earlier bouts: "brashness versus malevolence" for Sonny Liston; "holy wars" with Ernie Terrell and Floyd Patterson; and "the black prince on the lam" for his European fights with Karl Mildenberger, Henry Cooper, and Brian London. Now, with Quarry, Ali had cast himself as "Rimbrindt back from exile."[2]

The specific scripts are less important here than Kram's explicit recognition that boxing matches can function as cultural dramas or texts. The following spring Kram returned to this idea before Ali's first fight with Joe Frazier. In describing the roles that Ali and Frazier would be playing in the ring, Kram stood back to look at the history of boxing from this perspective:

Americans are the most curious in their reaction to a heavyweight title bout, especially one of this scope. To some, the styles and personalities of the fighters seem to provide the paraphernalia of a forum; the issue becomes a sieve through which they feel compelled to pour all of their fears and prejudices. Still others find it a convenient opportunity to dispense instant good and evil, right and wrong. The process is as old as boxing: the repelling bluff and bluster of John L. against the suavity and decorum of Gentleman Jim; the insidious malevolence of Johnson vs. the stolidity of Jeffries; the evil incarnate Liston against the vulnerable Patterson. It is a fluid script, crossing over religion, war, politics, race and much of what is so terribly human in all of us.

Heavyweight championship fights have always been culturally scripted; equally important, as Kram noted, is the fact that these scripts are read differently by different observers. Kram went on to describe some of the most prominent "readings" of the upcoming fight:

> The disputation of the New Left comes at Frazier with its spongy thinking and pushbutton passion and seeks to color him white, to denounce him as a capitalist dupe and a Fifth Columnist to the black cause. Those on the other fringe, just as blindly rancorous, see in Ali all that is unhealthy in this country, which in essence means all they will not accept from a black man. For still others, numbed by the shock of a sharply evolving society, he means confusion; he was one of the first to start pouring their lemonade world down the drain.
>
> Among the blacks there is only a whisper of feeling for Frazier, who is deeply cut by their reaction. He is pinned under the most powerful influence on black thought in the country. The militants view Ali as the Mahdi, the one man who has circumvented what they believe to be an international white conspiracy. To the young he is identity, an incomparable hero of almost mythological dimension.[3]

And so on. Black and white, conservative and liberal, young and old read the cultural text of Muhammad Ali in different ways. And my ramble through *Sports Illustrated* of the 1960s and 1970s confirmed that this was always the case. It's important to keep in mind both Ali's uniqueness *and* his typicality. Among the champions of our time Ali was uniquely enigmatic—a puzzle, a mass of paradoxes; this is how sportswriters repeatedly described him, as they obsessively attempted to unravel his mystery. Their own varied, conflicting interpretations were thus to some degree a consequence of Ali's resistance to simple explanation. In this range of interpretations, of course, Ali can also be considered typical: because of our diversity we Americans do not read *any* of our important cultural texts in identical ways. This may seem an obvious point, but its implications are important: no simple "dominant" ideology is imposed upon an unresisting public by the mass media. Sport in general, and perhaps Muhammad Ali in particular, can teach us how the media reach their diverse audience through multiple narratives.

The coverage of Ali's career in *Sports Illustrated* reveals an Ali who never fit a single role. Through the earliest years he was repeatedly termed a child: bragging, careless or casual about training, absurdly confident; a *willful* child with a short attention span, as unpredictable to his own managers as he was to the public. But against this sense of Clay as child stood the "remarkably calm and composed Clay" who entered the ring with the monster Sonny Liston in 1964, whose strategy had been "carefully rehearsed and meticulously perfected," who was driven by a deep sense of purpose, whose performance was remarkable for "the completeness of his ring wisdom." Tex Maule, the *SI* reporter whose words I've just quoted, commented that "the boasting and *calculated* gibes . . . had *seemed* the overweening confidence of a child" (my emphasis). Was Cassius Clay some kind of wondrous child of the gods or a canny ring technician whose childlike antics were meant to build interest in his fights and doubts in opponents' minds? Boxing fans answered that question in different ways, and at stake were beliefs about race, about what it takes to succeed in America, even about the relative importance of biology and self-determination in human lives.[4]

By the morning after the Liston fight, Cassius Clay was Muhammad Ali, a Black Muslim, forever altering the terms by which he would be considered, but not altering the conflicts among terms. Ali as vain self-promoter now competed with Ali as spokesman for black America; Ali as "that marvelous, whimsical, overweening and—when he turns the volume down—charming young man," with Ali as "black racist." Ali's Muslim connection was initially interpreted in terms of race, not religion; one writer dismissed his religious rantings as "the Allah routine." But the fighter—whether "a genius in his chosen craft" or simply a natural who did things in the ring that "no longer have any roots in intellection"—began to talk about dreams, about his sense of having been chosen for a purpose, about "divine things." The physical and the metaphysical, the natural and the supernatural, contended for reporters' and the public's attention. Following Ali's fight with Floyd Patterson in November 1965—in which the playful child had seemed cruelly contemptuous of his opponent, and of the audience as well—*SI*'s Gilbert Rogin mused: "What strange times we live in. What a strange, uncommon man is Clay. Who can fathom him? We can only watch in wonder as he performs and ponder whether, despite his truly affecting ways, he doesn't scorn us and the world he is champion of."[5] Playful or merely cruel, pug or prophet, an already puzzling Ali was becoming a more profound riddle.

In a five-part series in spring 1966, following Ali's challenge to his draft board, *Sports Illustrated* and Jack Olsen confronted the "enigma" of Muhammad Ali head-on: the incongruous mix of "bombast and doggerel," "hardheaded bigot[ry]," and "the conscience of a genuine objector." The most accessible champion in memory, to whom children flocked constantly, was also "the most hated figure in sport." His buffoonery too often crossed the boundary into nastiness. "His life is a symphony of paradoxes," Olsen wrote in the first installment of the series. In the third, an inquiry into the seeming hysteria of Ali's prefight and postfight rantings—temporary lunacy? an act? a psychological ploy? simple fear?—Olsen compiled a long list of the images that had become attached to Ali:

> Figuring out who or what is the *real* Cassius Clay is a parlor game that has not proved rewarding even for experts. Clay's personality is like a jigsaw puzzle whose pieces were cut by a drunken carpenter, a jumbled collection of moods and attitudes that do not seem to interlock. Sometimes he sounds like a religious lunatic, his voice singsong and chanting, and all at once he will turn into a calm, reasoning, if sometimes confused, student of the Scriptures. He is a loudmouthed windbag and at the same time a remarkably sincere and dedicated athlete. He can be a kindly benefactor of the neighborhood children and a vicious bully in the ring, a prissy Puritan, totally intolerant of drinkers and smokers, and a foulmouthed teller of dirty jokes.

Notice here—in 1966, two years after Ali changed his name—that Olsen still called him "Clay." The two names, Cassius Clay or Muhammad Ali, themselves conjured up conflicting interpretations of the heavyweight champion. Following his list, Olsen quoted Ali's physician, Dr. Ferdie Pacheco, who had heard it said that "there's 15 sides to Clay" but had decided that the fighter was "just a thoroughly confused person." Pacheco did not solve the riddle, of course, but only added a sixteenth possibility.[6]

The hero and villain of the late sixties became more thoroughly heroic in the seventies, yet without being reduced to a single dominant image. Following his world travels and campus lectures in the United States during his exile from boxing, Ali returned to the ring in 1970 as a spokesman "for 22 million black people," as "a symbol of black nationalism and antiwar sentiment," as a man fighting "not just . . . one man" but "a lot of men." Ali, who was once an "indefatigable consumer," now seemed to have turned ascetic. He had become a "patriarch," a "Prophet," a tool to be used however Allah wills—a serious man, driven by a sense of "divine destiny." But he was also a ring artist, "the ultimate action poet," and, in certain writers' more skeptical moods, still a fame junkie, con man, and nonstop showman.[7]

A sense of transcendent destiny runs through much of the writing on Ali from 1970 to 1975, the nature of the drama shifting from Broadway and Tin Pan Alley to Greek tragedy: Ali, the hero returned from banishment, fighting not just mortal opponents but mortality itself; Ali, once the golden child of the early sixties, after his defeat by Joe Frazier in 1971 now a man of suffering, of pain, of vulnerability; Ali the hero in the Underworld, in Sisyphean struggle against the Jimmy Ellises, the Buster Mathises, the Bob Fosters, the Floyd Pattersons (yet again—Ali doomed to clear obstacles once thought forever cleared), in his uphill quest to reclaim the championship that had once been his. In these fights Ali shows his old skills but seems too compassionate, seems to have lost his "will to kill." He is then shockingly defeated by Ken Norton, after which comes a further testing (by fate? by Allah?): Norton in a rematch; Frazier in a rematch but now not for the championship because Frazier has lost to a seemingly invincible George Foreman, the highest mountain yet up which Ali must roll his boulder. Ali seems blessed by the gods, by Allah, with his astonishing victory over Foreman in Africa, followed by the awesome *Götterdämmerung* of the third Frazier fight, the one in the Philippines. The fighter who danced and jabbed, and about whom cynics wondered whether he could truly punch and take a punch, became a fighter of stunning

power and an almost frightening courage to withstand the most brutal blows ever thrown in the heavyweight ring.

The question uppermost in writers' minds during this epic struggle to reclaim his stolen championship was What drove Ali? Clearly
he was driven, but was it by a simple lust for fame or by a truly transcendent destiny? Writers on the boxing beat, unaccustomed to
metaphysical speculations, now became serious philosophical inquir-
ers. And while Ali's popularity grew more general, the responses he
evoked continued to vary. The opposing possibilities of mortality and
transcendence defined the extreme limits of Ali's images in this period, culminating in a paradoxical kind of transcendent mortality in
Mark Kram's lyrical account of the third Frazier fight: "Once, so long
ago, he had been a splendidly plumed bird who wrote on the wind
a singular kind of poetry of the body, but now he was down to earth,
brought down by the changing shape of his body, by a sense of his
vulnerability, and by the years of excess. Dancing was for a ballroom;
the ugly hunt was on."[8] If Ali no longer danced and soared, in the
ugly hunt he was a dauntless hunter. Without explicitly echoing
Melville, Kram cast Ali as a Melvillean "Catskill eagle," who cannot
soar boundless and free but must fly within the gorge, yet that gorge
is in the mountains, high above where ordinary birds take wing. More
prosaically, when *Sports Illustrated* named Ali sportsman of the year
in 1974, George Plimpton proposed yet more ways to read the fighter,
attempting to explain how the triumph of so controversial a figure
could be so popular: "I think it was the sort of joyous reaction that
comes with seeing something that suggests all things are possible: the
triumph of the underdog, the comeback from hard times and exile,
the victory of an outspoken nature over a sullen disposition, the
prevailing of intelligence over raw power, the success of physical
grace, the ascendance of age over youth, and especially the confound-
ing of the experts. Moreover, the victory assuaged the guilt feelings
of those who remembered the theft of Ali's career."[9] The final phase
of Ali's career—the precipitous decline from triumph over Joe Frazier
in Manila in 1975 to defeat by Leon Spinks, Larry Holmes, and Trevor
Berbick in 1978, 1980, and 1981—was played out at times as farce
(the bizarre match with a sumo wrestler in Tokyo in 1976) or embarrassment, toward the end more often as tragedy: Ali, a man who "suf-
fers wonderfully from *hubris*," as Plimpton put it in 1974, now paying heavily for his pride and courage.[10]

In order to move toward some conclusions from this overview of Ali's cultural representations I want to return to Michael Jordan. Jordan, too, can be considered a "cultural text" in the way that I have been describing Ali. There is no single Michael Jordan in the public consciousness but many Michael Jordans: the fiercely competitive Jordan, committed to excellence; the selfish Jordan, who must have the ball and the spotlight; the Jordan as basketball artist and the Jordan as consummate winner; the various Jordans in his relations with his coach, his teammates, his family, his fans, his opponents, even his own image as it is marketed by Nike, Wheaties, and whoever else buys it. To these were added, when he retired from the Bulls, signed with the Whitesox, then rejoined the Bulls, a new medley: bored genius, self-deluded megalomaniac, intruder, exile, savior in his second coming. All of these "Jordans" generate narratives in which we explore issues of importance to us, narratives that are often closer to *our* concerns than to the star athlete to whom we attach them. This is simply one of the major functions of sport in our society.

But if Jordan is like Ali in this status as cultural text, Ali differed—and was perhaps unique—in two important ways. First, against the crush of media attention, Ali managed to maintain an amazing degree of control over the ways he was interpreted. *He* remained the principal author of his own cultural text. When *Sports Illustrated*'s Mark Kram reviewed Ali's "one-act play of infinite variations" (the occasion was his second fight with Floyd Patterson, in 1972), he described Ali as the producer of his own show; in the ring Ali seemed like a "drama coach" feeding Patterson his lines.[11] And it wasn't just the general public for whom Ali wrote his own scripts and enacted the dramas of his own creation. He also dictated to reporters, a group considerably less susceptible to illusions and delusions. He played for reporters the various roles that *he* wanted them to consider; he presented himself as an enigma that reporters became obsessed with figuring out, while never allowing them access to his essential mystery. Collectively, the reporters came to understand, as George Plimpton put it, that "so much of what Ali does is a game, a put-on," but both collectively and individually they never were exactly sure which part was put-on, which part serious.[12] In one of Howard Cosell's many interviews with Ali—one act in the vaudeville show they staged over most of Ali's career—Cosell and Ali bantered over who had created whom. The answer seems obvious: Ali was not a media creation but a self-creation who used the media brilliantly. In our world of sound bites and handlers, sport itself is resistant to mere manipulation. At the heart of sport, unlike most kinds of entertainment, lies something *real:* what the athletes themselves bring to the field or the ring. As Mark Kram wrote, in anticipation of Ali's third fight with Joe Frazier, "There is nothing contrived here. This is not an electronic toy conceived in network boardrooms and then sent out and made to look like a dramatic sporting conflict."[13] Within the world of sport, Muhammad Ali more successfully than anyone within memory resisted manipulation by others. As Kram wrote on another occasion, "Ali . . . dreams himself anew each morning."[14] Ali was the author of his own narratives, and, moreover, he transcended all attempts to explain him.

The second way I think Ali is different from other sports heroes lies in the kind of hero he was, and is. Having circled around it, I've arrived at the issue announced in the title of this essay: the question of Ali as a "hero" in an age in which the electronic media are capable of reaching billions of people everywhere in the world, but whose images are so overwhelmingly numerous and so dependent on novelty that the lifespan of even the most powerful images seems that of the firefly. I think that David Halberstam is correct in recognizing a new kind of fame: fame potentially of unprecedented reach, due to the transmission of images via satellite into every corner of the globe, but also fame of unprecedented brevity. That this fame will emanate from the United States, chiefly through commercials and images on consumer goods, also seems clear.

Michael Jordan is certainly a true "hero" of the satellite age: his fame is enormous, his fame is enormously marketed, and his fame will undoubtedly be fleeting. Although both his basketball artistry and his marketed image seemed unsurpassable at the end of 1991, they will of course be surpassed (his attempt at baseball already has altered the nature of his fame). The progression from oral to print to electronic cultures has meant the progressive shortening of the hero's endurance in popular consciousness. Muhammad Ali also had enormous fame, although he did not (could not?) market himself through product endorsements (if Michael Jordan is the first "new age athlete," perhaps Muhammad Ali is the last sport hero of the preceding era in which marketing was an adjunct of fame, not its principal form). It is worth noting that Ali remains a major hero in the developing countries of Asia and Africa, where Michael Jordan is virtually unknown. Where oral tradition remains strong, fame endures; heroes are passed on from generation to generation. Whether Ali's fame will transcend generations in the United States is uncertain, but for his own generation at least, Ali's fame has lasted, as has no other athlete's.

Where Ali chiefly differs from other sports heroes, however, is in something more fundamental: the very kind of heroism he represents. Halberstam's equation of heroism with fame runs counter to a definition of the hero that we associate with ages before the advent of the mass media—heroism as something more than celebrity, the hero as someone who embodies qualities we admire and wish to emulate, who ultimately represents his people in their highest aspiration. On these terms we might say that Jordan, too, is not just famous but also heroic; he embodies the dazzling grace, beauty, creativity, and competitiveness that feed the fantasies of children and inspire awe in adults. But Ali embodied that and more: the astonishing drama/melodrama/tragedy of his career gave his popular representations a kind of depth and resonance that the visual images of the electronic media cannot capture. Halberstam claims that Ali's religion and politics limited his fame. Certainly they made him a villain for many in the late sixties and early seventies, as they made him a hero to others; but they also gave moral substance to the image that emerged from the desperate fights of his comeback—the ones with Frazier and Foreman—during a politically more quiescent time, when history seemed to have proven him right in refusing induction into the army. The apparent moral courage of the draft resister and his identification with the underprivileged throughout the world deepened and enlarged the physical and psychological courage of the man who slugged it out with Joe Frazier for fourteen brutal rounds in Manila. If Ali's principles angered many in the 1960s, by the 1970s he could be admired for at least having principles. To think of Muhammad Ali in this way makes him seem an anachronism, a kind of hero perhaps no longer possible in the age of the spectacle.

Or—another possibility. Perhaps Muhammad Ali, as "cultural text," can represent a model for American culture as a whole for which we are desperately searching today. Through the 1960s, Ali was a hero to the young more than the old, to intellectuals more than blue-collar workers, to blacks more than whites, to militant blacks more than moderate and Christian blacks. By the mid-seventies, after the Foreman and Frazier fights, when Ali became almost universally admired, he continued to mean different things to different people. Mark Kram pondered the diversity of Ali's audience in the months following the third Frazier fight: "His followers cut across all class lines. There are the masses of poor, who see him as a symbol of escape from their own miseries, as an enemy of tyrannous governments. There are the moneyed, who must always be near success. There is the white middle class, that huge engine of society that once so rejected him but now jockeys for position with miniature cameras and ballpoint pens."[15]

I am led to think of this diversity among Ali's fans in relation to both our frequent agonizing over the immense power of the electronic media and our more recent agonizing over cultural diversity. These agonizings contradict each other. The media have been blamed for reducing all of us to an undifferentiated mass; we watch the same television programs, listen to the same music, read or watch the same news, supposedly think the same thoughts. On the other hand, we also know that advertisers, those who have most to gain by understanding the nature of this so-called mass audience, view us as dozens of distinct "markets," defined by age, race, economic status, education, and other criteria. We appear to be simultaneously an undifferentiated mass and a centerless nation of special interests. The current debates over cultural diversity are fed by both perceptions: a fear on the one side that an official American culture erases genuine differences, and a fear on the other side that we are losing all sense of a common culture.

Thinking about Muhammad Ali in these contexts leads me to two conclusions. What painfully divides us today is not the absence of a common culture but the uneven distribution of wealth and opportunity—the hard facts of American life that sometimes get lost in our debates over curricula and cultural representation. But in imagining a more just and equitable American society, we might envision an important role for sport in creating a genuine common yet diverse culture. Sport contributes importantly to what already exists as a common American culture: football, baseball, basketball, and boxing are cultural texts that we read in a variety of ways, yet they create a common interest that reaches across the boundaries that divide us. Muhammad Ali came to be a true "multicultural text," in which for over a decade we Americans, in all our diversity, were able to find important values. For most of Ali's boxing career his public images were inextricably tied to his race, and for part of that time they were bound to his racialist rhetoric. But at some point in the mid-seventies, this changed. Ali remained utterly racial yet simultaneously beyond race.

The world of sport regularly raises up a handful of heroes, who for a short time represent the fastest, the strongest, the most graceful, the most courageous, but who then yield their pedestals to the next set of heroes. The culture as a whole benefits, while the discarded heroes often become victims of their own fame, players in our modern version of an ancient tragedy. But in addition, on rare occasions, from the world of sport arises a Muhammad Ali, who not only is the prettiest, the loudest, and the greatest, but who reminds us of the deeper and broader possibilities of commitment and achievement, while still entertaining us and letting us dream.

Notes

1. David Halberstam, "A Hero for the Wired World," *Sports Illustrated,* December 23, 1991, 75–81.

2. Mark Kram, "He Moves Like Silk, Hits Like a Ton," *Sports Illustrated,* October 26, 1970, 19.

3. Mark Kram, "At the Bell . . . " *Sports Illustrated,* March 8, 1971, 20.

4. Tex Maule, "Liston's Edge: A Lethal Left," *Sports Illustrated,* February 24, 1964, 18–21, and "Yes, It Was Good and Honest," ibid., March 9, 1964, 20–25.

5. The quotations in this paragraph, with the exception of the last one, are from Gilbert Rogin, "Rabbit Hunt in Vegas," *Sports Illustrated,* November 22, 1965, 34–39. The final quotation is from Rogin, "Champion as Long as He Wants," ibid., November 29, 1965, 24.

6. Jack Olsen, "Hysteria Is a Sometime Thing," *Sports Illustrated,* April 25, 1966, 64. The series, under the title "A Case of Conscience," ran from April 11 to May 9, and letters from readers continued to be printed until June 6. These fifteen letters represented the magazine's readership, as constructed by the editors, their varied responses confirming the multiple Alis in the public consciousness.

7. For the account of Ali as the spokesman "for 22 million black people" and so on, and as the consumer turned ascetic, see Kram, "He Moves Like Silk, Hits Like a Ton," 16–19; George Plimpton, in "Watching the Man in the Mirror," *Sports Illustrated,* November 23, 1970, 80–102, re-

ports on the views of Ali as "patriarch" and "prophet"; Tex Maule and Morton Sharnik, in "It's Gonna Be the Champ and the Tramp," ibid., February 1, 1971, 14–17, comment on Ali's put-ons; and Kram, in "At the Bell . . . " 18–21, describes Ali as both "action poet" and man of "divine destiny."

8. Mark Kram, "'Lawdy, Lawdy, He's Great,'" *Sports Illustrated,* October 13, 1975, 26.

9. George Plimpton, "Return of the Big Bopper," *Sports Illustrated,* December 23, 1923, 101.

10. Plimpton, "Return of the Big Bopper," 97; see also Pat Putnam's accounts of the two Spinks fights and particularly of the Holmes fight, "Doom in the Desert," *Sports Illustrated,* October 13, 1980, 34–44.

11. Mark Kram, "Just Call Him Shubert Ali," *Sports Illustrated,* October 2, 1972, 24–25.

12. Plimpton, "Return of the Big Bopper," 98.

13. Mark Kram, "Manila—for Blood and Money," *Sports Illustrated,* September 29, 1975, 23.

14. Mark Kram, "Scenario of Pride—and Decline," *Sports Illustrated,* January 21, 1974, 23.

15. Mark Kram, "One-Nighter in San Juan," *Sports Illustrated,* March 1, 1976, 15.

2

The Wide World of Muhammad Ali: The Politics and Economics of Televised Boxing

Randy Roberts

America has accepted Muhammad Ali. The political controversies that once surrounded his conversion to the Nation of Islam and his stand on the war in Vietnam have died. He is today an aging celebrity, slower, quieter, calmer, and something of a national treasure. When he turned fifty in 1992, television celebrated the event with a special tribute. Singers sang, comedians joked, and tired Ali impersonations were trotted out, dusted off, and presented once again. The tribute was tame and respectful, lacking even a hint of a political edge. A quarter of a century earlier, Americans had watched Ali in a different, more politically charged, mood. Many wanted to see his mouth shut by a well-placed punch. Others wanted to see him "float like a butterfly, sting like a bee" and symbolically vindicate political stands with a victory in the ring.

Ali in his prime, Ali at fifty—the one constant was that he was "good television." He attracted the numbers, whether measured by ratings or shares. This essay tells the story of men and women in pursuit of those numbers and how Ali fit into and helped to shape their world. It is also the story of televised boxing and how Muhammad Ali changed the rules of that game, and indeed of all of televised sports.

The Emergence of Television and the Rise and Fall of Televised Boxing

Television was crucial to the life and career of Muhammad Ali. Indeed, Ali was one of the first American celebrities to grow up with television.

Ali was born in 1942, only three years after NBC's first televised sporting event, a baseball game between Columbia and Princeton played at Baker Field in New York. Television was largely set aside during World War II, as research-and-development money and scientific interest centered on the war effort. With VJ-Day, however, the mood of the country changed sharply. After four years of rationing and saving—of planting victory gardens, driving on worn tires, and drinking sugarless coffee—Americans were eager to spend. They wanted new cars with new tires; they pined for new houses with new electrical appliances. Just as radio had helped to stimulate the consumer splurge of the 1920s, television aided the consumer binge of the post–World War II era. Like radio, television suited the needs of America's secular trinity—producers, consumers, and advertisers. For manufacturers it was a perfect product because it encouraged Americans to purchase other products. And its acceptance came, as the television historian Eric Barnouw noted, with "surprising suddenness."[1]

Although television was quickly accepted, it did not at first spread uniformly across the country. The numbers speak for themselves. Between the end of the war and 1952, television's market was almost exclusively urban. The city's near-monopoly of the medium was aided by the Federal Communications Commission (FCC) "freeze" on new television station licenses between September 1948 and April 1952. When the freeze ended, America had 108 operating stations located in 63 cities, but most of the country's television receivers were in a handful of large urban centers. In 1949, for example, 41.6 percent of all receivers were in New York City, and another 40.9 percent were divided among Philadelphia, Washington, D.C., Boston, Chicago, Detroit, and Los Angeles. Most of the South, Southwest, and West was outside of television's market. Furthermore, in 1950 only 9 percent of American homes had televisions. Most people watched television in bars or the homes of friends.[2]

When limitations on television licensing ceased, so did the urban domination by the medium. The FCC moved swiftly to license new stations. In less than one year, it issued 70 new licenses, and by 1955 there were 422 stations in the country. The numbers continued to grow over the next decade. In 1958 America had 485 stations, a figure that grew to 572 by the end of 1965. In addition, the coaxial cable made coast-to-coast network broadcasting a possibility and permitted television to extend its reach into small-town and rural America. As television penetrated all sections of the county, the number of home sets multiplied. In 1955, 55.7 percent of all American households owned at least one television set. The percentage rose steadily—to 78.6 percent in 1957 and 85.9 percent in 1959. In 1966, the year Ali made his biggest impact on network television, the number had reached 92.8 percent. As a point of comparison, that same year only 80 percent of all American households had a telephone.[3]

The relentless spread and dramatic power of television triggered hosannas and howls from its defenders and critics. As Leo Rosten summed it all up, television was a "marvelous, exciting, depressing, promising, wonderful, deplorable miracle." But it was also something much more—and much less. David Karp expressed the essence of television better than anyone else: "TV is not an art form or a culture channel: it is an advertising medium." Its purpose is to push products and make money for manufacturers. "Obviously," Karp wrote about the leading network executives, "if their object is to make money—and they do make money—it seems a bit churlish and un-American of people who watch television to complain that their shows are so lousy. They are not supposed to be any good. They are supposed to make money."[4]

In the television business, success is the sum of the important numbers—the number of television sets, the number of viewers, the number of advertiser dollars. Numbers rule the empire. They determine what kind of programs make it to television and which ones stay on the air. They dictate how much a sponsor has to pay for advertising time and how much a network has to pay a performer. Corporation executives, as much as network leaders, dance to the numbers. From the late 1940s on, they shifted increasingly larger shares of their advertising dollars to television. By the mid-1960s, Procter and Gamble, one of television's leading sponsors, spent $148.8 million of its $167 million annual advertising budget for television air time. Although the dollar amounts were less, other companies spent an even higher percentage of their advertising budgets for television. Gillette, for example, earmarked 94.2 percent of its budget for television time, and the Consolidated Cigar Company—makers of Muriels and Dutch Masters—sent 98 percent of its budget to the networks.[5]

Gillette and Consolidated Cigar spent their money on television advertising because television provided the swiftest route to their primary market. In particular, televised sports attracted male viewers who smoked cigars and cigarettes, drank beer, used safety razor blades, and bought cars and insurance. From television's earliest years, sports programs provided the best arena for advertisers to woo male consumers. In the late 1940s and early 1950s, when most American men watched television with other men in bars, sports programming was ideal. Few men even suggested trying a nonsports program, for to do so would have risked immediate scorn and possible censure.

Given television's commercial purpose and the need to attract male viewers, it was guaranteed that network executives would tap the wellspring of sport. Not only were sports ideal from a marketing standpoint, they were near perfect from a programming standpoint as well. They came with their own heroes and villains, their own sets and props and plots. They supplied action, suspense, and drama. There was no need to introduce athletes or teams; viewers were familiar with the players and the sports. In television's early years, when programming was a major concern, sports provided an effective and profitable way to fill hours of air time.[6]

Still, sports presented a few problems. Stationary cameras and primitive audio systems made it difficult to capture the full complexity and drama of baseball and football. As Benjamin G. Rader has observed, "The essence of baseball involved an acute awareness of the entire playing field. The baseball fan not only enjoyed the isolated instances of action—the pitch, hit, catch, or throw; he also wanted to see the runner leading off the base, the signals of the third base coach, and the positions taken by the fielders. Only the fan in the stands, not the television viewer, could command all these perspectives." Before the development of instant replay, split screens, and more sophisticated cameras, television baseball focused on the dramatic action—the duel between the pitcher and the batter—at the expense of the more subtle action. As one critic summed up the experience, "People can't learn to watch baseball that way; they're just learning to watch television."[7]

Boxing and wrestling made for far better television. Both sports involved two men in a small arena. The action was direct and relatively simple to capture, and cameras could be positioned close to the ring to provide the viewer with an ideal vantage point. Like baseball, of course, televised boxing had its critics. A. J. Liebling, the sport's leading journalist, disliked watching boxing on television:

For one thing, you can't tell the fighters what to do. When I watch a fight, I like to study one boxer's problem, solve it, and then communicate my solution vocally. Some fighters hear better and are more suggestible than others—for example, the pre-television Joe Louis. "Let him have it, Joe!" I would yell whenever I saw him fight, and sooner or later he would let the other fellow have it. I get a feeling of participation that way that I don't in front of a television screen. I could yell, of course, but I would know that if my suggestion was adopted, it would be by the merest coincidence.

In addition, Liebling wanted other members of the fight cognoscenti to hear him: "You are surrounded by people whose ignorance of the ring is exceeded only by their unwillingness to face facts—the sharpness of your boxer's punching, for instance. Less malignant than rooters for the wrong man, but almost as disquieting, are those who are on the right side but tactically unsound." For Liebling, attending a boxing match was a form of human communication similar to a New England town meeting. He feared a growing privatization of life. "Television, if unchecked," he predicted, "may carry us back to a pre-tribal state of social development, when the family was the largest conversational unit."[8]

Although Liebling's criticisms were sound, he was not critical of television's technological coverage of fights. Watching boxing on television was inexpensive, convenient, and, most viewers agreed, satisfying. Sitting in a bar or a living room, one could watch a fight broadcast from thousands of miles away. The first championship fight the majority of Americans ever saw was on television. After watching the 1946 rematch between Joe Louis and Billy Conn—a fight that failed to live up to expectations—a columnist for the *Washington Post* observed, "Television looks good for a 1000-year run."[9]

During the late 1940s and 1950s, boxing was television's darling. Advertisers and television could not get enough of the sport. In 1954, for example, there was a prime-time fight televised nationally almost every night. On Monday, ABC televised matches from Eastern Parkway Arena in Brooklyn, and Dumont aired its own fights from St. Nicholas Arena in New York City. On Wednesday, CBS televised a bout. The "Gillette Cavalcade of Sports" Friday night fight from Madison Square Garden on NBC drew the most consistently high ratings. Finally, on Saturday, Ray Arcel and Dewey Fragetta promoted bouts televised by ABC. And those were only the *nationally* televised bouts. Weekly local fight shows were broadcast from Los Angeles, Montreal, Detroit, Mexico City, Hollywood, San Francisco, Philadelphia, and a dozen or more smaller cities. As Red Skelton, another television staple, joked, "The Monday fight, scheduled for a Tuesday this Wednesday, had been postponed till Thursday and rescheduled for Friday this Saturday because Sunday's a holiday."[10]

Although most series of televised boxing programs lasted only three or four years, the success of the shows pleased sponsors, television executives, and the people in the fight game. Everyone in boxing, from fighters and managers to matchmakers and promoters, reaped at least short-term profits. The most successful fight program, the "Gillette Cavalcade of Sports," sponsored by the Gillette Safety Razor Company, ran on NBC from 1944 to 1960. When the network canceled the program, Gillette jumped to ABC and sponsored the "Fight of the Week," also usually televised from Madison Square Garden, between 1960 and 1964. Gillette paid Madison Square Garden $25,000 for the first year, but by 1964 the Garden received that amount each week, and the total revenues exceeded fifteen million dollars. The guaranteed television money made it easier for matchmakers to schedule fights since they in turn could set standard rates for fighters. When the relationship ended in 1964, Harry Markson, boxing director at the Garden, remarked, "Let me say this, Gillette has been great to work with. Never a squawk. Never a regret. A wonderful sponsor."[11]

Nor did Gillette have any reason to squawk. "Gillette Cavalcade of Sports" and the "Fight of the Week" reached their targeted audiences. As a program title, the "Gillette Cavalcade of Sports" provided valuable sponsor identification and associated the rugged masculinity of boxing with Gillette's manly products. The slogan "Look sharp, feel sharp, be sharp," followed by "How're you fixed for blades?" entered into the national vocabulary and helped Gillette dominate the double-edge razor blade market. By 1963 Gillette controlled 70 percent of the market, compared to 22 percent for Schick and less than 3 percent for the American Safety Razor Company. In addition, in the early 1960s, when Gillette expanded into men's toiletries, the company used the weekly fight program to advertise its new products. Right Guard deodorant, Gillette foamy shaving cream, and Sun Up after-shave lotion were all hawked between the rounds of the fights. Even when the show's rating slipped in the late 1950s and early 1960s, Gillette remained quite satisfied with its sponsorship of boxing.[12]

For many of the years between 1944 and 1964, television executives were also satisfied with boxing. Production costs for televising a fight were low. In the mid-1950s, it cost the network about $50,000 to stage a fight. A variety show or a situation comedy would cost twice as much. For the investment, networks were rewarded with some of the highest ratings. The 1953 Rocky Marciano–Jersey Joe Walcott rematch for the heavyweight title captured 68.7 percent of the viewing audience, and the 1953 Kid Gavilan–Chuck Davey welterweight championship contest scored a 67.9 rating. As one network executive commented, "We not only get a bigger audience for less money than the big razzle-dazzle shows, but we get what practically amounts to a captive audience. A fight has to be a real smeller for anybody to tune it out."[13]

Like one of Gillette's double-edge razors, however, television could shave too close and draw blood. Jack "Doc" Kearns, a fight manager universally venerated for his wisdom, once commented, "You can't give it away and sell it at the same time." Although the statement applies equally to any number of commodities, Kearns was talking about his belief that televised fights would cripple live gates and kill small boxing clubs. His prediction came true during the 1950s. With championship fights on television, boxing fans stopped patronizing the neighborhood clubs where young fighters learned their craft. In 1952 there were about three hundred fight clubs in America; by the end of the decade there were less than fifty. Television—combined with the population flight from the inner city and changing leisure patterns—had closed most of the small fight clubs, and when they closed, boxers lost valuable training opportunities.[14]

The large arenas also felt the impact of television. Gates and ticket revenues declined dramatically. In 1943, thirty-three Madison Square Garden fights drew 406,681 fans, who paid $2,062,046 for tickets. Ten years later, thirty Garden fights attracted 152,928 spectators, who paid $629,775. Television revenues helped to offset the decline in ticket sales. In 1953 Madison Square Garden received $1,768,000 from the networks for broadcast rights to its fights. But the lack of paying customers took its toll on the Garden's concession business as well as the restaurants and hotels in the midtown area. In addition, of course, television revenues were not guaranteed. If the ratings slipped, television would desert the large arenas even faster than the fans.[15]

Toward the end of the 1950s, ratings for television shows began to decline. In 1953 a leading network boxing show would normally draw 31 percent of the available audience. By 1959 that figure had dropped to 10.6 percent. Part of the problem was oversaturation of the market. With fights televised almost nightly, the novelty of boxing wore thin. In addition, many of the best fighters were seldom seen on home television. Heavyweight champion Rocky Marciano, for example, fought only one of six title defenses on television. Promoters of his fights believed that they could make more money holding the contests in large outdoor ballparks and selling the film rights to newsreel and closed-circuit television companies. Moreover, new network programming cut into boxing's audience. ABC formed important partnerships with Walt Disney and Warner Brothers—giving them access to Hollywood movies—and CBS and NBC improved the quality of their shows. It was a different world from the late 1940s. By the late 1950s, boxing had to compete with popular television westerns—"Wyatt Earp," "Gunsmoke," "Wagon Train," "Death Valley Days," and many others—as well as with Hollywood movies rerun on television and such crime shows as "The Untouchables."[16]

One by one, the boxing shows were replaced by new programs. The biggest blow to the sport came, however, in January 1960 when NBC announced that it was dropping "The Gillette Cavalcade of Sports" Friday night fight, the longest-running sports program on television. "Anything we broadcast," an NBC executive told the press, "is our responsibility, and we felt we had adequate reasons not to continue the fights." Behind the vague and slightly imperious wording of the announcement were sound reasons. The year before, congressional investigations of fixed quiz shows had focused considerable attention on NBC's "Twenty-One," especially after Charles Van Doren, the show's all-American contestant and the summer replacement for Dave Garroway on NBC's "Today" show, confessed that he had conspired with the show's producers to rig his contests. With Congress turning its attention to professional boxing—a sport that clearly had very close ties to organized crime—NBC wished to avoid another scandal. Even though ratings remained fairly strong and Gillette was happy with the fight show, NBC, noted a leading advertising journal, was "squeamish about the gangster element which has tainted boxing" and wanted to become "associated with more respectable programs." In July 1960, NBC replaced its Friday night fight with a series entitled "Moment of Fear," described by one Brooklyn woman as "a worse program than most of the fights."[17]

NBC's decision to drop its fights changed the direction of televised sports. Neither Congressional investigations or declining ratings deterred Gillette. The men who purchased Gillette products liked the fights, and the company was upset with NBC's decision. As one Gillette official noted, "The audiences have been very loyal to us and to boxing and we don't like to deprive them of fights in the future." In the 1930s Gillette had controlled only 16 percent of the razor market. Then it had started to sponsor radio and television boxing and its market share increased to 70 percent. Poised to move into the lucrative men's toiletries field, Gillette wanted to maintain its high profile in boxing as well as other sports. Once it was clear that NBC would not reverse its decision on boxing, Gillette approached ABC with a deal. If ABC would pick up the Madison Square Garden weekly fight package, Gillette would shift the rest of its uncommitted advertising dollars—8.5 million—to ABC. ABC quickly agreed. Eight and a half million dollars was more than ABC had bid on sports during its history, more than the network's profits in 1959. The money allowed ABC, the poor sister of the industry, to become a player.[18]

ABC's capture of Gillette's advertising millions was less important for boxing than for other sports. To be sure, ABC honored its commitment. In the fall of 1960 it began to televise the Gillette-sponsored "Fight of the Week." The familiar opening music of the "Cavalcade of Sports" and Gillette's well-known slogan continued to be associated with boxing. But more important for ABC, the Gillette dollars provided a war chest that allowed the network to buy into other sports. ABC's first move was to outbid NBC for the rights to NCAA football games. Other acquisitions soon followed. ABC bought the rights to the American Football League, the Sugar Bowl, the Professional Golfer's Association championship, the U.S. Open, the U.S. Women's Open, the U.S. Men's Amateur, and AAU track-and-field events. A few years later, ABC also gained the rights to televise both the summer and winter Olympic Games. By 1965 it had replaced NBC as the leader in sports coverage, and by the mid-1970s ABC had become America's most watched network.[19]

The Roone Revolution

When in 1960 ABC began to acquire sports broadcasting rights, the network also commenced hiring the best talent possible. Their major acquisition was Roone Arledge, who moved to ABC from NBC in 1960 and produced ABC's NCAA football and American Football League telecasts. A product of Forest Hills, Queens, and Columbia University, Arledge was well prepared for the New York business world. Although he had won an Emmy Award at NBC for his production of Shari Lewis's puppet show "Hi, Mom," Arledge wanted to move into sports. He had produced a pilot entitled "For Men Only"—a magazine show featuring sports, adventure, and music—but NBC did not want the show. ABC did, and Arledge grabbed ABC's offer of "a nonspecific job somewhere in network production at a modest salary." Over the next twenty-five years, he became the driving force behind ABC Sports.[20]

Arledge believed that watching television should be an intimate adventure, that the viewer should feel a sense of participation in the experience. He employed this approach first in his NCAA football games. "What we set out to do was to get the audience involved emotionally," Arledge explained. "If they didn't give a damn about the game, they might still enjoy the program." Arledge used technology to achieve his goals. He put cameras on cranes, blimps, and helicopters to provide long shots of the stadium and the surrounding area, and he utilized hand-held cameras for closeups. He consigned three cameras to capture just the environment of the stadium. "We asked ourselves: If you were sitting in the stadium, what would you be looking at? The coach on the sideline, the substitute quarterback warming up, the pretty girl in the next section. So our cameras wandered as your eyes would." In addition, ABC engineers developed rifle mikes and instant replays to enhance the viewing experience. The object, as Arledge noted, was to take "the fan to the game, not the game to the fan."[21]

Arledge's ideal of televised sport as adventure was carried a step further in 1961 when "Wide World of Sports" premiered. A sports anthology show that emphasized exotic locations and interesting personalities more than the sports themselves, "Wide World of Sports" was a perfect series from a programming perspective. Since most of its shows were taped and edited before they were televised,

"Wide World of Sports" was not limited by seasonal schedules or weather. It realized Arledge's vision of "a year-around sports show that could fill the void [between sports seasons] and not have to worry about blackouts." The show's opening promised "the thrill of victory, the agony of defeat," and because it was carefully edited to increase the drama of sports, it delivered. Between 1961 and 1966, "Wide World of Sports" presented eighty-seven different sports, ranging from international track-and-field meets and championship skiing contests to demolition derbies and an Eiffel Tower climb. In the process, the show introduced Americans to remote regions of the world and flamboyant personalities. In terms of production, sports played a secondary role. Arledge commented, "We combined the techniques of documentary film making—so viewers could get to know the performers personally—with coverage designed to make you feel as though you are there."[22]

While Arledge was building ABC's sports empire, boxing—the sport that provided ABC's seed money—was largely forgotten. Gillette's "Fight of the Week" received little of Arledge's attention. Its presentation was straightforward and traditional. Don Dunphy, a skilled but colorless sports announcer, called the fights. He always centered his broadcasts on the fights themselves and tried to avoid controversy. Unlike "Wide World of Sports" or ABC's NCAA football coverage, the "Fight of the Week" did not attempt to bring the viewer to the fights by emphasizing the atmosphere surrounding the contest. Nor did the show create drama by developing the personalities of the fighters or the locale of the matches. Clearly, ABC's primary interest in boxing was Gillette's money.

ABC's one attempt to improve the technology of its boxing broadcasts had a tragic beginning. In early March 1962, Don Dunphy was called into ABC-TV studios for a demonstration of a videotape replay system that ABC engineers had recently developed. The innovation allowed ABC to replay in slow motion important parts of a fight between rounds. During the replays Dunphy could comment on the significance of the action. The system was technically perfect and was first used on the night of March 24, 1962, for the world welterweight title fight between Emile Griffith and Benny "Kid" Paret. It was a brutal battle. Several times the crafty Paret pretended that he was hurt, lulled Griffith into a making a mistake, and then punished his overconfident opponent. In the twelfth round, Griffith forced Paret into a corner and Paret once again appeared hurt. Griffith landed a cruel series of unanswered punches, and after a long delay the referee, Ruby Goldstein, pulled the two fighters apart. Unconscious, Paret slumped to the canvas. More than a week later, he died in Roosevelt Hospital without ever having regained consciousness. ABC used its new replay system to show the brutal last sequence on Dunphy's postfight show. The ratings for the postfight show were higher than they had been for the fight itself, but the Griffith-Paret fight injured the reputation of televised boxing.[23]

Throughout its history, boxing's popularity has taken extreme swings. At times, society has embraced the sport and feted its champions. At other times, reformers' demands for the abolition of boxing have gained broad followings. Often the popularity of the sport has reflected the popularity of the heavyweight champion. Given both the periodic shifts in popularity and the crucial role of the heavyweight champion, the years between 1960 and 1964 were depressed times. Boxing's reputation for honesty had never been high, but during the late 1950s and early 1960s it earned its label as the redlight district of professional sports. "Let me tell you about boxing," an associate of fight promoter Don King later told a reporter for the Chicago *Daily News*. "It's the most treacherous, dirtiest, vicious, cheatingest game in the world. . . . That's the nature of the business. It's a terrible business."[24]

Boxing's problems started at the top. Rocky Marciano, a popular heavyweight champion, retired in early 1956, and during the next eight years no heavyweight title holder emerged to replace Rocky in the public's imagination. Floyd Patterson, an earnest, decent man, was handled by a cautious manager who did not want his boxer to face the leading contenders. Instead of fighting the best in the division, Floyd battled a series of second-rate heavyweights, including one whose fight with Patterson was his first professional contest. On June 26, 1959, Ingemar Johansson, a handsome but limited Swedish fighter, knocked out Patterson, but a year later Floyd won back his title in a rematch with Johansson. Embarrassed at having to duck the leading contenders, in 1962 Patterson fought Sonny Liston, the top heavyweight contender, whose number of knockouts was rivaled only by the number of times he had been arrested. Liston knocked out Patterson in the first round and then repeated the task a year later in their rematch. Liston's criminal past—he had been a goon for the

St. Louis mob—and his continued close ties to gangsters, as well as his moody, sullen disposition, made him an unpopular champion and a poor representative for his sport.

Liston's personality was best captured in a story told by Red Smith, one of America's leading sportswriters. In 1965 Smith tried to interview Liston, but finding Sonny unresponsive, he started a conversation with Willie Reddish, Liston's trainer. In the course of their conversation, Smith and Reddish discovered that they had both been in Philadelphia during a particular time. "Oh, you were there then?" Reddish asked. "Willie," Smith replied, "I did ten years hard in Philadelphia." Although Liston had shown no interest in the conversation, he swung around on hearing Smith's last comment and asked, "Hard? No good time." Prison was never far from Sonny's thoughts or actions.[25]

Nor was prison far from the actions of many of boxing's other leading citizens. From the late 1940s to the early 1960s, organized crime played a leading role in professional boxing. Everyone who investigated boxing, from newspaper and magazine journalists to United States senators and governors, discovered—or confirmed—the close ties between organized crime and boxing's leading promoters, managers, and fighters. From New York, Boston, and Philadelphia to Chicago, Detroit, and Los Angeles, the story was the same: boxing was controlled by the mob. Frankie Carbo was the most important underworld figure in the sport, but he was joined by a host of other criminals. The breakup of the International Boxing Club, an organization that had monopolized the promotion of championship fights, had been an attempt to drive the mob out of boxing, but the maneuver was only partially effective. Even after Carbo was sent to prison in 1959, several of his associates remained active in boxing.[26]

Tragedies inside the ring compounded boxing's problems. The Griffith-Paret fight disturbed the conscience of the nation, and television magnified the event. Similar to its coverage of the Southern civil rights brutalities, television showed Americans the stark reality of one fighter beating another fighter to death. The last brutal seconds of the fight—Paret trapped in a corner, his head being jerked back and forth by the impact of Griffith's punches, and the fighter finally sinking unconscious to the canvas—outraged many Americans. A movement to ban boxing began immediately. *Sports Illustrated* called the movement "cheaply sentimental . . . shallow, gratuitous or, worse, opportunistic." One magazine editor asserted that "boxing is a fine and manly sport" and that "there is nobility in reasonable risk for gain and glory." Others disagreed. Boxing is "evil," commented one editor. The Vatican called professional boxing morally wrong; the New York State legislature formed a committee to investigate the sport; on his television show "Open End," David Susskind called boxing "ugly." As never before, the nation debated the future of the sport.[27]

Although the cries to abolish boxing subsided, they arose again less than a year later when Sugar Ramos killed Davey Moore in a featherweight championship fight. The contest was not as dramatic as the Griffith-Paret match. Moore absorbed a frightful beating, but he walked to his dressing room after the referee stopped the fight, and he conversed and joked with reporters: "I was off. . . . Just like you writers, if you'd only admit it, can't write a lick some days. Well, that was me tonight. I just wasn't up to my best." A few seconds after the last reporter left his dressing room, Moore complained that his head "hurts something awful" and then collapsed into a coma. He died three days later. Again, the chorus of protests. California Governor Pat Brown called for the abolition of the "barbaric spectacle." Headlines in Paris newspapers and the Vatican's *L'Osservatore Romano* condemned the sport. Even Pope John XXIII denounced boxing as "contrary to natural principles."[28]

Boxing was on the ropes. Senate investigations indicated that criminals controlled the sport. The heavyweight champion was a former thug. Medical studies charged that boxing led to severe brain damage. Ring deaths called attention to the brutal and dangerous nature of the sport and raised questions about any society that permitted men to engage legally in such an activity. In the spring of 1964 David Brinkley focused one of his highly rated television specials on boxing's problems. "Many think boxing is an ugly brontosaurus that has somehow survived beyond its time," Brinkley commented. During the course of the NBC program, Brinkley left no doubt that he stood firmly on the side of those who believed that dinosaurs had no place in the modern world.[29]

Even before Brinkley's special aired, ABC executives had sensed that the winds of reform were sweeping across boxing. Two days before Christmas in 1963, the network announced that it did not plan to continue the "Fight of the Week" after the new season began in

September 1964. ABC based its decision on a number of factors. Ratings, as well as the quality of boxers, had declined in the early 1960s, and the sport's gangland ties were bad for ABC's corporate image. Although Gillette was not surprised by ABC's verdict, it deeply regretted the move. "Our own organization has been so well satisfied with televised boxing as an advertising medium that we wish we could form our own network to continue it, but I'm afraid that's impossible," a Gillette vice president said. On September 11, 1964, Dick Tiger defeated Don Fullmer in the last fight of the series. After twenty years on the air, Gillette's fight of the week passed into extinction.[30]

Another factor prompted ABC's decision to cancel its fight show, although no one at the network mentioned it publicly. A new concept had started to exert influence in the industry: demographics. Increasingly network executives had become concerned with not only how many people watched a particular show but also who those people were. They focused on the cutting edge of the baby boom. By 1965 almost 41 percent of the nation's population was nineteen years old or younger. As a group, adolescents and young adults watched more television than any other age sector, and they spent millions of dollars on the products advertised on television. Advertisers were not blind to this fact. In the 1960s television began to gear its programs to the tastes of young, affluent, white Americans. Westerns, so popular in the 1950s, never really appealed to teenagers or young adults, and the shows all but vanished from television by 1970. The most popular horse on television in the 1960s was Mr. Ed. Such youth-oriented programs as "My Favorite Martian," "The Addams Family," "The Munsters," "Batman," "Shindig," "Hullabaloo," "Laugh In," and the "Smothers Brothers Comedy Hour" replaced the westerns. In "Leave It to Beaver," "The Adventures of Ozzie and Harriet," and "The Many Loves of Dobie Gillis," youths became the centers of families, replacing adults as the focus of interest and the font of wisdom. Noting the change in the industry, the television critic Les Brown commented, "For the first time in history, popular culture is not being handed down to the younger generation but handed up by it."[31]

Boxing was crushed by the industry's stampede toward the youth market. The demographics of boxing were all wrong. It appealed to older men—World War II veterans, not baby boomers—often from working-class and ethnic backgrounds, men who had limited disposable income and limited education. For many network executives, the problem was not boxing's ratings, it was boxing's audience. Popular cartoons suggested the problem, usually portraying the fight fan as a fat, beer-swilling man in a sleeveless undershirt sitting in an overstuffed chair in the middle of an unattractive room. Since he was often in need of a shave and constantly drinking, he might have been a good target for Gillette or Pabst Blue Ribbon Beer, but judging from his appearance and that of his home, he was a lightweight consumer. Everything about the Gillette "Fight of the Week" series ran counter to ABC's increasingly youth-oriented programming, and by the early 1960s, ABC's new philosophy had begun to pay dividends. "Bewitched," "My Three Sons," "The Addams Family," "Peyton Place," and "Shindig" were solid successes. In addition, Roone Arledge's sports programming, led by "Wide World of Sports" and college football, appealed to better-educated, more affluent sports fans. ABC, like David Brinkley, had decided that boxing had become a dinosaur in the age of demographics.[32]

The Louisville Lip

Ironically, the very year that ABC abandoned boxing, the sport entered the age of demographics and took on a new youthful appearance. On February 25, 1964, Cassius Clay, barely twenty-two years old, defeated Sonny Liston and became the world heavyweight champion. He was young, brash, and unique. Unlike Liston, there was no prison time in Clay's past, no shady underworld ties or suspicious connections. He had won a gold medal in the 1960 Rome Olympics and was managed by the Louisville Sponsoring Group, a collection of white millionaires. From the first, the Louisville businessmen sold Clay as a product—the new, improved, fresher athlete, a cross between Beaver Cleaver, Eddie Haskell, and Ricky Nelson. He was perfect for the youth market—honest but irreverent, sincere but boastful. As one member of the Louisville Sponsoring Group admitted, "You know it doesn't hurt sales in the Negro market if some of Clay's sponsors happen to be strongly identified with—shall we say—consumer products."[33]

Clay was made for television, but during the early phase of his career ABC did not capitalize on his unique qualities. To be sure, ABC quickly realized the public's interest in Clay and televised several of his matches on the Gillette "Fight of the Week." Clay's eighth professional fight, a match against Alonzo Johnson on July 22, 1961, was the Gillette fight of the week. So was his ninth fight, an October 7, 1961, contest against Alex Miteff. In 1962 Clay fought both Sonny Banks and Billy Daniels on the Gillette "Fight of the Week." But all the fights were presented in the standard format, emphasizing only the action in the ring. Even in the early part of his career, Clay was an outstanding boxer, but what separated him from hundreds of other outstanding fighters was not what he did inside the ring. It was what he did before, after, and between fights.[34]

What Clay did best, what would eventually make him great TV, was talk. He boasted, he predicted, he lectured, he teased, he insulted, he flattered, he hectored, he did everything but keep quiet. In a sport known for its monosyllabic men, Clay—or the Louisville Lip, as he came to be known—was something new. Not since Jack Johnson—who would also have made great TV—had a fighter said so much and generated so much controversy. Clay's mouth made him the most famous boxer in the 1960 Olympics, and a year after he turned professional his mouth had made him one of America's most recognized personalities. Whether he was chatting with Johnny Carson on late-night television, reading poetry at The Bitter End in Greenwich Village, or predicting the round that he would knock out his next opponent, Clay's activities outside the ring kept him in the news. Before he became champion, before he became Muhammad Ali, before he became the center of political controversies, he was a telecelebrity. And as a telecelebrity, Clay attracted a new audience to boxing. One new fan wrote to a boxing magazine, "Before Cassius Clay came along, I wasn't a least bit interested in boxing. Now you can't keep me away from my TV set when the fights are on—and that goes for the other people I know."[35]

Clay's style outside the ring was a composite of black culture and television culture. As the historian Lawrence W. Levine has demonstrated, black culture is richly verbal. Urban blacks, in particular, develop the skills of ritualized insults. Generally called the Dozens— but sometimes known as Signifying, Sounding, Woofing, Screaming, Cutting, or Chopping—these ritualized insults "involved symmetrical joking relationships in which two or more people were free to insult each other and each other's ancestors and relatives either directly or indirectly." "Your mother so old she fart dust," might be an opening line in a Dozens battle. "Least my mother ain't no railroad track, lay all around the country," might come the counterinsult. Once started, the contest is limited only by the power of one's imagination and verbal invention. Bouts of the Dozens developed the participants' verbal skills and self-discipline, for to resort to physical violence was to transgress the rules of the ritual and to lose face. Only a person whose mental and verbal skills were exhausted would throw a punch.[36]

Clay introduced television and white culture to a sanitized version of the Dozens. His poetry, his insults, his predictions, and his string of one-liners were all variations of the Dozens, all forms of verbal combat. His poems toyed with the language. Before he fought Sonny Liston, Clay recited a poem in which he described how he would knock Liston into orbit. The "Ode to Sonny" ended: "Yes, the crowd did not dream when they laid down their money / That they would see a total eclipse of the Sonny." He also invented names for his opponents: Liston was the "Big Ugly Bear," Floyd Patterson the "Rabbit," Joe Frazier the "Gorilla." Always maintaining his cool, Clay insulted and taunted his opponents inside and outside the ring. Unfamiliar with black culture and the Dozens, many white Americans misinterpreted Clay's actions. "Maybe I'm old fashioned," one man wrote Boxing Illustrated, "but I always thought a fighter had to prove himself with his fists, not with his mouth." In Clay's world, a man had to prove himself with both. And Cassius Clay, soon to be Muhammad Ali, excelled at both.[37]

If Clay's verbal skills were a product of his black heritage, his use of them was influenced by television. He did not care how white Americans interpreted him, as long as they did not ignore him. He drew inspiration from professional wrestling. In June 1961, a month before his first Gillette fight of the week, he met Gorgeous George. Both men were in Las Vegas for matches. Both agreed to a joint radio interview. Never humble, Clay soon discovered that he was not in the wrestler's verbal league. Clay told the interviewer that he would win his upcoming fight. Gorgeous George not only predicted victory but promised in the loudest possible voice, "I'll kill him; I'll tear his arm off. If this bum beats me, I'll crawl across the ring and cut off my hair, but its not going to happen because I'm the greatest wrestler in the world." Listening to George talk was like a visit to the mountaintop for Clay. He had received the Word, and the Word was words, plenty of them, loud and often. As George prognosticated,

Clay thought, "Man, I want to see this fight. It doesn't matter if he wins or loses; I want to be there to see what happens." He was there—and so were thousands of other people. At that moment, Clay realized, "I'd never been shy about talking, but if I talked even more, there was no telling how much money people would pay to see me."[38]

After meeting Gorgeous George, Clay turned up the volume of his self-promotion and engaged in an ever-escalating campaign of outrageous stunts. "To beat me," he said, "you have to be greater than great." He was so great, he pronounced, that just to win was too simple a task. To make his fights more interesting, he started to write poems in which he predicted the round that the fight would end. In his second Gillette fight of the week, he announced that he would knock out Alex Miteff in the sixth round. Then he did it. Other predictions followed: Willie Besmanoff in seven and Sonny Banks in four. Both fights ended in the designated round. Even when he was wrong, his quick mind and agile tongue corrected the mistake. He predicted that he would knock out Don Warner in five rounds, but he finished the job in four. When reporters asked him why he was wrong, Clay said that Warner would not shake hands with him before the fight so he subtracted one round for poor sportsmanship. By mid-1962, Clay's predictions generated as much publicity as the fights themselves. Late in the year, he fought the legendary former light heavyweight champion Archie Moore, a boxer whose agility with words equalled Clay's. "Don't block the aisle and don't block the door," Clay said. "You will all go home after round four." Moore could match Clay in the battle of words outside the ring, but once the fight started it was no contest. Moore went in four.[39]

Clay's behavior helped to divert some of the public's attention away from the ring deaths, congressional investigations of boxing, and revelations about the sport's ties to organized crime. But his antics could not save the Gillette "Fight of the Week." Shortly after Clay defeated Liston for the heavyweight title in 1964, the series left the air. But ABC eventually realized that although it could survive quite well without a weekly fight, it had no interest in separating from Cassius Clay. No sooner did Clay win the title than he moved off the sports page and on to the front page. After the Liston fight, Clay announced that he had converted to the Nation of Islam and changed his name. He became Cassius X Clay—the X indicated his lost African identity—then Cassius X, and finally Muhammad Ali. His friendship with Malcolm X, the leading spokesman for the Nation of Islam, became public, and Floyd Patterson offered to fight Ali for free in order to "take the title from the Black Muslim leadership." Cassius Clay had been outrageous; Muhammad Ali was political. The combination was great TV.[40]

Six weeks after the closed-circuit Clay-Liston fight, ABC showed the fight to its television audience on "Wide World of Sports." It drew a 13.7 rating—the percentage of all television homes in America tuned into the program. For a Saturday afternoon telecast of a prerecorded event, a 13.7 rating is outstanding. The rating suggested that Ali had transcended boxing, that he could draw an audience even in a difficult time slot. This point was reinforced a few months later when John Vrba, president of a company that put together TV hookup deals for special events, attempted to use the success of the Clay-Liston broadcast to convince advertisers to buy television time for the Floyd Patterson–Eddie Machen heavyweight fight. Although Patterson and Machen were leading contenders, the fight generated no interest among companies that made razor blades, shaving cream, cigars, cigarettes, pipe tobacco, automobiles, tires, gasoline, and beer. "There's no advertising interest in boxing, not even in a big bout like this one," Vrba concluded. But Ali was an exception to the rule. ABC's delayed broadcast of the 1965 Ali-Liston rematch and the Ali-Patterson bout (fought in late 1965 but not shown on "Wide World of Sports" until early 1966) again drew outstanding ratings.[41]

Political controversy and personal problems dogged Ali during 1964 and 1965. His conversion to the Nation of Islam intensified the normal pressures that came with winning the heavyweight championship. He met, married, and divorced Sonji Roi. He toured Africa, cut back on his training, ate too much, and watched his weight balloon to 231 pounds. He fought with his father, who resented the Muslim influence in Ali's life. He suffered from an incarcerated inguinal hernia and had to undergo a seventy-minute emergency operation. During the entire period, the press hounded him, searching for faults and refusing to call him Muhammad Ali. The pressure was constant, and Ali was occasionally moody, often unable to decide who was his friend and who his enemy. Jack Olsen, a white journalist who wrote for *Sports Illustrated* and followed Ali during this period, remarked, "If there was an ugly period with Ali, that was it."[42]

In 1966, however, Ali's problems intensified. On February 17,

1966, a Louisville draft board changed Ali's draft status from 1-Y ("not qualified under current standards for service in the armed forces") to 1-A (available for the draft). The decision confused and angered Ali. It threatened his career and conflicted with his religious and political beliefs. Reporter after reporter asked Ali for his comments, and finally the anger and frustration boiled to the top and he said, "Man, I ain't got no quarrel with them Vietcong." That was it. A truthful but ill-considered, off-the-cuff comment and he suddenly found himself at the center of one of the most bitter domestic battles in American history. No longer did journalists consider Ali just a boxer. They transformed him into—or more accurately, accepted him as—a political spokesman, a symbol of the social, political, and racial discontent in America. In Ali, the black struggle for equality fused with the reaction against the war in Vietnam. Indeed, Ali became a lightning rod for all of those conservatives discontented with the drift of American culture. "Clay is part of the Beatle movement," complained sportswriter Jimmy Cannon. "He fits in with famous singers no one can hear and punks riding motorcycles with iron crosses pinned to their leather jackets and Batman and the boys with their long dirty hair and girls with the unwashed look and the college kids dancing naked at secret proms held in apartments and the revolt of students who get a check from dad every first of the month and the painters who copy the labels off soup cans and the surf bums who refuse to work and the whole pampered style-making cult of the bored young." In short, for the athletic and political establishment, Muhammad Ali was the enemy.[43]

The mid-1960s was a time of enemies—and of heroes. America was divided. An enemy in one camp was a hero in the other. In Vietnam, American soldiers died fighting the army of Ho Chi Minh, while on college campuses some students hung posters of Ho in their dorm rooms. Ali was a symbol of this divided America. For the media he was something more—he was money in the bank. Newspapers, magazines, and television closely followed his efforts to gain a draft exemption on the basis of his religious convictions. They carefully detailed the successful attempts to strip Ali of his world heavyweight crown and prevent him from practicing his profession in the United States. Actively anti-Ali, the print media helped to create a climate of opinion so hostile to the fighter that he had to leave the United

States to defend his title. The controversy, however, made Ali an even more desirable commodity for ABC.

When Ali left the United States, ABC went with him. The timing was perfect. ABC needed something new. The success of the early 1960s had ended and the network was floundering; new shows came and went with frightening speed. Eventually, the network's remarkable failure rate prompted Milton Berle to say, "If [the government] wanted to end the Vietnam War, they should have scheduled it on ABC. It would have ended in 13 weeks." Sports was the company's only major area of success. Here recent technological changes in the industry offered exciting new possibilities. In 1962 the United States government had launched Telstar I, a communication satellite, into orbit. More improved communication satellites followed. By 1964 the Syncom III satellite was able to relay the two-hour opening of the Tokyo Summer Olympic Games back to the United States for live broadcast. Finally, the launching of the Early Bird satellite in 1965 made live telecasts between Europe and the United States relatively simple. ABC Sports quickly began to use the satellite technology. "Wide World of Sports" televised a series of live shows from Europe. In mid-1966 Roone Arledge observed, "We are approaching an era when live coverage of a sports event in Frankfurt will be no more unusual than the live coverage of a game show in a New York City studio."[44]

In spring 1966, Ali ventured to Canada to defend his title against George Chuvalo, a Canadian heavyweight renowned not so much for his boxing ability as for his talent for absorbing punishment. Ali had originally been scheduled to fight Ernie Terrell in Chicago, but after his comments about the Vietnam War, pressure mounted on Illinois authorities to prohibit the bout. Illinois Attorney General William Clark readily complied. Other states followed Illinois's example, and many movie theaters originally interested in the planned closed-circuit telecast backed off from the promotion. When Terrell announced that he was no longer interested in fighting Ali, the champion's managers began their search for another challenger and another country. The quest ended in Canada. The owners of Toronto's Maple Leaf Gardens agreed to stage the Ali-Chuvalo bout.[45]

The Ali-Chuvalo fight was a dreary pugilistic and financial bust. Chuvalo demonstrated ample courage but won only two of the fifteen rounds. One reporter commented that by the end of the bout, Chuvalo's face looked "like it was made up of a number of driving-range golf balls." His best punches landed below Ali's belt, and the majority of his blows connected with nothing but air. Promoters also took a beating. Protests against the fight in the United States crippled the closed-circuit market. Bob Arum, whose recently formed Main Bout, Inc., held the ancillary rights to the fight, remarked that Ali "in the U.S. is a dead piece of merchandise. He's through as far as big-money closed-circuit is concerned. If we can, we'll try to put [Ali's next fight] on home TV. . . . If not, we'll forget about it. The money we made on this one certainly wasn't worth the effort."[46]

Success came late for the Ali-Chuvalo bout. Three days after it was over, ABC aired a delayed broadcast of the match. Rather than treat the fight as simply another mediocre heavyweight championship contest, ABC transformed it into a newsmaking pseudoevent. The bout itself took a backseat to the activities in ABC's New York studios, where Ali, teamed with Howard Cosell, proudly showed the metal cup, dented from repeated low blows, that he had worn during the Chuvalo fight. In addition, Cosell discussed the political controversy surrounding the match, recounting how and why Ali was forced to defend his title outside the United States. Instead of trying to avoid controversy, Cosell courted it. While not agreeing with Ali's politics, Cosell struck the classic liberal pose of the defender of the rights of any person who took an unpopular stand. Ali's stand, Cosell suggested, was between Ali, his draft board, and perhaps eventually the courts of the United States; no person or organization had the right to deny his rights without due process. Ali and Cosell's performance helped to revolutionize television sports. Stuck with a boring fight that had been decided three days before, they ignored the athletic dimension of the event and turned the show into a political forum.[47]

Like Ali, Cosell was a man of many words. After a brief legal career and a sideline as a radio commentator, Cosell had moved full time into entertainment in 1956 when ABC used his "Sports Focus" show as a summer replacement for "Kukla, Fran, and Ollie." On radio and on television Cosell was a professional New Yorker. His voice alone— a nasal twang—piqued those living south and west of New York City, and he delivered his controversial opinions in a relentless staccato. At a time when sports announcers labored to overcome any trace of a regional accent, avoid controversy, and soothe the ears of their listeners—an age symbolized by the styles of Curt Gowdy, Jim

McKay, and Chris Schenkel—Cosell spoke with provocative intent. More than anyone else, he was broadcasting's answer to Muhammad Ali—brash, confident, overbearing, and loud. Roone Arledge recognized that Ali and Cosell formed a perfect duo, and both Ali and Cosell realized that they were good for each other's careers.[48]

Arledge's problem, of course, was getting the product to the people. Before Ali's comments about the Vietnam War, ABC could not compete with the closed-circuit market for a live heavyweight championship fight. The most ABC could buy was the delayed broadcast rights. But the howls of protest that surrounded Ali's controversial stand changed the unwritten practices that governed heavyweight championship fights. First, the protests altered the closed-circuit market, which included the thousands of individually owned theaters in America. Many of the theater operators bowed to the political pressure; they were unwilling to risk a potential boycott of both closed-circuit broadcasts and their regular movie fare. Second, the protests forced Ali to take his championship outside the United States. In the previous half century, only two heavyweight championship fights had been contested outside the United States. But now the rules had changed, and ABC saw its chance to win at the new game.

After the Chuvalo fight, Ali's managers scheduled his next three title defenses in Europe. Bob Arum's Main Bout, Inc., sold ABC the live telecast rights to all three fights, which would be relayed back to the United States via the Early Bird satellite for broadcast on "Wide World of Sports." Each show was tailored to attract the largest possible audience. Arledge knew from his experience televising football that the genuine fan would watch regardless of how the show was produced. But to attract the casual viewer, Arledge would have to offer something more. With this in mind, each fight showcased the personalities of the fighters, the location of the bouts, and the political controversy that enveloped Ali. The fight itself was only a part of the program.[49]

The first show pitted Ali against Henry Cooper in London's Arsenal Stadium. Few experts doubted that Ali would easily defeat Cooper. Although the two had fought before and Cooper had even knocked down Ali, the British fighter was a bleeder. He could, noted one journalist, "cut himself putting on his cap." Plagued by thin skin, it was almost certain that within five or six rounds Ali's punches would so cut Cooper that the referee would be forced to stop the fight. With that grim prospect in mind, ABC planned a telecast that had a long introductory segment. Instead of the old "Fight of the Week" format of one announcer and a short lead into the fight itself, Arledge placed three men in the telecast booth: Chris Schenkel called the fight and Howard Cosell and former heavyweight champion Rocky Marciano served as color commentators. As a lead into the fight, ABC had taped a thirty-minute introduction set to Roger Miller's popular song "England Swings Like a Pendulum Do" that featured footage of Ali, in a formal cutaway, top hat, and cane, walking the streets of London. It also contained shots of Ali and Cooper training for the fight and touched on several of the controversies surrounding the contest. By exploring the fighters' personalities and the scene of the fight, the introduction satisfied Arledge's ideal of taking the fan to the contest.[50]

Telecasting live, however, created problems. Five minutes into the pretaped introductory film package, ABC faced a crisis. In the last preliminary fight before the Ali-Cooper contest, Jimmy Ellis knocked out Lewina Waga in the first round. British boxing officials then notified Ali and Cooper that they had two minutes to make their way into the ring for their fight. If the fighters followed the rules, Cosell later commented, ABC's program would have been "down the drain." Chet Forte, the show's producer, told Cosell that he had to do something—anything—to delay the start of the contest. Fighting through the crowd, Cosell made his way back to Ali's dressing room. Explaining ABC's problem to Ali, Cosell pleaded with the champion to save the show. "How much time do you need," Ali asked. "Eighteen minutes," Cosell answered. Inside the darkened Arsenal Stadium, the crowd waited impatiently for the fighters to enter the ring. They clapped and stamped their feet. "It was almost ghoulish, all of us waiting in this unlighted, outdoor stadium, like some kind of mass seance," Cosell recalled. The fight started eighteen minutes late but exactly as ABC had planned. Ali had saved the show.[51]

Ali also won the fight. In the sixth round he opened a deep gash over Cooper's left eye near the small artery at the temple. Blood splattered on both fighters, and Ali, who hated the sight of blood, looked stricken. "Blood scares me," he said after the fight. "I was more desperate than anyone else when I saw Cooper bleeding so badly. . . . I didn't want that cut no worser." The referee agreed and stopped the contest. As a fight, the Ali-Cooper contest was a disappointment. The ABC coverage of the fight, however, was outstanding and received a

17.5 rating. (By comparison, the typical "Wide World of Sports" program of today receives a 4 to 5 rating.) Arledge's "up-close-and-personal" philosophy translated perfectly into the ring.[52]

Two and a half months after the Cooper fight, Ali returned to London for another title defense. His opponent, Brian London, had even less of a chance than Cooper to win. But once again, it was the show, not the fight, that was important to Arledge and ABC Sports. This time the long introductory segment was set to Frank Sinatra's recording of "A Foggy Day in London Town." The song had nothing to do with the fight, but it did capture the popular image of a wet, romantic London. Ali dutifully posed for shots to accompany the piece and spoke the lines ABC required.

London, who did not have the same grasp of American television as Ali, was less cooperative. Cosell and production assistant Joe Aceti traveled to Blackpool to get footage of London training and to interview the fighter. Finding London was a major task; interviewing him was an ordeal. Cosell, trying to introduce the element of controversy that was his trademark and address the question of a mismatch directly, began his interview, "Brian, they say you're a patsy, a dirty fighter; that you have no class; that you're just in there for the ride and the fast payday; and that you have no chance against Ali. Now what do you say to that?" London thought for a moment and pithily replied, "Go fuck yourself!" "No, no, no," Aceti explained, "those really weren't Howard's descriptions of you—they were the opinions of others." "Oh, I see," London said. But he didn't. He ruined the second take by answering Cosell's objectionable question: "Whoever said that can go fuck themselves." After Aceti explained the limitations that American television placed on four-letter words, London tried again. On the third take, he listened to the now-familiar question, wet his lips, and slowly answered, "Well, then, the people who said that—not you, but the people who said that—can go to hell!"[53]

London fought no better than he talked. Ali knocked him out in the third round. After the fight, the champion was charitable: "It was a hard fight until I caught him." In truth, it was a one-sided affair from the opening round. Reporters suggested that the match should never have been made, and that it was more of an exhibition than a championship fight. The controversy, however, was not reflected in the television ratings. The bout scored an impressive 12.9 rating and dominated its time slot as surely as Ali had dominated London.[54]

Ali and ABC returned to Europe in September. This time Ali fought Karl Mildenberger in Frankfurt. Although the fight was more competitive, the show was similar to the previous two. It featured Ali, Cosell, location shots, interviews, controversy, and a supporting cast that included an unimportant challenger. And once again, a high rating—13.5—indicated the success of the show. A few days before the fight, Cosell teased Ali, "I *made* you. . . . Where would you be without all the shows, without 'Wide World of Sports,' without me doing your fights, without the interviews in the ring? Yes, I made you." Of course, Cosell was wrong, and he knew it. He owed much of the success of his career to Ali. But both men were indebted to Roone Arledge's vision of sports broadcasting.[55]

The Ali-Mildenberger fight was the first satellite sports telecast transmitted in color. That fact was singularly appropriate. Ali's grace, muscle, and wit, teamed with Cosell's mouth and Arledge's mind, had taken boxing from the drab black-and-white world of small-screen televisions and local bars to the age of color. To the winning "Wide World of Sports" formula of colorful personalities and exotic locations, Ali added an aura of controversy. The result pleased Ali, Arledge, ABC, and the sponsors of "Wide World of Sports." Political pressures and Ali's draft troubles, however, would soon curtail the champ's television career. After the Mildenberger fight, Ali did not fight a live television match for seven years. But Arledge and Cosell did not forget the reasons that Ali generated high ratings. In a few years, "Monday Night Football" would recycle the Ali formula without Ali's hard political edge.[56]

Notes

1. Eric Barnouw, *Tube of Plenty: The Evolution of American Television* (New York: Oxford University Press, 1990), 99.

2. Arthur Frank Wertheim, "The Rise and Fall of Milton Berle," in *American History/American Television: Interpreting the Video Past,* ed. John E. O'Connor (New York: Ungar, 1983), 55, 69.

3. J. Fred MacDonald, *One Nation under Television: The Rise and Decline of Network TV* (New York: Pantheon, 1990), 59–62; David Karp, "Television Shows Are Not *Supposed* to Be Good," *New York Times Magazine,* January 23, 1966, 9; Wertheim, "The Rise and Fall of Milton Berle," 56.

4. Karp, "Television Shows Are Not *Supposed* to Be Good," 9, 40.

5. Ibid., 40.

6. Randy Roberts and James Olson, *Winning Is the Only Thing: Sports in America since 1945* (Baltimore: Johns Hopkins University Press, 1989), 95–111. In this paragraph and several others, I have reworked ideas and materials that I covered in *Winning Is the Only Thing*.

7. Benjamin G. Rader, *In Its Own Image: How Television Has Transformed Sports* (New York: Free Press, 1984), 54–55.

8. A. J. Liebling, *The Sweet Science* (New York: Grove Press, 1956), 15–19.

9. Roberts and Olson, *Winning Is the Only Thing*, 98–99.

10. "The Bittersweet Marriage of Boxing and Television," *TV Boxing*, Fall/Winter 1980, 6–8; Roberts and Olson, *Winning Is the Only Thing*, 95, 103; Tim Brooks and Earle Marsh, *The Complete Directory to Prime Time Network TV Shows, 1946–Present* (New York: Ballantine, 1992), 112–14.

11. Dan Daniel, "Gone Is Source of 15 Million: TV Income Ends After 20 Years," *The Ring*, October 1964, 16–17, 44.

12. Don Dunphy, *Don Dunphy at Ringside* (New York: Henry Holt, 1988), 166; Fred Danzig, "Besieged, but Still No. 1 in Blades, Gillette Eyes Men's Toiletries Field," *Advertising Age*, December 30, 1963, 6, 45; "ABC Ruling May End Gillette's 20 Years of Fight Sponsorship," ibid., 45; "Still Like Boxing TV, Gillette Tells Madison Sq. Garden," ibid., February 24, 1964, 14; "ABC-TV Is Fixed for Blades," *Broadcasting*, March 21, 1960, 32.

13. Joe Williams, *TV Boxing Book* (New York: Van Nostrand, 1954), 1–11.

14. "The Bittersweet Marriage of Boxing and Television," 6; Roberts and Olson, *Winning Is the Only Thing*, 106; Rader, *In Its Own Image*, 45.

15. Williams, *TV Boxing Book*, 8–11.

16. Charles Einstein, "TV Slugs the Boxers," *Harper's Magazine*, August 1956, 65–66; Bert Randolph Sugar, *"The Thrill of Victory": The Inside Story of ABC Sports* (New York: Hawthorn Books, 1978), 3–33; Roberts and Olson, *Winning Is the Only Thing*, 107.

17. "Gillette's Future as TV Sports Sponsor Cloudy," *Advertising Age*, February 1, 1960, 28; Barnouw, *Tube of Plenty*, 243–46; Roberts and Olson, *Winning Is the Only Thing*, 95–96.

18. "ABC Is Fixed for Blades," 32; Sugar, *"The Thrill of Victory,"* 46–49.

19. Rader, *In Its Own Image*, 100–116; Sugar, *"The Thrill of Victory,"* 34–85.

20. "Playboy Interview: Roone Arledge," *Playboy*, October 1976, 63–64; Sugar, *"The Thrill of Victory,"* 61–85; Roberts and Olson, *Winning Is the Only Thing*, 113–31.

21. Roone Arledge and Gilbert Rogin, "It's Sport . . . It's Money . . . It's TV," *Sports Illustrated*, April 26, 1966, 94–106.

22. "Playboy Interview: Roone Arledge," 78; Arledge and Rogin, "It's Sport . . . It's Money . . . It's TV," 94.

23. Dunphy, *Don Dunphy at Ringside,* 145–46; Gilbert Rogin, "The Deadly Insult," *Sports Illustrated,* April 2, 1962, 12–15.

24. "The Same Old Story," *Sports Illustrated,* April 4, 1977, 15.

25. Dave Anderson, ed., *The Red Smith Reader* (New York: Random House, 1982), 307.

26. "Professional Boxing," Hearings Before the Subcommittee on Antitrust and Monopoly of the Committee on the Judiciary, United States Senate, Parts 1–4 (1960–64); Barney Nagler, *James Norris and the Decline of Boxing* (Indianapolis: Bobbs-Merrill, 1964); Steven A. Riess, "Only the Ring Was Square: Frankie Carbo and the Underworld Control of American Boxing," *International Journal of the History of Sport* 5 (1988): 29–52; Jeffrey T. Sammons, *Beyond the Ring: The Role of Boxing in American Society* (Urbana: University of Illinois Press, 1988), 130–83. The best coverage and many of the most thorough investigations of boxing during this period are to be found in *Sports Illustrated.*

27. Rogin, "The Deadly Insult," 12–15; idem, "Still a Sweet Science," ibid., April 9, 1962, 19; idem, "Boxing," ibid., April 16, 1962, 5.

28. Morton Sharnik, "Death of a Champion," *Sports Illustrated,* April 1, 1963, 19–21, 79–81.

29. "Brinkley vs. the Brontosaurus," *Sports Illustrated,* May 4, 1964, 16.

30. "ABC Ruling May End Gillette's 20 Years of Fight Sponsorship," *Advertising Age,* December 30, 1963, 45; "Still Like Boxing on TV, Gillette Tells Madison Sq. Garden," ibid., February 24, 1964, 14; "The Big Television Decision—What It Means to You," *Boxing Illustrated and Wrestling News,* March 1964, 31–33; "Nat Fleischer Speaks Out," *Ring,* April 1964, 5; "Nat Fleischer Speaks Out," ibid., September 1964, 5, 47; "The End of an Era in Garden Boxing," ibid., November 1964, 7–15.

31. MacDonald, *One Nation Under Television,* 170–71.

32. Sugar, *"The Thrill of Victory,"* 3–85.

33. Huston Horn, "The Eleven Men Behind Cassius Clay," *Sports Illustrated,* March 11, 1963, 62–70.

34. "TV Fight of the Year," *Boxing Illustrated and Wrestling News,* January 1962, 26–27; "TV Fights of the Week," ibid., February 1963, 28–29.

35. "The Readers' Corner," *Boxing Illustrated and Wrestling News,* May 1963, 3; "The Night They Filled the Garden," ibid., June 1963, 42–45.

36. Lawrence W. Levine, *Black Culture and Black Consciousness: Afro-American Folk Thought from Slavery to Freedom* (New York: Oxford University Press, 1977), 344–58.

37. Thomas Hauser, *Muhammad Ali: His Life and Times* (New York:

Simon and Schuster, 1991), 62; "The Readers' Corner," *Boxing Illustrated and Wrestling News*, May 1963, 3.

38. Hauser, *Muhammad Ali*, 38–39.

39. Alan Goldstein, "Moore in Four (correct) Liston in Eight (?)," *Boxing Illustrated and Wrestling News*, February 1963, 6–10; Hauser, *Muhammad Ali*, 48–50; Dunphy, *Don Dunphy at Ringside*, 163.

40. Hauser, *Muhammad Ali*, 102; Huston Horn, "The First Days in the New Life of the Champion of the World," *Sports Illustrated*, March 9, 1964, 26–27, 54–57; "The Black Muslim Hope," ibid., March 16, 1964, 8.

41. "Doesn't Anyone Want to See a TV Fight?" *Broadcasting*, June 29, 1964, 44.

42. Hauser, *Muhammad Ali*, 80–139.

43. Ibid., 142–45.

44. Sugar, *"The Thrill of Victory,"* 30–31; Barnouw, *Tube of Plenty*, 308–14; MacDonald, *One Nation Under Television*, 167.

45. Hauser, *Muhammad Ali*, 146–47.

46. Gilbert Rogin, "A Battle of the Lionhearted," *Sports Illustrated*, April 11, 1966, 32–37.

47. Howard Cosell, *Cosell* (New York: Pocket Books, 1973), 195–96.

48. Sugar, *"The Thrill of Victory,"* 182–83.

49. Edwin Shrake, "Ready for a Little Bloodletting," *Sports Illustrated*, May 23, 1966, 74–78.

50. Ibid., 78; Sugar, *"The Thrill of Victory,"* 187–88; Cosell, *Cosell*, 197–98.

51. Sugar, *"The Thrill of Victory,"* 188–89; Cosell, *Cosell*, 197–99.

52. Edwin Shrake, "Blood at the Arsenal," *Sports Illustrated*, May 30, 1966, 20–23. All ratings are provided as a courtesy of ABC Sports. Interview with Mark Mandel, September 15, 1992.

53. Sugar, *The Thrill of Victory*, 189–90; Cosell, *Cosell*, 203–5.

54. John Lovesey, "If Cassius Can't Punch, Then London Isn't Down," *Sports Illustrated*, August 15, 1966, 16–19.

55. Martin Kane, "A Muslim Ministers to a Southpaw," *Sports Illustrated*, September 19, 1966, 34–35, 114–15; Cosell, *Cosell*, 206–7.

56. Hauser, *Muhammad Ali*, 154.

3

Muhammad Ali and the Revolt of the Black Athlete

Othello Harris

During the summer of 1991, *Sports Illustrated* published a series of articles under the title "The Black Athlete Revisited." These essays were a sequel to the renowned five-part series on the black athlete written by Jack Olsen in 1968. The first article began by stating that "in the 23 years since SI's groundbreaking examination of blacks in sports, things have changed. But how much?"[1]

Some of the contributors to the new study (including journalists, academics, and professional athletes) argued that there has been substantial progress in the treatment of African American athletes; others claimed that there has been little or none. However, I think most would agree that African American athletes themselves have changed in the last few decades. For years Joe Louis and Jesse Owens were the embodiment of the black athlete; they were heroes to many whites and African Americans. Yet, today's black athlete is unlikely to remind one of either Louis or Owens. During the 1960s a transformation took place in the institution of sport that mirrored the changes occurring in the larger society. The sports world witnessed an unprecedented revolution as African Americans demanded that the athletic establishment accept a new black athlete. One of the leaders—perhaps the catalyst—of this conversion was Muhammad Ali.

Sports Heroes before the 1960s

Perhaps if athletes were mere performers or entertainers the effect of their exploits would be minimal. But elite athletes transcend their on-field performances. They sometimes influence opinions about important social and political issues such as drug use, sexual behavior, and even foreign policy. In some cases their performances off the field are more important than their athletic accomplishments. Major social movements or social changes have accompanied sports figures' actions.

Jack Johnson, the first black heavyweight champion, the most visible black athlete, and perhaps the most visible African American of his time, forced changes in white perceptions of black Americans in and out of the ring. Until Johnson's reign as the heavyweight champion many whites believed that African Americans lacked the physical and mental ability to compete in sports (although white boxers who had fought black boxers knew better). With the exception of the world champion bicyclist Major Taylor (who abandoned the United States for Europe), few black athletes competed against whites during Johnson's era.[2] Black jockeys were becoming extinct,[3] baseball had already excluded African Americans,[4] and other black boxers were relegated to fighting for the "colored championships."[5]

For many people, Jack Johnson was *the* black athlete. Despite his boxing accomplishments, Johnson was best known for his behavior away from sport. His flamboyance, and especially his penchant for being intimately acquainted with white women, so infuriated whites that race riots accompanied his victories over white boxers. Laws were passed in some states forbidding interracial marriages, allegedly in response to Johnson's betrothal to a white woman. When white America regained the title with Willard's defeat of Johnson in 1915, the boxing establishment was careful to prevent another African American—especially another Jack Johnson—from wearing the heavyweight crown. For over two decades, black boxers were blocked from competing for the title.

Jesse Owens and Joe Louis were the two most prominent black athletes in the generation after Jack Johnson. Owens's performance in the 1936 Olympics, where he won four gold medals, and Louis's long reign as the heavyweight champion led to a new appreciation of black athletes. If Johnson's victories allowed white Americans to think that African Americans, like whites, had the physical capacity for sport, Owens's and Louis's victories caused many to believe that African Americans were *better* suited for some sports than whites.[6]

While their athletic performances were important, Owens's and Louis's social conduct was crucial to their gaining opportunities, whether related to sport or not. In an effort to win the admiration of the American public, they were instructed to behave unlike Johnson. Whites, from journalists to politicians, counseled Louis and Owens to be race ambassadors. For example, before fighting Primo Carnera in 1934, Louis received a letter from the governor of Michigan that advised:

> Destiny seems to have pointed you for a high rank in pugilism. Your ability to overpower others by skill and physical force is something of which you may be proud. . . . You'll have world prominence and money. They will mean little, Joe, if you do not use them as God intended that gifts of Nature should be used. . . . Your race, at times in the past, has been misrepresented by others who thought they had reached the heights. . . . The qualities which may soon make you a world champion should call to the attention of people the world over, that the good in you can also be found in others of your race. . . . So Joe, you may soon have on your strong hands the job of representative-at-large of your people.[7]

Similarly, Owens, at a welcoming party following his four-gold-medal performance in Berlin, listened as the mayor of Cleveland, Harold H. Burton, declared: "We are proud of Jesse because he is a clean gentleman wherever he goes. It is indeed an honor to have had him as our representative at the Olympics in Germany. By his high character, his clean living and attention to duty, he has brought credit and honor to his Race, to this the greatest city of the world, to his alma mater, Ohio State, to our great commonwealth, to this country at large."[8] The black athlete of this era was expected to be humble, obsequious, nonthreatening, and tolerant of demeaning stereotypes and characterizations.

Louis and Owens appeared to accept readily the role of race ambassadors; they adhered to the prescribed patterns of behavior for African Americans. Both were careful not to offend whites or to "embarrass" black Americans. Moreover, the press became their ally in shaping an image that countered Jack Johnson's. Newspapers printed the rules for Louis's conduct that had been established by his manager, John Roxborough, which included the admonishment that the champion never have his picture taken with a white woman.[9] Even Louis's mother declared, "I know that if Joe wins the championship he is going to make Jack [Johnson] feel ashamed of himself again."[10]

The behavior of Owens and Louis was considered unassailable, and it had social consequences. Each man was called "a credit to his race," which was thought to be the ultimate compliment a white could pay an African American. Many people, African American and white, have stated that the way Owens and Louis carried themselves opened doors for other blacks in sports and in the larger society. In 1946 when Jackie Robinson was chosen to break the color line in baseball, he was told that to emulate Joe Louis would be good for him and "the race." Countless others, including Muhammad Ali, were told or expected to do the same.

Clay/Ali as Role Model

For the young boxer Cassius Clay, Joe Louis was an idol. The press initially portrayed Clay as patriotic, as they had Louis. Clay told a Russian reporter at the 1960 Olympic Games, where he won a gold medal, that the "U.S.A. is the best country in the world, including yours." When reminded of racial inequality in America, he said, "Tell your readers we got qualified people working on that, and I'm not worried about the outcome." Reporters even compared Clay's comportment to Louis's, and Clay told an interviewer, "You know I'll be a credit to my race."[11] The mayor of Louisville, Kentucky, Clay's hometown, considered him a model for all youth: "If all young people could handle themselves as well as he does, we wouldn't have juvenile problems."[12]

But Clay was different from Louis. Louis was compliant, Clay was brash. As a boxer, Louis was quiet and workmanlike; he let his "fists do the talking." By contrast, Clay was loquacious; his prefight routine included reciting his own brand of poetry, which often demeaned his opponents, and predicted, with remarkable accuracy, the round of their defeat. Following a victory, Louis left the ring with his head bowed, seemingly embarrassed to have rendered an opponent helpless. But Clay stood over fallen rivals, taunting, dancing, and daring them to do battle with him.

Despite his dissimilarity to Louis, Clay was accepted by many and well liked by some, until he made an announcement that alarmed the boxing community. Two days after his defeat of Sonny Liston for the heavyweight championship, he informed the press that he had joined the Nation of Islam, a religious group headed by Elijah Muhammad. He later revealed he had dropped his "slave name," Cassius Clay, in favor of an Islamic name, Muhammad Ali.[13]

The Nation of Islam was a group hated and feared by many whites and some African Americans. Members believed that evil and destruction were the work of whites, as whites were inherently wicked; integration was undesirable; and God was a black man—all radical pronouncements in the 1960s. Detractors branded the Nation of Islam a hate group, an organization out of step with a country that was moving toward integration. The press denounced Ali's actions and others followed suit. Joe Louis considered Ali's conversion unacceptable. The former boxing champion Floyd Patterson declared "the Black Muslims" (as the Nation of Islam was commonly called) a menace to the United States and to "the Negro race." He further intoned, "The image of a Black Muslim as the world heavyweight champion disgraces the sport and the nation," and he promised to return the title to (Christian) America.[14]

The Nation of Islam and its supporters argued that they preached self-reliance and infused African Americans with black pride. Their goal was to break the mental chains that held blacks in bondage. Whites, they believed, would never grant true equality to people of color, making the quest for integration impractical.

Disillusionment with Ali, prompted by his association with the Nation of Islam, later turned to outrage when he declined to participate in the Vietnam War. In 1966 Ali's draft status was changed from 1-Y (not qualified for military service) to 1-A (qualified). When his request for conscientious objector status (on religious grounds) was denied, Ali maintained his position—he would not serve in the armed forces.

Following his refusal to be inducted into the service, the press and public turned against him. Ali was stripped of his title; his boxing career was, effectively, terminated. He was now considered to be unpatriotic, ungrateful, and a dangerous role model. On the last score the press and public were correct, at least in part; Ali did become a role model to many youths—athletes and nonathletes. He also ushered in the era of the new black athlete. Many of the changes in the sports world in the 1960s can be traced to his resistance to the sports establishment. Other black athletes would challenge the system much like he did.

A combination of factors placed Ali in a position to influence black athletes. First, he was visible. Ali was the heavyweight champion of the world—one of the most prominent positions in sport. Indeed, with his talent for getting media attention he was perhaps the most conspicuous athlete of all time.

Ali was also outspoken. There were many sportswriters, newspaper columnists, politicians, and others who disagreed with his anti-war position. Rather than go into hiding he confronted his adversaries. He was unwavering in his refusal to participate in the war, even when advised that he would not see action in Vietnam, that his role would be, like Louis's in World War II, that of a morale booster.

And, finally, Ali exhibited black pride. His religion, the Nation of Islam, taught that blacks were not *inferior* to whites; rather they were *superior* to them. Instead of praying to and "preaching" about a white God, Muslims believed that God was black, so being black was something to be proud of rather than something to apologize for. At a time when many African Americans were marching, protesting, and otherwise demonstrating to integrate nearly all-white facilities and institutions, these pronouncements were radical.

Ali's troubles with the government—the sentence for violating Selective Service laws and the lifting of his boxing license by states—were closely followed by many African Americans, both in and out of the sports world. To them he was an example of how black athletes are used by the system and discarded. He became an inspiration for the rebellion of the black athlete.

Black Athletes in the 1960s

Even as the heavyweight champion of the world, Ali was not immune to racism; he faced segregation in nearly all areas of his life away from the boxing ring, especially in the South. Ironically, many of his sympathizers, such as those white members of the press who admired Ali, participated in the Jim Crow system that victimized him. After interviewing Ali, or covering his fights, reporters retired to hotels and restaurants that were off-limits to their subject.[15] Perhaps unwittingly, those who patronized "whites-only" establishments helped to sustain the system of American apartheid. Of course, black exclusion from public accommodations was not unique to Ali. African Americans in college sport, although lauded by fans, found that their treatment mirrored Ali's.

For years black and white athletes had performed as a unit on the field but were treated differently before and after the games. In the 1930s and 1940s most African American collegiate athletes found

campus housing was denied them; they were refused service in restaurants and they were not allowed to stay at hotels with their white
teammates (not just in the South, but also in northern cities such as
Chicago and Buffalo). Perhaps most humiliating was the practice of
keeping black players out of games against southern teams. Southern custom required that teams with black players be gracious guests
by not fielding their African American players. On the other hand,
when northern teams played at home they were expected to be gracious hosts and, again, keep black players out of games against southern teams.[16] The first African American to play against a southern
college in this century was Harvard's Charles Pierce, who participated in a game against the University of Virginia in 1947.[17] Before him,
black players sat and watched (if they were able to attend the game
at all) while their teammates and fans acted as if nothing was amiss.

By the 1960s it was not uncommon to see black players competing
against, and sometimes for, southern schools, although some teams
and states held fast in their segregation practices.[18] But many of the
discriminatory practices continued, and others commenced. During
the sixties, African American athletes complained that they were denied service in restaurants, that they were forbidden to use the front
entrance in some hotels,[19] and that they were kept apart from teammates when traveling with the team.[20] Charges were also leveled
against coaches for restricting or curtailing social activities such as
interracial dating. And, black athletes had to endure coaches', players',
and sports administrators' derogatory, sometimes abusive, language.
In short, African American athletes were frequently demeaned by the
comments and stereotypes of whites associated with their teams.

While black athletes of earlier decades were inclined to ignore or
privately complain about their treatment, black athletes in the sixties began to confront racial injustice. Accommodationists were on
their way out. A new black athlete was evolving, one who, like Ali,
was assertive, defiant, proud of his or her blackness, and willing to
sacrifice athletic rewards and profits to maintain dignity.[21] The sports
world would be permanently altered.

Exploitation

If one question came to dominate discussions about the treatment
of black athletes in America, especially black collegiate athletes, it was

whether African Americans were exploited for their athletic ability. Many argued that African Americans were indebted to sport for providing opportunities to succeed that were absent in most other societal institutions. From this point of view the sports world was due praise, not admonishment, for its conduct toward African Americans; it had taken many men and a few women out of the "ghettoes" and afforded them a chance for upward mobility.

George McCarty, athletic director at the University of Texas at El Paso (UTEP), undoubtedly had this in mind when he said: "In general, the nigger athlete is a little hungrier, and we have been blessed with having some real outstanding ones. We think they've done a lot for us, and we think we've done a lot for them."[22] The assistant athletic director at UTEP, in defending his program and McCarty, said: "This was the first institution in Texas—right here—that had a colored athlete, and George McCarty, our athletic director, was the coach who recruited him."[23] In return for their "benevolence" toward African Americans, sports administrators, coaches, and fans expected homage. Blacks who did not exhibit the proper amount of deference found themselves under attack from whites.

For example, when Elvin Hayes, star basketball player at the University of Houston, turned down an opportunity to play for the Houston Mavericks (ABA), electing instead to play for the San Diego Rockets (NBA), he was considered to be an "uppity nigger" by University of Houston fans. *Sports Illustrated* reported that a cab driver said of Hayes, "I used to think he knew his place, but now he is acting like one of your smart-ass Northern jigs." "He should be more grateful to the people who made him," said a reporter, "he *was* a credit to his race" (emphasis mine).[24] Obviously this reporter felt sport, and more specifically, the University of Houston basketball program, *made* Elvin Hayes.

The other point of view in the debate about the exploitation of black athletes was that sport had provided insufficient opportunities for the advancement of African Americans. Black athletes were alienated; they found few activities on or off campus that were open to them, and, for many, educational experiences were almost nonexistent. Furthermore, professional sport aspirations were, for most, unrealized.[25] To quote the sociologist Harry Edwards, black athletes began to understand that, once their athletic abilities are impaired by age or injury, only the ghetto beckons and they are doomed once again to that faceless, hopeless, ignominious existence they had supposedly forever left behind. At the end of their athletic career, black athletes do not become congressmen, as did Bob Mathias, the white former Olympic decathlon champion, or Wilmer Mizell, ex–Pittsburgh Pirate pitcher. Neither does the black athlete cash in on the thousands of dollars to be had from endorsements, either during his professional career or after he retires.[26]

Like other African Americans, black athletes faced discrimination everywhere except on the playing field (and sometimes there). Their response was to challenge the system. Of course, protest was not new in the 1960s; in 1968 there were protests against American involvement in the Vietnam War, demonstrations for civil rights, a Poor People's March led by Dr. Martin Luther King, Jr., and similar events. But athletes seldom had been leaders or even participants in the fight for social change. The black athletes of the 1960s were different; they would take a stand. They would fight injustice for other athletes and for the black community. Although the black collegiate athlete used different methods, he or she had in mind the same goals as Ali—the elevation of the status of all African Americans.

Perhaps the first victory in the black collegiate athlete's struggle for equality was the forced cancellation of a football game between San Jose State University (SJSU) and the University of Texas at El Paso in 1967. Harry Edwards and others had demanded a chance to discuss their grievances about racism at SJSU with the school president. When they were ignored, a rally was held where conditions for eradicating injustice were set out; it was announced that the first home football game of the season would be disrupted if those conditions were not acted upon. The administration took the threats of danger seriously and would not allow the game to be played. (The rumor that the football stadium would be burned to the ground if the teams attempted to play probably had something to do with the administration's decision to cancel the game.) Black students—athletes and nonathletes—realized the power of the new weapon they had unleashed against racism. The movement spread to other colleges around the country.

By the end of 1967 sentiment had begun to build for a black athletes' boycott of the 1968 Olympics. The list of demands included the expulsion of South Africa and Rhodesia from the games (because of their apartheid policies), the appointment of blacks to the Olympic team's coaching staff and the United States Olympic Committee, and the resignation of the International Olympic Committee chairman, Avery Brundage (who was widely believed to be racist and anti-Semitic). However, the number-one demand was the restoration of Muhammad Ali's title and boxing licenses, which had been taken away when he refused to be inducted into the armed forces. According to Harry Edwards:

> Ali is probably the single greatest athletic figure of this century in terms of the black community, largely because he turned around the image of the black athlete. . . . [During the 1960s] our legitimacy and access were pretty much on track, but we were still struggling for dignity and respect from the sports mainstream and American society. The principals in that struggle were people like Tommie Smith, John Carlos, and Arthur Ashe. But the greatest figure in that regard was Muhammad Ali. And because of the impact of sports on American society, there was a carryover of dignity and pride from Ali's efforts that accrued to all black Americans.[27]

The Olympic Boycott

In December 1967 the Olympic Boycott for Human Rights (OBHR) claimed that black athletes who had attended the Black Youth Conference in Los Angeles had agreed unanimously to boycott the 1968 Olympic Games; many of them were prominent college athletes. However, by the summer of 1968, the ranks of those committed to the boycott had declined precipitously. Edwards attributed this to the fact that 1968 was an election year and there were numerous other protests—antiwar, civil rights, and the Poor People's March—vying for media coverage.[28] With the media downplaying the proposed boycott, support began to dissipate.

Another reason for the diminishing interest in a boycott among athletes was that many had worked for years to position themselves for a try at a gold medal. For a number of them, participation in the Olympic Games was the pinnacle of their athletic life, especially in track and field, where no "professional" opportunities awaited them. Still, a few athletes—including Lew Alcindor (now Kareem Abdul-Jabbar), Elvin Hayes, and Mike Warren, all considered to be among the top collegiate basketball players—decided to reject invitations to participate in the games.

There was, in the end, no organized boycott of the Olympic Games. Black athletes were encouraged to protest individually America's treatment of people of color, and some of the more courageous did just that. Most memorable were Tommie Smith and John Carlos, who each raised a black-gloved clenched fist in a "black power" salute as they stood on the victory stand after the 200 meter dash. Their gesture prompted a stream of hate mail but also engendered feelings of pride in many African Americans. The boycott was not successful but the black athletic revolt had begun. As Arthur Ashe remembered, Ali was at the forefront of the movement:

> I really believe that, if Ali hadn't done what he did [joining the Nation of Islam, speaking out for black pride, opposing the war], Harry Edwards wouldn't have gotten a fraction of the support he got in 1968 to boycott the Mexico City Olympics. Tommie Smith and John Carlos wouldn't have raised their fists. Ali had to be on their minds. He was largely responsible for it becoming an expected part of the black athlete's responsibility to get involved. He had more at stake than any of us. He put it all on the line for what he believed in. And if Ali did that, who were the rest of us lesser athlete mortals not to do it? I know, he certainly influenced me later in 1967 when the Davis Cup draw came up and lo and behold, the United States was supposed to meet South Africa in the third round. . . . There's no question that Ali's sacrifice was in the forefront of my mind.[29]

In upholding his beliefs, Ali was willing to give up the rewards that accrue to a heavyweight champion. The Nation of Islam's position was that believers were forbidden to participate in wars alongside nonbelievers. As Ali stated, "We are not, according to the Holy Qur'an, to even as much as aid in passing a cup of water to the wounded."[30] His adherence to religious teachings resulted in the loss of his heavyweight title, a three-and-a-half-year expulsion from professional boxing, and the forfeiture of movie, record, and product endorsement contracts.[31] Other black athletes who considered embracing an antiestablishment position could expect a similar fate.

When Smith and Carlos raised their fists during the playing of the national anthem they put the sports world on notice that black athletes would fight injustice no matter the price. They had been warned of serious reprisals against those participating in demonstrations, and they knew the penalty for insubordination would be severe. After all, there had been precedents. Black athletes at colleges such as the University of California at Berkeley, the University of Texas at El Paso, and Oklahoma City University had been suspended from teams and even lost their athletic scholarships because they boycotted games or practices. Other athletes, even at Ivy League schools such as Princeton, quit teams rather than submit to mistreatment and exploitation.[32] The president of UTEP said of black athletes who refused to compete against Brigham Young University because of the Mormon doctrine of black inferiority: "A whole lot of pushing has been done by Negroes, and that pushing is going to hasten the day when your Negro comes close to equality. But I think in this case they paid a hell of a price to win their point. . . . This is a price that no college athletes in this country have ever yet paid for a point on this issue. They were laying down their collegiate athletic lives, and they surely knew it."[33]

Smith and Carlos were also laying down *their* athletic lives. They knew that their actions would be condemned by the press and that their participation in professional sport would be curtailed. For their actions the two athletes were suspended from the Olympic team, expelled from the games and from Mexico, and banished from further amateur competition for life.[34] On the other hand, demonstrations such as George Foreman's—he proudly waved the American flag after his victorious heavyweight bout for the gold medal—were praised by the Olympic Committee and Americans. Foreman, in part because of his display, was considered one of the heroes of the games and was warmly received by Americans when he returned home. Smith and Carlos were not so fortunate.

Tommie Smith had been drafted by a professional football team, the Los Angeles Rams, but to maintain his amateur athletic status as an Olympian he wasn't permitted to sign a professional contract until after the games. Following his gesture at the games, professional teams avoided him. He managed to play on the Cincinnati Bengals' taxi squad for three years, but he likely sacrificed his professional sport opportunities and salary by his actions at the Olympics. Carlos also found no professional sport offers awaiting him, even though he and Smith were now considered two of the fastest men in America. However, Jim Hines, who won a gold medal in the 100 meter dash and made no gesture, signed a professional football contract after the games. "Good behavior" was rewarded by the sports establishment.

A New Black Athlete

From the turbulence of the 1960s, from the struggles of Ali, Smith and Carlos, and other black collegiate and professional athletes, a new black athlete emerged. This athlete came to resemble Ali more than Louis or Owens. Perhaps it was merely a sign of the changing times—that African Americans were becoming more assertive, more likely to challenge the existing social order, because this was an age of assertiveness and challenges to the system. However, I would argue that Ali, more than the athletes who preceded him (with the possible exception of Jack Johnson), *shaped* rather than simply reflected the times.

Like Johnson, Ali was a rebel, but a very different kind of rebel. While Johnson was hated, in part, because of his penchant for white women, fine clothes, partying, and drinking, Ali did not flout conventional morality—at least not in such conventional ways. Rather, Ali was unpopular because of his association with a militant black organization, the Nation of Islam, and his position on a number of issues, including the Vietnam War. In a society that was moving, perhaps reluctantly, toward integration, he was comfortable with separation—but he endorsed racial separation in the name of autonomous black power.

Whereas Louis and Owens fit neatly into the social space allotted to African Americans, Ali went beyond white limits of acceptability in his beliefs and behavior. Pride in his blackness was taken as a sign of arrogance, and his embrace of Islam and his name change were interpreted as indications of contempt for whites, both serious indictments for an African American in the 1960s. More than anyone else, Ali made sports into contested political ground for blacks, and athletes who followed would find it easier to challenge the sports establishment. As Kareem Abdul-Jabbar stated: "He gave so many people courage to test the system. A lot of us didn't think he could do it, but he did and succeeded every time. . . . there's no doubt in my mind the public acceptance of what I did was greater because Muhammad lay the groundwork before me. He was, and is, one of my heroes."[35] While the problems of discrimination, social isolation, academic neglect, and ill-treatment by coaches and others didn't disappear during the sixties and seventies, African American athletes were more inclined to confront coaches and administrators than they had been in earlier years. They knew their services were needed; some of their demands had to be met.

In the struggle against injustice in America, black athletes were not without a role model. Ali was a shining example to them. As Edwards says in *The Revolt of the Black Athlete:*

> Special mention is due to Muhammad Ali. For in a very real sense he is the saint of this revolution in sports. He rebelled at a time when he, as an athlete, stood alone. He lost almost everything of value to any athlete—his prestige, his income, and his title. But he maintained and enhanced the most crucial factor in the minds of black people everywhere—black dignity. . . . Young blacks and old revere him as a champion in the struggle for black liberation. . . . for a significant proportion of people—black people in particular—he is still champion and the warrior saint in the revolt of the black athlete in America.[36]

Muhammad Ali continues to influence contemporary athletes. Perhaps they don't think of Ali as they challenge the sports world's coveting of the accommodating and docile athlete. But he has made it acceptable for today's athletes to be more assertive and less concerned about humility. Ali paved the way for the new black athlete.

Notes

1. William Oscar Johnson, "The Black Athlete Revisited: How Far Have We Come?" *Sports Illustrated,* August 5, 1991, 38–41.

2. Andrew Ritchie, *Major Taylor: The Extraordinary Career of a Champion Bicycle Racer* (San Francisco: Bicycle Books, 1988).

3. Frederic C. Jaher, "White America Views Jack Johnson, Joe Louis, and Muhammad Ali," in *Sport in America: New Historical Perspectives,* ed. Donald Spivey (Westport, Conn.: Greenwood Press, 1985), 239–62.

4. Robert Peterson, *Only the Ball Was White* (N.Y.: McGraw-Hill, 1970).

5. A few black boxers in the lower weight categories were able to compete against whites for titles near the turn of the century (e.g., George "Little Chocolate" Dixon, Joe Walcott, and Joe Gans). However, most athletic events forbade interracial competition. (See Elliott J. Gorn, *The Manly Art: Bare-knuckle Prize Fighting in America* [Ithaca, N.Y.: Cornell University Press, 1986].)

6. This notion of black athletic superiority, which few believed in before Johnson's reign, continues to flourish today. It is apparent when

sports announcers analyze the feats of black athletes in physical terms (e.g., "he's a 'natural' athlete") and those of white athletes in cerebral terms (e.g., "he doesn't have the physical skills, but he more than makes up for it with his knowledge of the game"). Seventy or eighty years ago, most believed in black athletic *inferiority*. Owens and Louis helped to change this perception.

7. Chris Mead, *Champion: Joe Louis, Black Hero in White America* (New York: Penguin Books, 1985), 56.

8. William J. Baker, *Jesse Owens: American Life* (New York: Free Press, 1986),125.

9. Mead, *Champion,* 52.

10. Jaher, "White America Views," 161.

11. Robert Lipsyte, *Sportsworld: An American Dreamland* (New York: Quandrangle Books, 1975).

12. Jaher, "White America Views," 169.

13. Thomas Hauser, *Muhammad Ali: His Life and Times* (New York: Simon and Schuster, 1991), 102.

14. Ibid., 139

15. See Hauser, *Muhammad Ali,* 54, for examples of acquiescence to Jim Crow practices by whites who associated with Ali.

16. See my "African American Predominance in Sport," in *Racism in College Athletics,* ed. D. Brooks and R. Althouse (Morgantown, W.Va.: Fitness Information Technology Press, 1993), 53–54.

17. Art Rust, Jr., and Edna Rust, *Art Rust's Illustrated History of the Black Athlete* (Garden City, N.Y.: Doubleday, 1985), 240.

18. Mississippi was slower than most other states to desegregate athletics. Mississippi State University sat out the NCAA basketball tournament in 1959 and 1961 rather than play against black athletes. Similarly, the University of Mississippi's football team decided against participating in a bowl game in 1961 to avoid an integrated contest. Today, the basketball and football teams at both universities are like those at many southern schools—predominantly black. In 1992 Mississippi State University hired an African American head basketball coach.

19. Even in places like New York City, for prestigious events like the New York Athletic Club track meet, black athletes complained of having to use the freight elevator.

20. During a trip to Texas in 1959, Oscar Robertson, the star of the University of Cincinnati's basketball team, had to stay at a black college, while the rest of the team stayed in Houston.

21. I am not arguing that all or even most black athletes exhibited these characteristics. What was striking, however, was the number of athletes who took on these characteristics in an institution that has long

been regarded as being very conservative. That a large number of prominent athletes were at odds with the owners and managers of sports institutions made noncompliance more acceptable.

22. Jack Olsen, "The Black Athlete: A Shameful Story; Part 1, The Cruel Deception," *Sports Illustrated,* July 1, 1968, 15. As an interesting aside, when African Americans complained about McCarty's use of the term "nigger," he said that because of his southern upbringing he couldn't say (pronounce) "Negro" and he couldn't remember to say "colored."

23. Jack Olsen, "The Black Athlete: A Shameful Story; Part 3, In an Alien World," *Sports Illustrated,* July 15, 1968, 30.

24. Ibid., 20.

25. Stacking—the practice of having black athletes compete against each other for the same position, such as running back or wide receiver, thereby reserving other positions for whites—and team quotas for black players limited the number of openings in professional sport for African Americans.

26. Harry Edwards, *The Revolt of the Black Athlete* (New York: Free Press, 1969), xxvii.

27. Hauser, *Muhammad Ali,* 449.

28. Harry Edwards, *The Struggle That Must Be* (New York: Macmillan, 1980).

29. Hauser, *Muhammad Ali,* 205.

30. Ibid., 155.

31. Lipsyte, *Sportsworld,* 91.

32. Edwards, *Revolt of the Black Athlete,* Appendix B, 144–62.

33. Olsen, "In an Alien World," 42.

34. Edwards, *The Struggle That Must Be,* 204.

35. Hauser, *Muhammad Ali,* 178.

36. Edwards, *Revolt of the Black Athlete,* 89–90.

4

Some Preposterous Propositions from the Heroic Life of Muhammad Ali: A Reading of *The Greatest: My Own Story*

Gerald Early

> The scenes I have in mind are ones of violence, specifical-
> ly ones of preposterous violence. By "preposterous" I mean
> so exaggerated that most of the audience know full well
> that what they are watching is make-believe. The scenes are
> caricatures—often literally cartoons—of recognizable se-
> quences. By "violence" I mean more than a force directed
> against an object. . . . I mean a force directed against a vic-
> tim, usually a specific human being.
>
> —James B. Twitchell, *Preposterous Violence*

There is no more suspect literary genre in America than the autobiography: always self-serving, often falsified, and more than likely a
wretched piece of writing in the bargain—a form, a skeptic might say,
that confesses all while telling nothing. The autobiography stands
as a kind of amalgam of the cunning of the mountebank and the
faltering of the do-it-yourselfer. It can blend the patently false with
the scathingly true. Nowadays, especially, one is forced to ask if it is
a literary genre or a pop culture device for self-advertisement.

Of all literary genres, it is the autobiography that seems most richly
and strikingly American, offering as it does three features that are
endemic to the American national character: private confession as
public narrative; the invention or reinvention of the self; and personal history as salvation dramaturgy. Most of all, the autobiography
is democratic; anybody can write one, as long as one is famous
enough to justify its publication (and even fame or notoriety is not
a prerequisite for writing an autobiography). The genre is open equal-

ly to the canaille and to the elite, to the hoi polloi and to the intelligentsia. It is the only literary genre that is opened, without question, to the nonliterary.

All of these features have made the autobiography a particularly attractive and endearing literary form to African Americans, a people who have been, historically, especially interested in confessing the nature of their lives, reformulating their identities, and demonstrating the course of salvation history as providing a teleological meaning for their oppression. The slave narrative, a form of autobiography popular from 1830 to 1860, is the genesis of African American letters in the United States. It formally complicated the American autobiography by making it explicitly political (and subversive) literature while serving the conventional forms and practices of bourgeois morality. Because of the peculiar cultural tensions that are both expressed and resolved by the way that blacks have structured autobiography to serve them, and because of the historical weight given in the collective black imagination to autobiography as the expression of freedom and protest, this literary genre is probably even more attractive to African Americans than to other Americans.[1]

In this essay I will consider autobiography as the conjunction of African American political and personal expression and pop culture self-advertisement. Naturally, black American autobiography, like its white counterpart, has become a convenient genre for the famous in popular culture. However, autobiographies of figures in popular culture serve less as assessments of careers in the limelight than as ratification of celebrity status. This essay will look at the autobiography of Muhammad Ali, *The Greatest: My Own Story* (New York: Random House, 1975), as a literary and self-consciously political construct. I intend to take seriously, in other words, a work that has been undeservedly dismissed.

Probably the most famous athlete of his time, black or white, and debatably the most famous American of his era, Ali was not unique as a black or as a boxer in writing his autobiography. Virtually every noteworthy fighter from John L. Sullivan and James J. Corbett to Floyd Patterson and Henry Armstrong has written an autobiography, partly to cash in on his fame, partly to show the world that he was not simply a brute but a thoughtful man who considered boxing an honorable profession. I will examine Ali's autobiography, not as a true or "authentic" picture of the fighter, but as a tactical or strategic representation of his politics and his political image as America's most famous, most fanciful, most physically striking, and most "far-fetched" dissident. Particularly important here, Ali's autobiography addresses the political meaning of black masculinity, a natural obsession for a black prizefighter, the most perverse and the most telling symbol of the masculine-as-performance in American culture.

First, a word about the truth or biographical accuracy of the autobiography: In his oral history *Muhammad Ali: His Life and Times,* Thomas Hauser provides a disclaimer of *The Greatest:*

> In 1976, Random House had published the Ali "autobiography," written by Richard Durham. Given Ali's popularity, the book had enormous potential but it was plagued by problems from the start. Ali was uninterested in the project, and spent relatively little time with Durham. Indeed, he never read his "autobiography" until after it was published. Moreover, even though Durham was an editor for *Muhammad Speaks,* before any material was submitted to Random House, each page had to be approved and initialed by Herbert Muhammad.[2]

Hauser does not mention the fact that Toni Morrison was the editor of *The Greatest.* Moreover, he gives little account of Richard Durham himself, a man of considerable interest in his own right as the long-time Marxist-oriented editor (he was not a Muslim) of *Muhammad Speaks.*[3] Generally, I think Hauser's comments about *The Greatest* can be dismissed as inaccurate, perhaps even self-serving, as, after all, his book was meant to supplant it. Morrison constructed *The Greatest* from a box of audio tapes that Durham supplied. He taped an enormous number of conversations that Ali had with a number of people. Naturally, Herbert Muhammad approved the final product. (Apparently, a clique from the Nation of Islam hovered around the project.) Yet there are portions of the book that have more of a Marxist stamp than a Nation of Islam flavor, suggesting Durham's influence. Finally, a wretched film version of *The Greatest* was made in 1977 in which Ali played himself. Despite the fact that the film failed critically and financially, it further validated the book, *The Greatest,* as *the story* of Ali's life.

Something momentous happened to the jazz trumpeter Miles Davis in 1954, the year that signaled his ascent from a promising musician of intriguing if narrow gifts to one of the major innovators in American music. As he puts it in his autobiography: "Anyway, I really kicked my [drug] habit because of the example of Sugar Ray Robinson; I figured if he could be as disciplined as he was, then I could do it, too. I always loved boxing, but I really loved and respected Sugar Ray, because he was a great fighter with a lot of class and cleaner than a motherfucker. He was handsome and a ladies' man; he had a lot going for him. In fact, Sugar Ray was one of the few idols that I have ever had."[4] Davis continues about his own boxing lessons a few pages later:

> I had convinced Bobby McQuillen that I was clean enough for him to take me on as a boxing student. I was going to the gym every chance I could, and Bobby was teaching me about boxing. He trained me hard. We got to be friends, but he was mostly my trainer because I wanted to learn how to box like him. . . .
>
> So Bobby was teaching me Johnny Bratton's style, because that was the style I wanted to know. Boxing's got style like music's got style. Joe Louis had a style, Ezzard Charles had a style, Henry Armstrong had a style, Johnny Bratton had a style, and Sugar Ray Robinson had his style—as did Muhammad Ali, Sugar Ray Leonard, Marvelous Marvin Hagler, Michael Spinks, and Mike Tyson later. Archie Moore's peek-a-boo style was something else.

But Davis returns to Sugar Ray Robinson as heroic image and role model:

> But you've got to have style in whatever you do—writing, music, painting, fashion, boxing, anything. Some styles are slick and creative and imaginative and innovative and others aren't. Sugar Ray Robinson's style was all of that, and he was the most precise fighter that I ever saw. . . .
>
> The reason I'm talking so much about Sugar Ray is because in 1954 he was the most important thing in my life beside music. I found myself even acting like him, you know, everything. Even taking on his arrogant attitude.
>
> Ray was cold and he was the best and he was everything I wanted to be in 1954.[5]

What we first notice about this confession of hero-worship is how, on one level, it is plainly preposterous. No musician, especially a trumpeter, could possibly take boxing lessons in any serious way, not if he expected to continue to make a living as a musician. One playful punch in the mouth and Davis's career could have ended. Yet Davis did just this for a number of years. It is ironic that when his career began its upward arc in the mid-1950s, that when trumpet playing should have begun to mean the most to him, he placed himself most at risk by playing around with boxing, trying to emulate a star boxer. Perhaps there was a masculine bit of brinkmanship in Davis's pursuit of boxing, reminiscent of the sort of brinkmanship that characterized the actions of the successful black jazz musician, from his fiercely competitive jam sessions to his rebellion against respectable bourgeois convention through taking drugs, and his rebellion against racist conventions through dating white women.

The year 1954 signaled a change not only for Davis but for the country at large. It was the year of the *Brown v. Board of Education* desegregation decision and the beginning of our country's profoundly painful and exceedingly ambivalent adventure in a national policy of racial integration. However, the *Brown* decision was based upon the idea that segregation had damaged blacks, left them bereft, alienated, and without a culture, thoroughly marginalized; it had made blacks, in fact, believe in their own environmentally induced and politically reified degradation and inferiority as both inevitable and natural. Davis, a product of the highly creative, chauvinistically masculine, disciplined though—paradoxically—self-destructive world of itinerant professional black musicians, decided to graft himself onto and draw inspiration from another equally creative, disciplined, brutally masculine, self-destructive world, that of the itinerant black professional prizefighter, making a linkage through an idea or concept that he calls "style" or that we can more accurately call "stylization." By stylization, I mean the conjunction of fashion with not only an explicit, if inchoate, sense of political self-consciousness, but the conjunction of fashion and political self-consciousness with method and discipline that is ultimately expressed as the triumph of will. Davis's belief in a black stylization, indeed, a series of black male stylizations that are individual yet wedded through bonds and rituals of blackness and masculinity, is clearly a refutation, however unconscious, of assumptions underlying integration in 1954. For Davis, the Negro was not "sick" nor was he "deprived," nor was he "defeated" by his segregated status, as many historians and sociologists argued during these years. In fact, Davis, using Ray Robinson as a source of inspiration for kicking drugs, demonstrates that if the

Negro is sick, it is only through the example of other Negroes, through identification with them, that he will get well. It is all a matter of recognizing the styles, knowing the stylizations, and realizing—as Davis did throughout his career, remaining the technically limited trumpeter of the middle register—that the center is the margin.

In his 1970 autobiography, *Sugar Ray,* Robinson describes the young, brash, 1960 Olympic gold medal winner Cassius Clay as a lovesick groupie who called the middleweight champion "the king, the master, my idol." Everyone who knows the career of Ali is aware that Robinson was the inspiration—one might say, the masculine aesthetic model—for Ali during his amateur and early professional career. Ali wanted to be a heavyweight version of Robinson. Yet the interpretation of the politicized dimension of black masculine stylization was where Ali and Robinson parted company. It was a distinction that extended even to the way each man wore his hair: Robinson was a longtime wearer of the process, or "do," the style of the apolitical and quasi-nihilistic street-corner black; Ali wore a very modest Afro that seemed a compromise between the 1960s outsized sculptures of hair design as protest and autonomy, and the genteel, uplift tradition of the respectable middle-class black. (Ali always wore more hair in the 1960s and 1970s than was standard for the rank-and-file member of the Nation of the Islam, a conservative organization built on the ideas of a present-centered religion, petit bourgeois respectability, and an identification with the East.)

In Robinson's chapter on Cassius Clay[6] (the fact that he entitled the chapter using Ali's former name suggests either Robinson's contempt for the Muslims and Ali's conversion, or Robinson's emphasis on Ali's boyish and boylike quality, which the name "Clay" evokes), he tells how he sent Bundini Brown, a former Robinson handler, to work for Ali, how he offered advice for Ali in his fight against Liston, how he was asked by one of Ali's millionaire backers to look after the young heavyweight, and how frightened Ali was about his looming problems with the military.

But in Ali's *The Greatest,* Robinson is treated much more summarily: "Years later, when we became friends, [Robinson] would shake his head sadly over 'what might have been' if he had taken me on. Now, looking back, I'm glad he didn't. I respect Sugar Ray in the ring as one of the greatest of all times. But he stayed out of what I call the real fighting ring, the one where freedom for black people in America takes place, and maybe if he had become my manager he might have influenced me to go his way."[7] Ali does not mention that Robinson actually sent Bundini Brown to him, only that Brown had once worked for him.

In the account of his first marriage, Ali talks about battling with Sonji Roi, who was then his wife, over the length of a dress she was wearing at a party (she was not a Muslim, indeed, was a sometime singer, sometime model, occasional escort). While he and his wife are arguing in a locked room, Robinson bangs on the door. Ali warns him ominously: "Listen, I'm gonna open this door in a second, and if you ain't gone, I'm gonna whip you good. You ain't nothing but a middleweight, so go on, mind your business."[8] Here, Robinson is bluntly belittled and dismissed; Ali suggests by his taunt that, in an anxiety-of-influence confrontation, he has superseded his idol.

There are at least two apparent reasons for the difference in the way black male stylization operates in the instance of Robinson and Miles Davis and that of Robinson and Ali. First, Davis can afford to adopt Robinson as a model because the two men are not in the same profession.[9] There is a sense of competition between Ali and Robinson, although weight difference would preclude their fighting each other professionally, simply because both are boxers and both are particularly noted for their innovative styles. Second, there is the generational difference. In 1954, Davis was twenty-eight and Robinson was thirty-three. In 1964, Ali was twenty-two and Robinson was forty-three, a has-been, his glory days having occurred in Ali's adolescence.[10]

But another way to think about generations is to consider the year 1955 and the death of Emmett Till, a black Chicago teenager on a summer vacation visiting relatives in Mississippi, who was murdered for speaking in a sexually suggestive way, or, more colloquially, "getting fresh," with a white woman. Ali writes:

Emmett Till and I were about the same age. A week after he was murdered in Sunflower County, Mississippi, I stood on the corner with a gang of boys, looking at pictures of him in the black newspapers and magazines. In one, he was laughing and happy. In the other, his head was swollen and bashed in, his eyes bulging out of their sockets and his mouth twisted and broken. His mother had done a bold thing. She refused to let him be buried until hundreds of thousands marched past his open casket in Chicago and looked down at his mutilated body. I felt a deep kinship to him when I learned he was born the same year and day I was. My father talked about it and dramatized the crime.

In this telling, Till's murder and Ali's coming of age merge:

> I couldn't get Emmett out of my mind, until one evening I thought of a way to get back at white people for his death. That night I sneaked out of the house and walked down to Ronnie King's and told him my plan. It was late at night when we reached the old railroad station on Louisville's West Side. I remember a poster of a thin white man in striped pants and a top hat who pointed at us above the words UNCLE SAM WANTS YOU. We stopped and hurled stones at it, and then broke into the shoeshine boy's shed and stole two iron shoe rests and took them to the railroad track. We planted them deep on the tracks and waited. When a big blue diesel engine came around the bend, it hit the shoe rests and pushed them nearly thirty feet before one of the wheels locked and sprang from the track. I remember the loud sound of ties ripping up. I broke out running, Ronnie behind me, and then I looked back. I'll never forget the eyes of the man in the poster, staring at us: UNCLE SAM WANTS YOU.
>
> It took two days to get up enough nerve to go back there. A work crew was still cleaning up the debris. And the man in the poster was still pointing. I always knew that sooner or later he would confront me, and I would confront him.[11]

In this obviously fictionalized account, Ali brings together a number of major themes related to his obsessions about black masculine stylization. The passage on one level seems confused: at first, Till and Ali "were about the same age"; later, the text says that Ali and Till were born on the same year and day. In fact, Ali was born in January 17, 1942, and Till was born July 25, 1941, roughly a six-month difference. But both were teenaged black boys in the 1950s, one of whom lived in the South and the other who frequently visited there. And while it may be that the young Cassius Clay paid scant attention to the school desegregation decision of 1954, he would have been, as a black male in the throes of puberty, sympathetically and imaginatively riveted to a sex case involving a black boy transgressing the white-woman taboo.[12] This taboo fascinates Ali the autobiographer: in several places in the book, he speaks of his "purity" in not being tempted to have affairs with the white women who throw themselves at him. This assertion, of course, he was to repeat on many public occasions. Also, in the book, Ali gives accounts of two crazed, hysterical white women, Miss Velvet Green, who followed Ali from fight to fight, praying for his defeat, and the other, a friend of the family of Jerry Quarry—the white boxer Ali fought in October 1970 when he returned from exile—who dreamed that she had made love to Ali during his training and so weakened him as to make him incapable of beating Quarry. Finally there is the long recital (told in *The Greatest* just before the account of the Oscar Bonavena fight) of the horrible castration of Judge Aarons, a black southerner attacked for his alleged violation of a white woman.[13]

Till's sexual audacity represented a certain inchoate protest, absolutely daring and preposterous in its bravado, that ultimately, through the ritualized response of white male violence and mutilation, reinvented for young Clay and the entire country the mythic status of the black male as expendable demon. The Till case is seen by many historians and culture analysts as the political stimulant for the social protest and civil disobedience that formed an important aspect of the civil rights movement. Understood in this light, the episode that Ali relates clearly shows how Till, not Robinson, as many of Ali's biographers and sportswriters have claimed, shaped his black masculine style as a *politicized* expression. The Till murder leads Ali to mutilate an army induction sign, the icon of the government and of white male authority. This episode confirms that within the young Clay were the seeds of his self-stylization as the black heavyweight champion, Muhammad Ali, although that was a name he did not take on publicly until he won the title. It also confirms Ali the dissident as actor in the national tragedy of expendable youth. Identification with Till means that Ali was identified not only with social protest but with youthful social protest. For most people who were sympathetic to his antidraft stance, the tragedy of his three-and-a-half-year exile from boxing was how he so daringly and romantically threw away his "boxing youth." It was only through this gesture that Ali, like Till through his death, could expose the absolutely preposterous hysteria of white male racism.

Later in the autobiography, Ali discusses his own historical consciousness in relation to both black male stylization and his profession:

Angelo kept telling me, "You're not like any of them old fighters." I know better. Who I am is what those who came before me made it possible for me to be. Just ahead of me were some of the best fighters the world ever saw, like Joe Louis, Sugar Ray Robinson, Henry Armstrong, Archie Moore, Johnny Bratton, Kid Gavilan, Sandy Saddler, Jersey Joe Walcott, Ezzard Charles, Floyd Patterson, Chalky Wright, Jimmy Carter, and others who had new styles and powerful punches.

I used to hang around the gym and hear the pros talk about famous old fighters and their feats, and it sounded more exciting and daring to me than any tales of the Wild West: stories about Black Deacon, Tiger Flowers, Boston Tar Baby, Kid Chocolate, Joe Gans, Battling Siki, and others just as good who fought all across the country, almost always in places where the audience wanted to see them stomped. For a black fighter in those days, just to climb in the ring—as the films showed Jack Johnson doing, with crowds screaming for his "lynching"—was a brave deed.

Ali's homage to the skills of his black predecessors slipped naturally into a discussion of the racism surrounding the ring:

Jersey Joe said to me once, "Sometimes it felt like I was in a KKK convention whipping the Grand Wizard while they were still putting up 'White Supremacy Forever' signs."

I hired Harry Wyle a few months before he died. Wyle, who had seen them all, almost since the days of Joe Gans, used to take black fighters from town to town, sleeping in cars because no hotel would house them, sending a white associate into restaurants to bring out food because no restaurant would serve them, training in church basements and coming into the stadiums shielding their water buckets from spit, with the audiences screaming, "Kill the coon! Kill the coon!" as they passed on their way up to the ring. . . .

"There was no region fairer than any other," Dick Sadler, who developed George Foreman and who was once a brilliant boxer, said. "The South didn't allow black to fight white. The North was bad. The West was terrible and the East was disgraceful.

"In one place I had to cover my fighter's head with a wicker basket in between rounds to protect him from beer cans and bottles thrown when he was winning over a local white boy. It was hard for a black athlete to make a dollar in those days. We were totally barred from big, popular sports like baseball or football or basketball. Boxing was all."[14]

Ali, like most fighters, is endowed with a profound sense of the history of his profession, its details imparted as masculine pedagogy in the oral history of the old men instructing the young boys. Historically, the great black fighter is the racial rebel and the racial martyr. Ali, in effect, with his own career, is both the synthesis and the synecdoche for the entire range of black male stylizations represented by boxing. As Muslim dissident and black "self-determining" male presence, he synthesized both the rebel and the martyr. As a black athletic champion whose every competition, every success, was a veritable political statement against the white status quo and white privilege, he symbolized, as did Jackie Robinson, the struggle of blacks in white society.

The Greatest opens and closes with episodes of two Ali bouts: his March 31, 1973, loss to Ken Norton and his October 30, 1974, victory over George Foreman to recapture the heavyweight title he had lost to Joe Frazier on March 8, 1971. The two episodes are, in effect, Ali's own conclusive recognition of the meaning of black male stylizations in American culture, and the meaning of style, for Ali, operates on two levels. Ali was always bothered by Norton's awkward style, his "foot in the bucket" shuffle, his loping, odd-angled punches. The California boxer, whom Ali eventually defeated in two very close rematches, represented a backward, "unsophisticated," if effective, competitive boxing style. But Norton also represented a politicized stylization of masculinity that modern prizefighting, since the introduction of the Negro to competition in the heavyweight championship with Jack Johnson in 1908, has used with near-teleological pretension. Ali, of course, reinvented that stylization within his own politically charged eschatological vision as the world's most famous Muslim athlete and America's most romantically preposterous dissident. That the Negro, as an apolitical being, could be used to represent white interest and that the prize ring symbolized the dramatic conflict of a larger set of politics was what Ali revealed in this fight; indeed, he showed that a Negro who was apolitical was, by virtue of his sheer inability to understand himself as a being with a political nature and political interests to protect, automatically a pawn for whites. In short, the apolitical black boxer was inadvertently a political expression against Ali's assertion of himself as a political being in his own interest. Ali writes that the white crowd roared after the fight: "'That loud-mouth's finished! Norton beat that nigger! Norton beat that nigger!'" Then, Ali continues: "Only this morning Norton was a 'nigger' like me. But tonight he's The Great White Hope."[15]

As with virtually all of Ali's black opponents from Sonny Liston on, Ali depicted Norton simultaneously as the white folk's nigger for blacks and the Great White Hope for whites. In effect, he became both the black with an invisible white skin and racially traitorous heart—a mime turned minstrel—and the black with a black skin and a white heart, as whites condescendingly termed the nineteenth-century Australian black heavyweight Peter Jackson. In both cases, Norton was made a mulatto, transformed into a representation of something less than pure, a grotesque that only America's racial phobias could have taken seriously. Norton is, in essence, a miscegenated presence, an unspeakable demon of the sort that Thomas Dixon imagined in his crazed 1905 novel *The Clansman,* and that D. W. Griffith reimagined so tellingly in his 1915 film *The Birth of a Nation.* But this miscegenated being is now a horror for the blacks, not the whites.

Ali, by contrast, became the true black heart beating in the breast of white American popular and urban cultures: he was in effect both the totem for and the miniaturization of an idealized black city itself and its New Negro invention—bravely masculine, young, for racial uplift and racial consciousness, against white hegemonic pretensions, theologically and morally fervent. He was the migratory southern black turned New Negro militant, symbolizing the migrant black as mythic urban settler. If, for the whites, the black's racial purity was a sign of his biological degeneracy, then, for the newly conscious, political Negro, the black's lack of racial purity was, symbolically, a sign of political degeneracy. In the drama of the quest for their rights, black folk, among themselves and later for the country at large, redefined race largely as a state of mind, a state of consciousness; race was not concerned merely with identity but with identification, a matter of the heart's allegiance with the community. We are reminded of James Weldon Johnson's description of Harlem in his *Black Manhattan* (1930): "So here we have Harlem—not merely a colony or a community or a settlement—not at all a 'quarter' or a slum or a fringe—but a black city, located in the heart of white Manhattan."[16] Ali is the heart of the heart; he moved the black male as a symbol of an idealized black city to the very center of white American culture.

We recall that Norton literally beat the loudmouth by breaking his jaw, which impaired America's most famous speechifier's ability to perform discourse, an ability that first brought him to the attention of both Main Street and Madison Avenue, distinguishing him from nearly every other fighter, black or white, in history, and that ultimately condemned him when his speech became more than mere chatter or the ritualized challenge of male insult. The opening sequence of Ali's autobiography is largely built around the ambiguity of his defeat to Norton, which brought up questions of whether he was finished as a fighter. The defeat was even politically ambiguous because, as Ali puts it, Norton was not one of the "internationally qualified monsters" like George Foreman or Joe Frazier but a "local boy,"[17] an unknown fighter from the provinces, one might say, whose victory may have signified the reduced challenge to the white civic order of Ali's own black nonconformity.

Ali ends the book with his fight against Foreman, where he regains the title and where all the ambiguities of the black masculine stylizations of the Norton fight are resolved. That resolution comes largely because Ali reinvents the fight as a replication of his first championship bout with Sonny Liston, which defined in precise terms the mythology of his own masculinity against the mythology of Liston. Ali describes the prebout confrontation with Foreman in the ring as that preposterous pop culture synecdoche for moral violence, the American western gunfight: "Our eyes are locked like gunfighters' in a Wild West movie. Angelo and Bundini rub my shoulders. Sandy and Archie stand with George. In his eyes, I see Sonny Liston glaring at me ten years ago at Miami Beach, a fresh, powerful, taller, stronger Liston. Now I think this will answer the question critics have been asking since I first won the title from an 'aging Liston': Could I have defeated a young Sonny Liston?"[18]

So much is Ali convinced that this is the reinvention of the Liston championship fight, that he mistakenly refers to the referee Zack Clayton as the same man who officiated the Liston rematch in Lewiston, Maine; in truth, that fight was refereed by the former champion Jersey Joe Walcott.

Ali also portrays Foreman as a mythic representation of antiblack interests more than he ever did Norton, the local boy, because Norton was never champion when Ali fought him: "I think of who I am and who my opponent is. Who is he? He is White America, Christianity, the Flag, the White Man, Porkchops. But George is The Champion, and the world listens to The Champion. There are things I want to say, things I want the world to hear. I want to be in a position to fight for my people. Whatever I have to do tonight, George will not leave Africa The Champion."[19]

Ali, moreover, has found his voice, the same voice that bothered Liston to distraction. Despite warnings from the referee when both Ali and Foreman are receiving instructions, Ali continues his stream of masculine taunt: "I keep talking. Too much is at stake to stop this fight. Too much has gone into making it; a billion people around the world are watching it. I'm not worried about the referee. After all, he knows I will not neglect my work while I lecture George."[20]

Opening the book with the Norton fight, where his jaw is broken, and ending with the Foreman match, where he regains his title partly through masculine rhetorical rituals, Ali frames his autobiography with his ability to speak, with the symbolic suggestions of black male stylization through ordinary masculine insult speech made political by context and by who utters it. Ali conquers black male stylizations, as he does Norton and Foreman, even as he recreates them.

In the circularity of the autobiography, Ali is, finally, Odysseus returning home from the black male exile: in the opening of the book he comes home to Louisville after the Norton fight, and at the end he has returned to his spiritual home, Africa, to reclaim his birth-right—the title—which he has lost through his enforced exile in America. That exile has a particular significance for him as a member of Elijah Muhammad's Muslims, who called American blacks "the lost-found Nation." As Elijah Muhammad wrote in his 1965 work, *Message to the Blackman in America:*

> It has been for the past 6,000 years that we had to wait for the proper time to learn just who is Our Father, for the false god (the devil) would not dare tell us lest he lose his followers. Naturally, the child will leave a foster father for his real father, especially when he is a good father. The real father by nature loves his own flesh and blood regardless of how it looks or acts, for it is his own child.
>
> So it is with us, the so-called Negroes, "lost-found members of the Asiatic nation." He who has found us is Our Father, the God of love, light, freedom, justice, and equality. He has found his own, though His own does not know Him. They (the so-called Negroes) are following and loving a foster father (the devil) who has no love

for him nor the real father but seek to persecute and kill them daily. He (the devil) makes the lost and found children (the American so-called Negroes) think that their real father (God) is a mystery (unknown) or is some invisible spook somewhere in space.[21]

Like the heroes of other noteworthy black male autobiographies, such as Frederick Douglass's *Narrative,* Booker T. Washington's *Up from Slavery,* Richard Wright's *Black Boy,* Claude Brown's *Manchild in the Promised Land,* Jackie Robinson's *I Never Had It Made,* Floyd Patterson's *Victory Over Myself,* or *The Autobiography of Malcolm X,* Ali clearly sought something quasi-political, quasi-religious, and hugely millennialistic in the end: to return to the land of the true father, in an attempt to reckon with the underlying conflict that informs the ritual of black masculine stylization, namely, father deprivation. "Whose little boy are you?" is the question James Baldwin poses literally and metaphorically in his masterpiece on the Black Muslims, *The Fire Next Time,* not just for himself but for all black men. It is a question that has a central position in a culture where black paternity has historically been questioned and where black authority has been culturally undermined. Father-deprivation, real or imagined, explains the system of black male stylizations as both male competitive jousting and as fraternity, as a system that promotes and thwarts brotherhood.[22] As in other black male autobiographies, *The Greatest: My Own Story* tells how masculine rites are negotiated and reinvented beyond the frame of filial piety. Yet it tells too of the search for male honor of which only filial piety is the guarantor.[23] This is the symbolic and stylized expression of the preposterous yet real heroism of the black American male.

Notes

The passage that forms the epigraph for this chapter comes from James B. Twitchell's *Preposterous Violence: Fables of Aggression in Modern Culture* (New York: Oxford University Press, 1989), 3.

1. For more on African American autobiography as a literary and cultural genre see, for instance, Robert Stepto, *From Behind the Veil: A Study of Afro-American Narrative,* 2d ed. (Urbana: University of Illinois Press, 1991); Stephen Butterfield, *Black Autobiography in America* (Amherst, Mass.: University of Massachusetts Press, 1974); William L. Andrews, *To Tell a Free Story: The First Century of Afro-American Autobiography, 1760–*

1865 (Urbana: University of Illinois Press, 1986); Charles T. Davis and Henry Louis Gates, eds., *The Slave's Narrative* (London: Oxford University Press, 1985); Sidonie Smith, *Where I'm Bound: Patterns of Slavery and Freedom in Black Autobiography* (Westport, Conn.: Greenwood Press, 1974); and Joanne Braxton, *Black Women Writing Autobiography: A Tradition within a Tradition* (Philadelphia: Temple University Press, 1990).

For general treatments of autobiography see, for instance, Roy Pascal, *Design and Truth in Autobiography* (Cambridge, Mass.: Harvard University Press, 1960); James Olney, ed., *Autobiography: Essays Theoretical and Critical* (Princeton: Princeton University Press, 1980); Albert E. Stone, *Autobiographical Occasions and Original Acts: Versions of American Identity from Henry Adams to Nate Shaw* (Philadelphia: University of Pennsylvania Press, 1982); and Thomas G. Couser, *American Autobiography: The Prophetic Mode* (Amherst, Mass.: University of Massachusetts Press, 1979).

On the specific issue of truth and falsehood in American autobiography, see Timothy Dow Adams, *Telling Lies in Modern American Autobiography* (Chapel Hill: University of North Carolina Press, 1990).

2. Thomas Hauser, *Muhammad Ali: His Life and Times* (New York: Simon and Schuster, 1991), 343.

3. For more on Durham and the editorship of *Muhammad Speaks* see "Elijah," in Leon Forrest's *Relocations of the Spirit* (Wakefield, R.I.: Asphodel Press, 1994). Forrest worked for several years as a non-Muslim editor for *Muhammad Speaks* and knew Durham well.

4. Miles Davis and Quincy Troupe, *The Autobiography* (New York: Simon and Schuster, 1989), 174.

5. Ibid., 180, 181, 183.

6. Sugar Ray Robinson and Dave Anderson, *Sugar Ray* (New York: Viking, 1970), 335–50.

7. Muhammad Ali and Richard Durham, *The Greatest: My Own Story* (New York: Random House, 1975), 53–54.

8. Ibid., 194, 195. For a more detailed discussion of the issue of masculine jousting and generational contest in African American male autobiography, see David L. Dudley, *My Father's Shadow: Intergenerational Conflict in African American Men's Autobiography* (Philadelphia: University of Pennsylvania Press, 1991).

9. Within the jazz fraternity, Davis was known for being both a harsh critic of many of his fellow players—following a competitive urge, to be sure—and an instructive nurturer of new or unappreciated talent. Ali, too, in boxing, was harsh with his black opponents, yet he promoted them as fearsome competitors, worthy of being taken seriously as fighters. He was appreciated by his fellow heavyweights because he gave so many an opportunity to fight for the title and he brought out their

best as fighters. It should be remembered that both Davis and Ali, as young men, were trying, in different ways, to bring respectability to disreputable professions, ones that were largely written about by whites.

10. By 1964, when Ali won his title, Robinson had been middleweight champion five times, losing the title for the last time in 1960, and he had fought nearly two hundred professional bouts, a staggering number, not to mention the ninety fights he had as an amateur. It is no wonder that his physician felt that the mental illness, perhaps Alzheimer's disease, that Robinson suffered at the end of his life was partly induced by the punishment he took in the ring.

11. Ali and Durham, *The Greatest,* 34–35.

12. Ali was never especially political, growing up, and certainly never envisioned his future run-in with the government over the draft. This passage sounds a great deal like Durham. It must be remembered that when Ali refused to be drafted, it was not a political protest against the Vietnam War or against the government's right to draft men to fight.

13. See *The Greatest* for accounts of Miss Velvet Green (163–64), Quarry's white woman friend (332–33), and Judge Aarons (340–46).

14. Ali and Durham, *The Greatest,* 324–25.

15. Ibid., 21.

16. James Weldon Johnson, *Black Manhattan* (1930; New York: Da Capo, 1991), 3–4. James Weldon Johnson was one of the prime movers and shakers behind the New Negro Renaissance (or Harlem Renaissance) as well as one of the earliest users of the term "New Negro" (1906). During his days as a popular songwriter, he was also a good friend of Jack Johnson, a man about whom he had decidedly mixed feelings.

17. Ali and Durham, *The Greatest,* 19.

18. Ibid., 403.

19. Ibid., 400.

20. Ibid., 404.

21. Elijah Muhammad, *Message to the Blackman in America* (Chicago: Muhammad's Temple No. 2, 1965), 4–5.

22. There is something very blueslike in the ethos of both jazz and prizefighting as systems of black male stylization. First, we have the idea of the jazz musician or boxer as an agent of affirmation in the face of adversity. We also have the idea that this adversity is largely induced by the inescapable vagaries of human life and so can never truly be defeated, for the vagaries are endless and one simply endures them. For more on this idea, see Albert Murray, *Stomping the Blues* (New York: Vintage Books, 1982), and Ralph Ellison, *Shadow and Act* (New York: Vintage Books, 1972), esp. 24–44, 45–59.

23. There is no greater indication of the tension between fathers and

sons in Ali's life than his conversion to Islam, which meant his rejection of his father's Christian beliefs and his name as well. Ali was originally named after his father, Cassius Marcellus Clay, Jr. In *The Greatest,* he transforms the issue to one of conflict between a black son and a fictive white father, when he discusses, at some length, the white antislavery Kentuckian Cassius Marcellus Clay and Henry Clay (38, 40–41).

5

Victory for Allah: Muhammad Ali, the Nation of Islam, and American Society

David K. Wiggins

"I envy Muhammad Ali," declared Bill Russell, the basketball great, following a well-publicized meeting between the famous boxer and several other prominent black athletes in Cleveland during the summer of 1967. "He has something I have never been able to attain and something very few people I know possess. He has an absolute and sincere faith."[1] Russell's assessment of Ali's religious belief, which came just a month prior to the fighter's conviction for refusing induction into America's armed forces, was entirely accurate; Ali embraced the Nation of Islam with great fervor and has shown unquestioning devotion to Muslim leadership and complete faith in Allah throughout his adult life. Even after being suspended from the movement during the late 1960s, Ali never wavered from his commitment to Allah or to the religious teachings of Elijah and Wallace Muhammad.[2] He willingly submitted to the rigid discipline of a movement designed to control the total behavior of its members.[3] In doing so, he rejected many of the essential values of American society to which other middle-class citizens adhered and set himself apart as perhaps the most influential and significant athlete in history.

Ali's conformity to the dictates of Muslim philosophy was a primary reason for his influence on the black community and the broader American society. Muslim doctrine gave him the faith and single-mindedness necessary to combat injustices in American society. Much of the black community's adulation for Ali stemmed from his refusal to seek a middle ground while he simultaneously pursued athletic success and maintained beliefs that were often antithetical to those found in sport. Ali was not universally endorsed by the black community because he rejected Christianity and talked of racial separation. But he satisfied the wishes of the Muslim leadership by being recognized as an autonomous, proud black man who was not dependent on the heavyweight championship for his sense of self-worth or his livelihood. He became the movement's most important symbol of black masculinity, a man of heroic stature who came to represent the struggle for civil rights in a society torn by racial divisions and by war.

To many in the white community, Ali's membership in the Nation of Islam was both frightening and detestable. His involvement with a group that advocated separation of the races was reprehensible to whites who expected black champions to concentrate on boxing and refrain from speaking out on racial and political issues. Rather than acquiescing to the sport establishment and assuming the subservient role traditionally assigned black athletes, Ali acted "inappropriately" by showing contempt for white authority and values. Instead of being appreciative for his many opportunities, Ali had the audacity to call America an oppressive society and insist on a separate homeland for blacks. Ali was considered a traitor for refusing induction into military service on religious grounds, instead of rallying around the flag.

Ali ultimately attained an honored position among broad segments of American society and won grudging admiration from even the most conservative blacks and whites. The transformation of much of the Nation of Islam into a more orthodox Islamic religion, along with improved race relations, resulted in a growing respect for Ali that transcended race and eventually led to his becoming one of the world's most revered persons. The aging Ali, more appreciated than ever because of his contributions to boxing and his unwillingness to sacrifice his religious principles, endeared himself to a wide audience by abandoning the idea of racial separateness and supporting integration and the democratic process. Ali's changing beliefs, while criticized by Muslims who continued to hold a racialist position, seemed to be natural for a man whose fundamental generosity and racial tolerance was never subsumed by rhetoric about black superiority and white devils. Once feared and despised because of his religious faith, Ali became a beloved figure lionized by people of all races and backgrounds.[4]

Acceptance of Allah and the Nation of Islam

Ali became involved with the Nation of Islam long before it was known to the American public. The young Cassius Clay first heard of Elijah Muhammad and his followers during a Golden Gloves boxing tournament in Chicago in 1959. Two years later in Miami, Clay met a follower of Muhammad named Sam Saxon (now known as Abdul Rahaman) who convinced him to attend a meeting at the local Muslim temple. This meeting, as Clay would later proclaim, was a turning point in his life. Saxon, along with two other Muslim ministers, Jeremiah Shabazz and Ishmael Sabakhan, inculcated Clay with Muslim philosophy and the teachings of Elijah Muhammad. They taught him that Allah was a black man who, in contrast to the white man's Jesus, was a "powerful prayer-answering God" genuinely concerned about the plight of the oppressed black masses. They explained to him that blacks had been brainwashed, led to believe that anything of value was always white rather than black. They told him that Elijah Muhammad was the only black leader in America with enough courage to tell the truth about the white man. And they assured him that the solution to the black man's suffering was separation of the races rather than integration.[5]

Though cautious at first about what he heard, Clay was enthralled by the Muslim doctrines and gradually embraced them with great passion. He seemingly found comfort in the elaborate rules of behavior prescribed by the Nation of Islam. As with members of more orthodox religions, there was a side to Clay that relished leaving decisions to higher authorities who dictated what to eat, how to pray, what clothes to wear, and how to spend free time. He was enamored with the Nation's work ethic. He believed strongly in the group's insistence that its members engage in hard, honest labor, practice thrift and sobriety, refrain from gambling and idleness, and adhere to principles of good nutrition and personal hygiene. Clay also believed in the Nation of Islam's more extreme teachings, which claimed that there was no heaven or hell, that Christianity was a religion organized by the enemies of the black community, and that white civilization was a genetically engineered devil race.[6]

Moreover, Clay was infatuated with Elijah Muhammad, the self-professed Messenger of Allah who assumed leadership of the Nation of Islam in 1934 following the sudden disappearance of his mentor, the spiritual founder of the movement, W. D. Fard.[7] In Muhammad, Clay found a surrogate father, a powerful man who would teach him the ways of the world and nurture his latent sense of social and political responsibility. Clay was awakened, most noticeably, by Muhammad's talk of black pride in the face of white domination. Inspired by Muhammad's dreams of a separate black nation and powers of a glorious African heritage, Clay could now take pride in his own negritude and align himself with other blacks to overcome the effects of white oppression that had lingered since childhood. Like many other blacks at this historical moment, he was outraged by the crimes committed against blacks by white Americans.[8]

Clay initially tried to shield his allegiance to the Nation of Islam from the American public. There was a heavyweight championship in his future, and Clay, aware that many people hated and feared the Nation, believed that knowledge of his ties to the movement would jeopardize his chances for a title fight. He spent the next couple of years quietly entering Muslim meetings through the back door and keeping talks with other believers secret.[9]

Despite his good intentions, Clay's attempts at religious privacy were destined to fail as his star rose in boxing. In the months leading up to his championship fight with Sonny Liston in Miami, newspapers reported Clay's attendance at Muslim rallies across the country and speculated about his level of involvement in the black nationalist movement. As Thomas Hauser noted, Clay's interest in the Nation of Islam first came to public notice in September 1963 when the *Philadelphia Daily News* reported his appearance at a local Muslim gathering. Some five months later, the *New York Herald Tribune* ran a front-page story describing Clay's involvement in a Muslim rally, noting rather prophetically that the young fighter's presence at meetings of the Nation of Islam lent the group immediate prestige. Two weeks after the appearance of the *Herald Tribune* column, the *Louisville Courier-Journal* published an interview in which Clay expressed his agreement with the Muslims' opposition to integration and announced his refusal "to impose myself on people who don't want me."[10]

Any remaining doubts about Clay's religious leanings were laid to rest by activities at the young fighter's training camp in Miami. He was accompanied virtually everywhere by clean-shaven, conservatively dressed Muslims with short-cropped hair, men who looked more like uniformed guards than boxing fans. One black man who stood out from the rest, conspicuous for both his light skin and reddish hair, was Malcolm X, the brilliant and controversial Muslim minister. Malcolm was in town at the request of Clay, who had invited the famous Muslim leader and his family to Miami as a sixth wedding anniversary present. The two men had established a close friendship, which extended back to 1962 when Clay and his brother, Rudolph, journeyed to Detroit to hear a speech by Elijah Muhammad.[11]

Malcolm's stay in Miami was not a typical wedding anniversary celebration. Although attempting to enjoy the excitement surrounding the championship fight, Malcolm found himself embroiled in turmoil and controversy. Recently suspended from the Nation of Islam by Elijah Muhammad, Malcolm X was not welcomed by everyone in Miami. He and his Muslim friends cast a shadow over the whole affair. The fight's promoter, Bill MacDonald, believed that the Muslim presence had alienated the local community and caused sluggish ticket sales. Worried about financial losses, MacDonald, with the help of Harold Conrad, a boxing promoter and friend of Clay's, convinced Malcolm to leave Miami until the day of the fight.[12]

In truth, Malcolm's decision to leave Miami was as much a result of pressure from the Muslim leadership in Chicago as anything else. He showed some vestiges of respect for Elijah Muhammad by disassociating himself publicly from Clay's camp. Muhammad feared that Malcolm's presence in Miami would ultimately be an embarrassment to the Nation of Islam. Muhammad expected Clay to be defeated by the heavily favored Sonny Liston, and any association of Malcolm X or other members of the Nation of Islam with the losing fighter would reflect negatively on the movement. Perhaps the best indication of the Nation of Islam's approach to the fight was the fact that no writers from the organization's official publication, *Muhammad Speaks,* were in Miami to cover the fight.[13]

Malcolm returned to Miami in time to offer Clay encouragement just prior to his battle with Liston on February 25, 1964. He tried to convince Clay of the symbolic importance of the fight, that it was no ordinary heavyweight championship bout between two black gladiators but an encounter pitting the "cross and the crescent" in the prize ring for the first time. "It's a modern Crusades—Christian and a Muslim facing each other with television to beam it off telstar for the whole world to see what happens," Malcolm wrote in his autobiography. "Do you think Allah has brought about all this intending for you to leave the ring as anything but the champion?"[14]

Armed with a belief in his own ability and the power of Allah, Clay made short work of Liston. He made the "Big Bear" look amateurish, pummeling his face and wearing him down until he refused to answer the bell for the seventh round. The real excitement, however, did not take place until the following morning at a Miami Beach press conference. Responding to a question about his rumored membership in the Nation of Islam, Clay explained that he was no longer a Christian but a believer "in Allah and in peace." "I know where I'm going," said Clay, "and I know the truth and I don't have to be what you want me to be. I'm free to be what I want."[15]

At a second press conference the following morning, Clay could not have been more direct about his religious affiliation. He told those in attendance that "Islam is a religion and there are 750 million people all over the world who believe in it, and I'm one of them. I ain't no Christian."[16] That same day, Elijah Muhammad acknowledged Clay as a member of the Nation of Islam. "I'm so glad that Cassius Clay was brave enough to say that he was a Muslim," Muhammad told a cheering crowd at the Nation of Islam's annual convention in Chicago. "I'm happy that he confessed he's a believer. Clay whipped a much tougher man and came through the bout unscarred because he has accepted Muhammad as the messenger of Allah."[17] Several days later, Clay was again seen in the company of Malcolm X, this time in New York touring the United Nations and taking in a film of the championship fight.[18] Finally, on the night of March 6, Elijah Muhammad provided the ultimate affirmation of Clay's status in the Nation of Islam by announcing in a radio broadcast from Chicago that he was giving the fighter the name Muhammad Ali. Muhammad thereby repudiated the champion's "slave name" and bestowed upon him a name that signified his rebirth as a proud black man in racist white America.[19]

The Movement's Leading Symbol of Black Pride

The American public reacted swiftly to Ali's membership in the Nation of Islam. The initial disbelief expressed by many white Americans quickly turned to disdain. Northern liberals, veteran sportswriters, southern conservatives, and ordinary citizens expressed both fear and loathing toward Ali because he had joined a movement that

advocated separation of the races, denounced Christianity, celebrated negritude, and accused America of being a racially oppressive society. The new champion provoked trepidation among white Americans because of his membership in a group that was willing to
confront civil authority, rebel against social norms, and engage in
militant acts of defiance. Ali was a threat because he belonged to a
religious organization that challenged white supremacist ideology
through a celebration of black intellect, culture, and physical beauty. Perhaps most important, Ali was denounced because he joined a
group that challenged the authority associated with the dominant
conceptions of the sacred in America. The champion deserved to be
vilified, many believed, because he had turned his back on the Christian God and pledged faith in Allah as the source of all power, wisdom, and authority.[20]

Segments of the black community, while sometimes hesitant to
speak out too loudly against the new champion for fear that criticism
would be construed as racial disloyalty, were disturbed by Ali's membership in the Nation of Islam for many of the same reasons expressed
by white Americans. Both Joe Louis and Floyd Patterson were troubled by Ali's rejection of the Christian religion, believing the ties
between the heavyweight championship and the black separatist
group would ultimately prove fatal to boxing.[21] Perhaps no member
of the black community was more appalled by Ali's new religion than
his own father, Cassius Marcellus Clay, Sr. The elder Clay despised
the Muslims, not so much for their religious beliefs but because he
believed they were exerting too much control over his son and had
designs on his money. He told the sportswriter Pat Putnam prior to
the Liston fight that the Nation of Islam had brainwashed Cassius
and his younger brother, Rudolph. "They have ruined my two boys,"
said Clay senior; "they should run those Black Muslims out of the
country before they ruin other fine people."[22]

Negative reactions to Ali's membership in the Nation of Islam were
quickly countered by Elijah Muhammad. He realized the symbolic
importance of a Muslim heavyweight champion and proceeded to
orchestrate a public relations campaign that transformed Ali into the
movement's leading example of black pride. He used the controversy surrounding Ali to his own advantage, branding criticism of the
heavyweight champion as religious persecution and hatred of Muslims. With Malcolm X now defrocked and discredited within the

Nation, Ali could step in as a charismatic leader who would spread the word. He could serve as an example of righteousness for blacks who had been instilled with a false sense of racial inferiority by white Christian Americans. Elijah Muhammad envisioned Ali as the Nation of Islam's model citizen, a beautiful black man who would lend credibility to the movement, embodying Muslim ideals and the Islamic way of life. In one of his first discourses on Ali in *Muhammad Speaks,* Elijah Muhammad declared that America hated the new champion because he had given up the life of a Christian, sought the "hereafter and not the world," courageously elevated himself "to the side of the true god," and had "shaken off the slavemaster's ways." "The heavyweight champion's name," proclaimed Muhammad, "will live forever."[23]

Shortly after receiving Muhammad's blessings, Ali embarked on a trip to Africa. Arranged by Osman Karriem, a close friend of Malcolm X, the month-long tour was ostensibly intended to provide Ali with some rest and remove him from the controversy surrounding his recent religious conversion. In truth, the trip served more as a promotional tour for the Nation of Islam and as an opportunity for Ali to nurture ties with his black brethren and gain a sense of his cultural heritage. *Muhammad Speaks* covered the trip in great detail and was always careful to mention that the enthusiastic reception of Ali by the African countries indicated their approval of Elijah Muhammad.[24]

Ali's trip was marked by a number of memorable moments, but none of them seemed to affect him so deeply as his chance meeting with Malcolm X in Ghana. After months of quarreling with Elijah Muhammad over a variety of issues, including Muhammad's supposed sexual misbehavior and financial transgressions, Malcolm had embarked in early spring 1964 on a pilgrimage to Mecca. While in the lobby of Ghana's Hotel Ambassador preparing for his return to the United States, Malcolm bumped into Ali, who had just come back from a morning walk around the city. Accounts of the unexpected meeting differ, but observers agree that the encounter was awkward and strained.[25] Having once respected and genuinely admired one another, the two men were now headed in opposite directions, a split caused by their conflicting racial ideologies and religious beliefs.

Malcolm's pilgrimage to Mecca helped to solidify his already changing view of the Nation of Islam by convincing him that true Muslims believed in the brotherhood of all people irrespective of color. His travels through the Muslim world had given him "a new insight into the true religion of Islam" and a better understanding of America's entire racial dilemma.[26]

The change in Malcolm did not stop him from caring for Ali. Distraught at the prospect of losing Ali as a friend, Malcolm claimed he had tried to avoid the encounter at the Hotel Ambassador because it might prove embarrassing for the heavyweight champion, who had undoubtedly been prohibited by the Nation of Islam from associating with him. After his return to the United States, Malcolm sent a telegram to Ali imploring him "to make sure he'd never let his enemies . . . exploit his reputation."[27] For Malcolm, it was obviously difficult to stop being a spiritual adviser to his former student even if that student had chosen a different path to fulfillment.

Ali, for his part, cemented his strong allegiance to Elijah Muhammad and the Nation of Islam by virtue of his trip to Africa. His sojourns in Ghana and Egypt, in particular, heightened his sense of black separateness and his belief in the righteousness of Muhammad's cause. Unlike Malcolm, Ali did not gain faith in the brotherhood of all men. "In America," Ali explained to a Ghanese audience, "everything is white—Jesus, Moses and the angels. I'm glad to be here with my true people."[28] Osman Karriem perhaps said it best when he noted: "I'll remember that trip to Africa as long as I live, because that was where I saw Cassius Clay become Muhammad Ali."[29]

For Ali, coming face to face with Malcolm meant confronting the Nation of Islam's chief apostate. The heavyweight champion believed that Malcolm had forgotten his degraded past and that Muhammad had transformed him from a hustler and pimp into a proud and committed black man. When asked about Malcolm's telegram warning him of possible exploitation at the hands of his enemies, Ali showed his disgust by commenting to reporters about his former comrade's appearance in Africa: "Did you get a look at Malcolm? Dressed in that funny white robe and wearing a beard and walking with that cane that looked like a prophet's stick? Man he's gone. He's gone so far out he's out completely. Nobody listens to Malcolm anymore."[30]

Ali was right that nobody listened to Malcolm anymore. On February 21, 1965, Malcolm was murdered while delivering a speech at the Audubon Ballroom in New York City.[31] Ali had no public response to the death of one of the most controversial figures in American history. He let Elijah Muhammad and Malcolm's own brothers, Philbert and Wilfred, vilify the slain black leader, whose "foolish teaching brought him to his own end."[32] At the Nation of Islam's annual Savior's Day Convention in Chicago, shortly after Malcolm's death, Ali cheered on Elijah Muhammad as the leader announced: "We didn't want to kill Malcolm and didn't try to kill him. They know I didn't harm Malcolm. They know I loved him."[33]

Ali's much-publicized association with Malcolm tended to overshadow the relationship he had forged with Herbert Muhammad, the third son of Elijah Muhammad. Shortly after capturing the heavyweight title from Sonny Liston in 1964, Ali found himself in the company of Herbert Muhammad, who had been asked by his father to shield the new champion from hangers-on and other people with questionable motives. Elijah Muhammad, who always preferred to stay behind the scenes and who recognized the advantages of working through an intermediary, wanted Herbert to guide Ali so as to protect the interests of the Nation of Islam as well as the champion himself. He did not want people preying on Ali, taking money out of the pockets of the heavyweight champion who was expected to give over a portion of his yearly earnings to the Nation of Islam. Perhaps most important, he wanted to ensure that the public image he was trying to cultivate for Ali was going to be protected and promoted in the appropriate fashion.[34]

Herbert Muhammad, who operated both *Muhammad Speaks* and a small photography studio in Chicago, had journeyed to Africa with Ali and increasingly spent time with him on their return to America. Ali hardly made a move without first consulting Herbert, seeking his advice on everything from legal issues to religious doctrine. The two men became close friends and eventually formed a business partnership (Herbert became Ali's manager) that proved financially beneficial to both of them and, by extension, to the Nation of Islam.[35] "He [Herbert] has made it possible for me to help change the history of manager/boxer relationships," noted Ali in the acknowledgments to his autobiography, "and is forever encouraging me not only to give the best performance to the people, but to be concerned with the progress of the people and to stand for the principles of peace, justice and equality—to show that in a profession which is mainly known for brutality and blood, a man can have nobility and dignity. It is not only I who owes Herbert Muhammad a debt of gratitude, it is the entire boxing and athletic world."[36]

Testing Ali's Religious Convictions

The alliance between Ali and Herbert Muhammad coincided with the controversy over the champion's opposition to the Vietnam War and his refusal to enter military service. Of all the factors in the debate over Ali's draft status, perhaps the central issue was his membership in the Nation of Islam. In February 1966, Ali created a national furor when he requested deferment from military service due to financial hardship and on various procedural grounds.[37] Once deferment was denied, Ali appealed his 1-A reclassification and fought for exemption from the draft before various boards and courts of justice. He then decided, however, to abandon his original argument for deferment and to seek exemption from military duty based on conscientious objector status. From spring 1966 until his conviction on draft evasion charges on June 20, 1967, Ali went through a number of appeals to overturn his 1-A reclassification, with the central questions usually focusing on his membership in the Nation of Islam: Was Ali's objection to military service based on political and racial considerations rather than on religious grounds? Was the Nation of Islam a true religion?[38]

Ali spelled out his religious convictions and opposition to the war on August 23, 1966, at a special hearing before retired circuit court judge Lawrence Grauman, who was brought in to determine the merits of the heavyweight champion's request and to make a recommendation to the Kentucky Appeal Board. Under oath, Ali testified that he sincerely believed in the teachings of Elijah Muhammad and the Holy Qur'an, which forbade true Muslims from participating in wars "on the side of nonbelievers." He illustrated the depth of his faith by pointing out that he would not have risked losing large sums of endorsement monies nor sacrificed his public image unless he was genuinely committed to the Nation of Islam.[39]

Lawrence Grauman surprised most people by concluding that Ali was sincere in his religious opposition to war and should be granted conscientious objector status. Grauman's recommendation was countered by the Department of Justice, which claimed in a written communiqué to the Appeal Board that Ali's opposition to the war was based on political and racial considerations rather than religious beliefs. The appeal board ultimately sided with the Department of Justice, and Ali's claim for conscientious objector status was rejected.[40] Eight months later, Ali's 1-A classification was upheld by the National Selective Service Presidential Appeal Board. On April 28, 1967, during induction ceremonies in Houston, Ali refused to take the customary one step forward signifying entrance into the army. In a written statement, he rejected induction because he was "a minister of the religion of Islam."[41] Ten days later, Ali was indicted by a Federal Grand Jury in Houston for refusing induction.[42] Finally, on June 20, 1967, he was found guilty of draft evasion by a twelve-person jury that returned its verdict after only twenty minutes of deliberation. Mort Susman, head of the United States Attorney's Office for the Southern District of Texas, expressed the belief of many people when he declared shortly after the verdict had been returned "that he had studied the Muslim order and found it as much political as it is religious."[43]

Susman's beliefs about the Muslim order seemed to strike at the heart of Ali's problems with the United States government. Because he belonged to a movement that was not considered a legitimate religion, Ali found it difficult to convince anyone that he deserved the same status as conscientious objectors who came from the Mennonite Church and other Christian groups. Ali's claim of pacifism was contradicted by the Nation of Islam's blending of radical social and political philosophy with religious doctrine. The Muslim militancy invoked hostile responses from a society that granted legitimacy only to those religions that complied with societal norms such as accommodation and submissiveness. Ali had to convince people of the sincerity of his religious beliefs while belonging to a movement that was overtly political, one that took uncompromising positions on racial issues and insisted on a separate state for black Americans. The burden of proof ultimately rested with Ali since the government would not accord Muslims the same constitutional and legal rights enjoyed by more traditional faiths. Because the Nation of Islam merged religion and politics, Ali was unable to enjoy the benefits granted other faiths and could not avoid the hardships that typically befell members of secular protest movements.[44]

The Nation of Islam took no official position on Ali's draft status and his struggles with the United States government. But it took a keen interest in Ali's fight for conscientious objector status and used the whole affair to help legitimize its own goals, stir up an already angry black community, and point out the injustices and hypocrisy of white America. *Muhammad Speaks* ran one article after another reporting the wide-ranging support for Ali from individuals and groups around the world, including the philosopher Bertrand Russell, the civil rights activist Floyd McKissick, and Martin Luther King, Jr. It also began describing Ali's religious commitment in greater detail, referring to him more frequently as a great Muslim minister as well as the heavyweight champion of the world. Though unable to sway the courts directly, the Nation of Islam realized it was essential to portray Ali as a man who performed clerical functions if his fight for conscientious objector status was to be taken seriously. In a March 3, 1967, column titled "World Champion Moves Step Closer to Full-time Task as Muhammad's Minister," the newspaper announced that Ali "took complete charge" of the Muslim mosque in Houston because the regularly assigned minister was on a temporary leave of absence. "Reaction to the young athlete's assumption of his spiritual duties," noted the newspaper, "was not only highly favorable among the believers, but exclamations of admiration were many among leaders of the black community here [Houston]—many of whom jammed into the temple to hear Muhammad Ali expound upon the teachings given him by the Honorable Elijah Muhammad, the Messenger of Allah."[45]

Elijah Muhammad dealt with Ali's military status with uncharacteristic openness. Careful not to incriminate himself in any wrongdoing, Elijah Muhammad, who had served time in jail for draft evasion during World War II, nurtured Ali's public identification with the Nation of Islam while maintaining that the fighter's refusal to be inducted into military service was done independently of anyone else. In a rare and carefully orchestrated interview broadcast by the major networks in May 1967, Muhammad announced that Ali's refusal to be inducted into the armed forces was the champion's own decision and an indication that he had learned the truth about himself and the status of blacks in American society. When asked if Ali sought his advice on the draft, Muhammad responded by saying that "every one of my followers is free to make his own choice. I gave him no more advice than I gave the faithful ones who followed me to the penitentiary in 1942." When asked if he thought Ali should be excused from the draft because he was a Muslim minister, Muhammad noted that he himself was a minister when he went to jail and that the United States government "does not excuse you for righteousness because by nature, it is against righteousness." When questioned as to whether Ali was being mistreated at the hands of the government simply because he was a Muslim, Muhammad replied: "It can't be anything else. Muhammad Ali is harassed to keep the other mentally sleeping so-called Negroes fast asleep to the fact that Islam is a refuge for the so-called Negroes in America."[46]

Notwithstanding these comments, in the late 1960s and early 1970s Muhammad willingly stepped aside as an ever-increasing number of people began speaking out on behalf of Ali and his right to freedom of religion. Attitudes had changed. The hatred and disdain once directed at Ali gave way to genuine respect as a result of the increasing dissatisfaction with the war, a consensus on civil rights, gradual acceptance of athletes' struggles against racism, and the Nation of Islam's diminishing antiwhite rhetoric. In addition, Ali's willingness to suffer the loss of fame and fortune for his ideals had garnered him adherents of all colors and from different strata of society. Sportswriters, entertainers, politicians, Christian leaders, business people, orthodox Muslims, and more conservative black organizations such as the Congress of Racial Equality (CORE) praised Ali's courage. Articles in such major publications as *Christian Century, Newsweek, Sports Illustrated,* and *Esquire* commended him for maintaining his sincerity and dignity in the face of persecution from America's power structure, which unfairly took his title and denied him the right to make a living.[47]

It was in this atmosphere that Ali's battles with the government finally drew to a close. In April 1971 his draft evasion case came up before the United States Supreme Court. During oral argument, Solicitor General Erwin Griswold contended that Ali was not truly a conscientious objector because he had claimed on several occasions that as a member of the Nation of Islam he would not go to war unless it was declared by Allah. Five of the eight justices agreed with Griswold and decided Ali should go to jail. The members of the majority were especially worried that a vote in Ali's favor would result in hordes of blacks joining the Nation of Islam in an effort to avoid military service.[48]

Chief Justice Warren Burger selected Justice John Harlan to write the majority view. In preparing the draft opinion, however, two of Harlan's clerks told him they were convinced that Ali's religious beliefs did qualify him for conscientious objector status. They suggested that Harlan read the *Autobiography of Malcolm X* and Elijah Muhammad's *Message to the Blackman in America* to gain a greater understanding of the Nation of Islam. Harlan took their advice and was transformed by the two books, enough to change his vote and convince him that the government had mistakenly characterized Ali as a racist and distorted the Black Muslim religion. Harlan's change in position put the vote at 4 to 4, but it still meant that Ali would go to jail.[49]

Equally divided decisions by the justices were never accompanied by an opinion, meaning that Ali would go to jail without knowing why his conscientious objector status had been denied. To resolve the stalemate, Justice Potter Stewart suggested that Ali could be set free because of a technical error made by the Justice Department. Stewart noted that the draft appeal board had never indicated the specific reasons for denying Ali conscientious objector status. It was possible, therefore, that the denial contradicted the government's previous acknowledgment before the Supreme Court that Ali's opposition to the war was sincere and based on religious training. A decision based on a technicality would ensure that the ruling in the case would not establish a precedent or expand the classification under which others could assert conscientious objector status. After much debate, the justices agreed to go along with Stewart's compromise and voted unanimously to set Ali free. The decision was announced on June 28, 1971, ending Ali's five-year struggle against the United States government.[50] "I thank Allah," Ali said after hearing about the decision in Chicago, "and I thank the Supreme Court for recognizing the sincerity of the religious teachings that I've accepted."[51]

Suffering the Wrath of Elijah Muhammad

One of the ironies of Ali's struggle against the United States government was that his status within the Nation of Islam had changed dramatically between the time he was found guilty of draft evasion in June 1967 and the point four years later when the Supreme Court finally granted his freedom. In early 1969, Howard Cosell asked Ali during an ABC television interview if he thought he would return to the ring soon. Ali responded, in effect, by telling Cosell he would return to boxing because he needed the money.[52]

Ali's comments angered Elijah Muhammad. In an April 4, 1969, column in *Muhammad Speaks,* entitled "We Tell the World We're Not with Muhammad Ali," the Messenger explained that he wanted everyone to know that Ali had "stepped down off the spiritual platform of Islam to go and see if he can make money in the sport world." In stating his intentions to return to boxing, noted Muhammad, Ali had "plainly acted the fool to the whole world," placed "his hopes and trust in the enemy of Allah (God) for survival," and showed his love for "sport and play," which the "Holy Quran teaches him against."[53]

Muhammad continued to blast Ali in the next issue of *Muhammad Speaks* and announced that the champion was "out of the circle of the Brotherhood of the Followers of Islam for one (1) year" and would be referred to as Cassius Clay rather than recognized "under the Holy Name Muhammad Ali." Muhammad showed the extent of his indignation by publishing statements of support for his actions from two of Ali's closest associates, Herbert Muhammad and John Ali. Herbert declared to the world that he was "no longer manager of Muhammad Ali (Cassius Clay)" nor was he "at the service of anyone in the sports world." The Nation of Islam's national secretary, John Ali, in a much lengthier declaration of support for the Messenger, announced that he was "with the Honorable Elijah Muhammad in his defense of Islam against the reckless statements by Muhammad Ali." He noted that the boxer's need to fight in order to pay off debts resulted from the champion's "own ignorance and extravagance." Ali had failed to follow the teachings of Elijah Muhammad, who advised all of his disciples to be prudent in handling their money. "Neither Messenger Muhammad, the Nation of Islam nor the Muslims," stated John Ali, "have taken any money from Muhammad Ali. In fact, we have helped Muhammad Ali. Even Muhammad Ali's sparring partners made better use of their monies than Muhammad Ali who did not follow the wise counsel of Messenger Muhammad in saving himself from waste and extravagance."[54]

Ali's difficulties with the Nation of Islam obviously resulted from a number of interrelated factors. Elijah Muhammad was always suspicious of organized sport, believing it greatly harmed the black community. Like many others, he argued that white America had intentionally encouraged blacks to participate in games in order to divert their attention from the real source of their problems and to keep them from advancing as a civilized people. Sport, and the associated evils of gambling, drunkenness, and crime, was another tool used by white Christian society to keep blacks in a state of confusion and ignorance. In his book *Message to the Blackman in America*, Elijah Muhammad stated that "poor so-called negroes are the worst victims in this world of sport and play because they are trying to learn the white man's games of civilization. Sport and play (games of chance) take away the remembrance of Allah (God) and the doing of good, says the Holy Quran. Think over what I am teaching, my people, and judge according to justice and righteousness."[55]

While Muhammad's feelings about the "white man's games of civilization" seemed genuine, it was not Ali's participation in sport or boxing per se that drew his wrath. Muhammad was troubled more by Ali's departure from the party line as interpreted by himself and articulated by his ministers. Like Malcolm X a number of years earlier, Ali had failed to overcome his own impulses and adhere to the Nation of Islam's exclusive code of behavior. He mistakenly expressed a dependence on white society rather than having faith that Allah would provide him with the material goods and other necessities required for an abundant life. Such attitudes revealed Ali's self-absorption and his lack of complete trust in Muhammad, the Nation of Islam, and its doctrines. It also angered Muhammad since it left the impression that the Nation of Islam had taken advantage of Ali by funneling the heavyweight champion's earnings into its own coffers. Muhammad was troubled by any comments, including those from Ali himself, that might confirm rumors that the Nation of Islam had stolen the champion's money and was not looking out for his best interests.[56]

Muhammad's suspension of Ali, then, was his own attempt to rehabilitate the champion. He wanted to ensure a public image for Ali that fit his own needs as Messenger of Allah and those of the Nation of Islam. He was intent on guaranteeing that Ali mold himself to the requirements of the Nation of Islam and project an image of himself as an autonomous, proud black man. Muhammad ingeniously passed off Ali's success as evidence of black superiority and as a means to pay homage to Allah. At the same time he minimized the importance of the heavyweight title, which whites had once held up as a symbol of racial superiority. Muhammad believed that Ali had to be seen first as a Muslim. Otherwise, Ali would appear to be just the latest in a long line of black heavyweight champions, a mere gladiator serving entertainment-hungry white America.[57]

The severity of Ali's suspension by Elijah Muhammad became

evident when he was ignored in *Muhammad Speaks,* the publication that in previous years had filled its pages with literally hundreds of photographs and stories of the champion. The newspaper did not mention anything about Ali for three years, completely ignoring his triumphant return to the ring against Jerry Quarry in 1970 and his initial bout with Joe Frazier one year later. He would not be mentioned in the newspaper again until February 4, 1972, and even then it was apparent he was not back in Elijah Muhammad's good graces. Responding to a series of questions about Ali's status in the Nation of Islam, Muhammad said in that issue that the Muslim fighter was "full of sport and he goes along with sport, too, but I think in his heart he wants to be good. As far as certain duties or posts as he used to hold as teaching the ministry," continued Muhammad, "I do not know when that will take place."[58]

Muhammad's suspension of Ali had obviously evolved into a deep dissatisfaction with the fighter that would never be completely eradicated.[59] Meanwhile, Ali seemed to gravitate toward boxing with greater urgency. He needed the money from boxing to pay off debts and stay abreast of alimony payments, but the sport also provided him with many of those things that had initially attracted him to the Nation of Islam. He was lured by the asceticism and discipline of boxing. He found sustenance in comradeship with his fellow fighters, his entourage, and the boxing world in general. He craved the attention, intense excitement, and respect that boxing brought him. As a fighter he was taken seriously, given a feeling of specialness and an unparalleled degree of adulation. He was enticed by the mystique of the ring, relishing the struggles in the sacred circle against men who were also striving for acclaim and immortality. The ring provided him with unparalleled opportunities for transcendence of self, peak experiences, and emotional "highs."[60]

Ali's status in the Nation of Islam was made most apparent by the kinds of relationships he established during the early 1970s. Although Herbert Muhammad continued to serve as his manager and confidant, Ali was no longer surrounded by Muslims who looked after his every move and protected his interests. Cassius Clay, Sr., became a more visible member of his son's entourage, which was now sprinkled with larger numbers of nonbelievers and attendants. Ali's press conference following his well-publicized return fight against Jerry Quarry was noteworthy in that he shared the podium with Mrs.

Martin Luther King, Jr., and the Reverend Ralph Abernathy, "who presented him with the Dr. Martin Luther King Memorial Award for his contributions to human rights and equality."[61] Bundini Brown, whom the Muslims hated for his womanizing, heavy drinking, and other assorted vices, had returned to Ali's camp, reading poetry and clowning with the champ. Ali also chose to relocate his wife and three daughters to Philadelphia after living close to Elijah Muhammad in Chicago for a number of years.[62]

These changes never stopped Ali from openly expressing faith in the Muslim religion. Nor did they hinder the Nation of Islam from eventually breaking its silence on the champion and cashing in on the publicity generated by his success in the ring. Although his relationship with Elijah Muhammad would never be the same, Ali continued to praise the Messenger and Allah at every opportunity. He told inmates at a New York correctional facility during the latter part of 1974 that the only man who could stop blacks from wrongdoing was Elijah Muhammad. "I am a follower of the Honorable Elijah Muhammad. We are peaceful people. We don't hate nobody. We are just trying to clean up our people and unite."[63]

The Nation of Islam began publicizing Ali's accomplishments more frequently as the 1970s progressed. Elijah Muhammad's deteriorating health resulted in gradual changes in the daily operations of the Nation of Islam, which in turn resulted in a resurrection of sorts for Ali. The champion seemed to resume a more prominent position in the Nation of Islam. He was revitalized as the movement's greatest symbol of black pride by virtue of his ring triumphs and his outspokenness on racial issues. Ali's rehabilitation was best reflected in the extended coverage that *Muhammad Speaks* devoted to his trip to Jamaica following his regaining of the heavyweight championship from George Foreman in 1974. Reminiscent of the coverage he received during his tour of Africa ten years earlier, Ali's every move in Jamaica was detailed by the newspaper. It was another promotional tour for the Nation of Islam, with Ali again the main attraction.[64]

From the Nation of Islam to the World Community
of Al-Islam in the West

Ali's involvement with the Nation of Islam changed significantly following his trip to Jamaica. On February 25, 1975, Elijah Muhammad passed away, ending a forty-one-year reign as leader of the Nation of Islam. He was succeeded by his son, Wallace D. Muhammad, who took the organization in an entirely different direction through a series of policy changes and modifications in philosophy. Wallace, who had been suspended from the Nation of Islam by his father on several occasions and had considered Malcolm X one of his good friends, transformed the movement in many ways, including changing its name to the World Community of Al-Islam in the West. He reinterpreted his father's contributions to the organization, acknowledged the positive contributions made by Malcolm X, refuted the notion of black racial superiority, ceased to ask for a separate state for blacks within America, honored the American Constitution, and advocated the adoption of orthodox Islamic practices.[65] In his first official interview, Wallace Muhammad proclaimed that the World Community of Al-Islam in the West would no longer dwell on the past atrocities of white America and would accept people of all races into membership.[66]

The changes made the movement more palatable to an American public that had begun to appreciate both Muslim doctrine and the demands of the black community. For some members of the movement, however, the modifications brought about by their new leader were sacrilegious. The enormous sense of racial pride instilled in black Americans and the many other contributions made by Elijah Muhammad, including his emphasis on self-help and moral uplift, appeared to be cast aside in favor of a program that was focused more on integration than on continuing the fight for justice and freedom of opportunity. Louis Farrakhan, the former professional musician and calypso singer who became one of the Muslim organization's leading ministers, was so troubled by Wallace Muhammad's changes that he eventually mounted a public campaign against the new leader and rebuilt the Nation of Islam based on the early principles of Elijah Muhammad. Believing that blacks had not yet achieved liberation, Farrakhan began promulgating his beliefs through publication of the *Final Call,* taking the name of a newspaper put out by Elijah Muhammad in 1934.[67]

Ali's response to the changes made by Wallace Muhammad were the opposite of Farrakhan's. Instead of resisting, Ali almost immediately expressed his support for the new policies, which were similar to those suggested by Malcolm X some ten years earlier. Nearly everywhere he went, Ali carefully rationalized the practical utility of

Elijah Muhammad's old programs while paying homage to Wallace Muhammad and declaring enthusiasm for the new changes in the movement. He now de-emphasized race and exalted the deeds of humankind, stopped talking of a separate black state and praised America as the greatest country in the world, spoke of the bonds of brotherhood in the Muslim faith, and avoided any mention of white devils. A perfect illustration of Ali's changing attitudes was an interview he did on May 2, 1976, on the CBS program "Face the Nation." In the interview, which was published in its entirety in the *Congressional Record*, Ali noted that it was necessary for Elijah Muhammad to speak of white devils because during much of the first half of the twentieth century, black Americans "were being castrated, lynched, deprived of freedom, justice, equality, raped." Because of improved racial conditions in society, continued Ali, "Wallace Muhammad is on time. He's teaching us it's not the color of the physical body that makes a man a devil. God looks at our minds and our actions and our deeds."[68]

Ali had no sooner declared his support for the World Community of Al-Islam in the West when Wallace Muhammad began chiding him for his continued involvement in boxing. Like his father, Wallace was concerned about the image the fighter was projecting. He was particularly alarmed by the unsavory people and temptations associated with boxing. He was troubled by Ali's illicit associations with women because they called to mind his own father's indiscretions and could prove embarrassing to the World Community of Al-Islam in the West.[69] Wallace was saddened, moreover, by the potential tarnishing of Ali's reputation brought on by inferior performances in the ring and worried about the harm the sport was inflicting on his physical well-being. Wallace argued that boxing provided much-needed income for the participants and necessary pleasure and excitement for blacks in this country, but he hated to see Ali struggle against opponents who would have been no match for him earlier in his career.[70]

Other Muslims, as well as millions of fans of both races, would eventually join in calling for Ali's retirement from the ring. People were heartbroken by the champion's diminishing abilities and the punishment he absorbed with each successive fight. As they witnessed the erosion of Ali's physical skills, people who had identified with the champion because of his triumphs and stands against social injustice were reminded of their own frailty. To see Ali flounder in the ring was tragic for his followers because he had touched the hearts of so many. He was much more than an athlete or celebrity or entertainer. He had won respect and adulation because he combined incredible abilities as a boxer with moral courage and a social conscience. Nassar Akbar, an inmate in a Michigan prison, captured the prevailing mood when he asked: "Do you, Brother Ali, wish to bring tears to our eyes, sadness to our hearts by returning to the fight game? Or would you like to see smiles on the faces of your brothers and sisters?"[71]

Ali failed to heed the advice of his supporters and continued to fight without any apparent regard for his physical well-being. He remained addicted to the excitement of the ring, but the fights he entered only damaged him further. The long march to destruction finally ended when Ali retired from boxing following his defeat at the hands of Trevor Berbick in 1981. After more than a quarter century of lacing up the gloves and doing battle in the squared circle, Ali now faced life without boxing.[72]

Ali's retirement from the ring allowed him more time to work on behalf of Wallace Muhammad and the World Community of Al-Islam in the West.[73] He was involved throughout the 1980s in everything from helping to promote the annual Muslim-sponsored Patriotism Day parade, and distributing religious literature on the streets, to being a member of the Muslim Political Action Committee (MPAC) and raising funds for the Sister Clara Muhammad School Educational Fund. Interspersed with these activities was his involvement with several Muslim-related businesses, including the marketing of "Muhammad Ali Ummmee Brand Seafood Sausage."[74] Ali even found time to visit the White House and present Ronald Reagan with a copy of Wallace Muhammad's *Prayer and Al-Islam.*[75]

Further evidence of Ali's commitment to the World Community of Al-Islam in the West came when he took on Louis Farrakhan and the resurrected Nation of Islam. He was appalled by Farrakhan's continued belief in racial superiority and separatism. In 1984, for example, Ali took Farrakhan to task for his derogatory remarks about Jews and made every effort, as did Jesse Jackson, then a presidential candidate, to dissociate himself from the new leader of the Nation of Islam. At an Independence Day celebration in Washington, D.C., Ali chastised Farrakhan for his recent anti-Semitic remarks and misrepresentation of true Islam. "What he teaches is not at all what we believe in," noted Ali when asked to comment about Farrakhan's controversial remarks. "We say he represents the time of our struggle in the dark and a time of confusion in us and we don't want to be associated with that at all."[76]

Ali's dissociation from Farrakhan resulted from his involvement in a religious movement that now stressed a more democratic decision-making process and spiritual fulfillment even while it put less emphasis on controlling the total behavior of individual members. Al-Islam in the West was sympathetic to the capitalistic system, committed to the United States Government, and open to nonblack peoples.

Without the tight reins of control and almost mesmerizing influence of Elijah Muhammad, Ali now exercised more freedom of thought. He had been transformed from a black rebel into a conservative American who favored steady progress for his people within American society. The emphasis Ali once placed on racial separateness and black solidarity had been undermined by the very things they were meant to produce; namely, equal justice and more freedom of opportunity for black Americans. Ali had inspired and helped foster pride among the most deracinated African Americans by spreading the belief in white devils and in the superiority of blacks. He now discarded those notions yet maintained a strong sense of racial consciousness, adhered to the distinctive creed of Islam, and embraced a more disparate group of individuals.[77]

Commitment to Boxing and Faithfulness to the Muslim Religion

The changes in Ali's religious beliefs capped a long spiritual journey marked by steadfast devotion and commitment. Though renowned for his sexual appetite and enjoyment of worldly pleasures, Ali was unwavering in his faithfulness to the Muslim religion and his belief in Allah. He derived strength and a sense of freedom from unquestioning obedience to Muslim leadership and belief in the omnipotence of Allah. His commitment to the Nation of Islam also supported him in his own quest for a sense of identity and racial consciousness. His loyalty to the movement gave him the confidence necessary to express pride in his blackness and the merits of black culture. He shed the humility and accommodating attitude typically associated with black athletes and defiantly rebelled against the limitations imposed by American society.

The Nation of Islam benefited as much from Ali's membership as did the fighter himself. Elijah Muhammad might have preached black separatism, railed against the evils of commercialized sport, and viewed boxing with disdain, but he had recognized the value of having Ali as a member of the Nation of Islam. Muhammad knew that what ultimately set Ali apart from anyone else in history was that he was both a Muslim and the heavyweight champion of the world, a combination that would attract unprecedented attention for the Nation of Islam, act as an uplifting force in America's black community, and cause impassioned responses in a society that placed unremitting faith in the power of sport to break down racial barriers. Ali could be held up as a symbol of unlimited possibilities for black achievement even while he was portrayed as a proud black man who received his basic sustenance from the Muslim religion. He proved invaluable to the Nation of Islam because he encouraged believers to rebel against social oppression and helped to create unity among competing factions.

Ali's importance to the Nation of Islam can be measured to a large extent by his influence on both the black and white communities in this country. His membership in the Nation of Islam, along with the heavyweight championship, elevated him to hero status of almost mythic proportion among many black Americans. Even those blacks who were appalled by the Nation of Islam's extremism and segregationist policies were infused with racial pride because of the champion's boldness in upholding a religion that accused America of everything from crass materialism to racial oppression. By embodying Muslim ideals, triumphing in the ring, and refusing to acquiesce to either the sport establishment or the broader American society, Ali helped invert stereotypes about blacks and inspired members of his race whose daily lives were often filled with drudgery and belittlement. Black Americans of every age group, economic class, political affiliation, and religious denomination were inspired by Ali's refusal to sacrifice his principles when the clash came between individual success in sport and the imperatives of group action.

Although he garnered respect from white Americans for his great boxing skills and even for the courage of his convictions, large segments of the dominant culture were appalled by Ali's membership in a movement that talked of "white devils," scorned Christianity, refused to fight for their country, and believed in black racial superiority. To many whites, Ali was a traitor, pure and simple, an ingrate who had turned his back on America and joined forces with hate-filled blacks who worshiped an unfamiliar god and refused to abide by the guiding principles of this country. They believed that Ali was a misguided soul who had been taken in by manipulative charlatans interested merely in self-aggrandizement rather than true religion. It was inconceivable to many whites that Ali could criticize a country that had provided him with limitless opportunities and the chance to secure wealth beyond that of ordinary citizens.

The transformation of the Nation of Islam following the death of Elijah Muhammad, along with the winding down of the war in Vietnam, the lessening of racial tensions, and other societal changes, would eventually lead to greater admiration of Ali by members of all races. Refusing to join forces with Louis Farrakhan and other blacks who remained loyal to Nation of Islam policy, Ali adhered to the orthodox Islamic religion adopted by Wallace Muhammad and the World Community of Al-Islam in the West. In so doing, Ali assumed an honored place in the public consciousness and became less threatening to many Americans. Like the World Community of Al-Islam in the West, Ali seemingly evolved from a revolutionary who was intent on promulgating social upheaval to a conservative American more concerned with spiritual salvation than racial confrontation.

The discipline, self-help, and strict moral code Ali was expected to observe as a member of the Nation of Islam would be forcefully transmitted into his new religion. Finding himself in an atmosphere more favorable to African Americans, and armed with a transformed religiosity, Ali shed his racism to speak of the brotherhood of man and the power of God. His new religious beliefs did not sit well with blacks who continued to worship at the shrine of Elijah Muhammad, but it was a relatively smooth transition for the heavyweight champion, who realized that the promise of freedom in American society served to diminish the belief in racial separatism. Ali had helped to liberate African Americans psychologically. He now involved himself in the uplifting of all people through the promotion of Islam. For Ali, separatism had given way to integration, devils and saints were now members of both races, and Christians were no longer responsible for all the evils in the world.

Notes

I would like to thank Elliott Gorn, Steven Hardy, Steven Riess, and Randy Roberts for their cogent comments and suggestions on an earlier version of this manuscript.

1. Bill Russell with Tex Maule, "I'm Not Worried about Ali," *Sports Illustrated,* June 1, 1967, 19–21. See also *Muhammad Speaks,* June 16, 1967; Muhammad Ali, with Richard Durham, *The Greatest: My Own Story* (New York: Ballantine, 1975), 208–9.

2. For secondary accounts that touch upon Ali's relationship to the movement, see Jeffrey T. Sammons, *Beyond the Ring: The Role of Boxing in American Society* (Urbana: University of Illinois Press, 1988); Don Atyeo and Felix Dennis, *The Holy Warrior: Muhammad Ali* (London: Bunch Books, 1975); Budd Schulberg, *Loser and Still Champion: Muhammad Ali* (Garden City, N.Y.: Doubleday, 1972); Frederic Cople Jaher, "White America Views Jack Johnson, Joe Louis and Muhammad Ali," in *Sport in America: New Historical Perspectives,* ed. Donald Spivey (Westport, Conn: Greenwood Press, 1985), 145–92; Thomas Hauser, *Muhammad Ali: His Life and Times* (New York: Simon and Schuster, 1991).

3. Still one of the best analyses of Muslim philosophy is C. Eric Lincoln, *The Black Muslims in America* (Boston: Beacon Press, 1973).

4. Jaher, "White America Views Jack Johnson, Joe Louis, and Muhammad Ali," 145–92; Randy Roberts and James Olson, *Winning Is the Only Thing: Sports in America since 1945* (Baltimore: Johns Hopkins University Press, 1989), 163–88; Sammons, *Beyond the Ring,* 184–223.

5. Hauser, *Muhammad Ali,* 92–93.

6. Ibid., 84–89.

7. *Muhammad Speaks,* May 22, 1964.

8. Ali, *The Greatest,* 35.

9. Hauser, *Muhammad Ali,* 97.

10. Ibid., 83.

11. Ibid., 97–98. Information about Malcolm X's stay in Miami and involvement with Ali prior to the fight can also be gleaned from Malcolm X and Alex Haley, *The Autobiography of Malcolm X* (New York: Ballantine, 1990), 305–8, 407–11; George Plimpton, "Miami Notebook: Cassius Clay and Malcolm X," *Harper's Magazine,* June 1964, 54–61; Robert Lipsyte, "Cassius Clay, Cassius X, Muhammad Ali," *New York Times Magazine,* October 25, 1964, 29, 135, 140–42; Bruce Perry, *Malcolm: The Life of a Man Who Changed Black America* (New York: Station Hill Press, 1991), 245–50.

12. Hauser, *Muhammad Ali,* 66–67.

13. See Malcolm X and Haley, *Autobiography of Malcolm X,* 306.

14. Ibid., 306–7. The FBI busily charted the meetings between Malcolm X and Clay while the two men were in Miami. See Claybourne Carson, *Malcolm X: The FBI File* (New York: Carroll and Graf, 1991), 71, 248–50, 255.

15. *New York Times,* February 27, 1964.

16. Ibid., February 28, 1964. See also U.S. Congress, Senate, "Civil Rights and Cassius Clay," 88th Congress, 2d Session, *Congressional Record,* February 28, 1964, 4006–10; *Louisville Courier-Journal,* February 27, 1964; *Raleigh News and Courier,* February 28, 1964.

17. *Muhammad Speaks,* March 13, 1964.

18. "Cassius X," *Time,* March 13, 1964, 78; "Cassius X," *Newsweek,* March 16, 1964, 74.

19. *New York Times,* March 7, 1964. One of the ironies is that Ali's "slave name," Cassius Clay, was taken from a famous Kentucky abolitionist who served as Abraham Lincoln's bodyguard for a time and later as his ambassador to Russia. See U.S. Congress, Senate, "Civil Rights and Cassius Clay," 4006–10.

20. Don Atyeo and Felix Dennis, *The Holy Warrior: Muhammad Ali,* 57; John Cottrell, *Man of Destiny: The Story of Muhammad Ali, Formerly Cassius Clay* (London: Frederick Muller, 1967), 154, 180–86.

21. Martin Kane, "The Greatest Meets the Grimmest," *Sports Illustrated,* November 15, 1965, 36–41; *New York Times,* March 8, 1964; *Muhammad Speaks,* December 3, 1965.

22. *Kansas City Call,* February 14, 1964. See also *Baltimore Afro-American,* February 15, 1964; *Miami Herald,* February 7, 1964.

23. *Muhammad Speaks,* April 24, 1964.

24. Ibid., May 8, 1964; June 5, 10, 19, 1964; July 17, 1964. See also "Muhammad Ali in Africa," *Sports Illustrated,* June 1, 1964, 20–25.

25. For details of the chance meeting, see Malcolm X and Haley, *Autobiography of Malcolm X,* 359; Bruce Perry, *Malcolm: The Life of a Man Who Changed Black America,* 270; Peter Goldman, *The Death and Life of Malcolm X* (Urbana: University of Illinois Press, 1979), 178.

26. Malcolm X and Haley, *Autobiography of Malcolm X,* 339–40.

27. Perry, *Malcolm,* 271.

28. "Muhammad Ali in Africa," *Sports Illustrated,* June 1, 1964, 20.

29. Hauser, *Muhammad Ali,* 112.

30. Quoted in Perry, *Malcolm,* 271. See *New York Times,* May 18, 1964.

31. Malcolm X and Haley, *Autobiography of Malcolm X,* 434–39.

32. Ibid., 450.

33. Ibid.

34. Hauser, *Muhammad Ali,* 119.

35. Ibid., 150–52.

36. Ali, *The Greatest,* 8.

37. Hauser, *Muhammad Ali,* 144.

38. Ibid., 144–70. See also *Muhammad Speaks,* March 25, 1966; May 5, 19, 1967; June 23, 30, 1967.

39. Hauser, *Muhammad Ali,* 154–55.

40. Ibid., 155.

41. Ibid., 169.

42. Ibid., 173.

43. Ibid., 179.

44. See Oliver Jones, Jr., "The Black Muslim Movement and the American Constitutional System," *Journal of Black Studies* 13 (June 1983): 417–37.

45. *Muhammad Speaks,* March 3, 1967. See also *Muhammad Speaks,* April 14, 28, 1967; October 20, 1967; November 10, 1967.

46. Ibid., May 12, 1967.

47. See Jaher, "White America Views Jack Johnson, Joe Louis, and Muhammad Ali," 175.

48. Bob Woodward and Scott Armstrong, *The Brethren: Inside the Supreme Court* (New York: Simon and Schuster, 1979), 136–39.

49. Ibid.

50. Ibid.

51. See Sammons, *Beyond the Ring,* 216.

52. See Peter Wood, "Return of Muhammad Ali, a/k/a Cassius Marcellus Clay Jr.," *New York Times Magazine,* November 30, 1969, 32–33, 116, 123, 133–32; Robert Lipsyte, "I Don't Have to Be What You Want Me to Be, Says Muhammad Ali," *New York Times Magazine,* March 7, 1971, 24–25, 54–59, 62, 67.

53. *Muhammad Speaks,* April 4, 1969.

54. Ibid., April 11, 1969; see also April 25, 1969.

55. Elijah Muhammad, *Message to the Blackman in America* (Chicago: Muhammad Mosque of Islam No. 2, 1965), 246–47.

56. See Hauser, *Muhammad Ali,* 81–82.

57. *Muhammad Speaks,* April 4, 11, 1969.

58. Ibid., February 4, 1972.

59. Hauser, *Muhammad Ali,* 193.

60. Those closest to Ali frequently discussed the fighter's devotion to boxing. For comments from his trainer, Angelo Dundee, see Hauser, *Muhammad Ali,* 460–61.

61. Lipsyte, "I Don't Have to Be What You Want Me to Be," 67.

62. Ibid.

63. *Muhammad Speaks,* January 3, 1975.

64. See, for example, *Muhammad Speaks,* January 17, 24, 1975.

65. For information on changes in the movement, see the *Washington Post,* July 5, 1977; Lawrence H. Mamiya, "From Black Muslim to Bilalian: The Evolution of a Movement," *Journal for the Scientific Study of Religion* 21 (1982): 138–52; Zafar Ishaq Ansari, "W. D. Muhammad: The Making of a 'Black Muslim' Leader (1933–1961)," *American Journal of Islamic Social Sciences* 2 (1985): 245–62; Clifton E. Marsh, *From Black Muslims to Muslims: The Transition from Separatism to Islam, 1930–1980* (Metuchen, N.J.: Scarecrow Press, 1984).

66. *Muhammad Speaks,* March 21, 1975.

67. Mamiya, "From Black Muslim to Bilalian," 138–52; Askia Muhammad, "Civil War in Islamic America," *The Nation,* June 11, 1977, 721–24; David Gates, "The Black Muslims: A Divided Flock," *Newsweek,* April 9, 1984): 15+; "The Farrakhan Formula," *National Review,* November 1, 1985, 19–20; *Washington Post,* July 5, 1984.

68. U.S. Congress, Senate, "Muhammad Ali Faces the Nation," 94th Congress, 2d Session, *Congressional Record,* May 4, 1976, volume 122, 12372–75.

69. *Bilalian News,* June 1, 1979.

70. See *Bilalian News,* October 15, 1976; June 1, 1979.

71. *Bilalian News,* April 11, 1980.

72. See Hauser, *Muhammad Ali,* 430.

73. Ibid., 500.

74. *Muslim Journal,* December 4, 1987.

75. Ibid., November 18, 1988.

76. *Washington Post,* July 5, 1984.

77. See Jaher, "White America Views Jack Johnson, Joe Louis, and Muhammad Ali," 145–92; Roberts and Olson, *Winning Is the Only Thing,* 163–88; Sammons, *Beyond the Ring,* 184–233.

6

Muhammad Ali and the Age of Bare-Knuckle Politics

Thomas R. Hietala

To categorize any era with a slogan or symbol is to risk caricaturing the time. Yet both professional and amateur historians habitually apply shorthand descriptions to the past in order to reduce its complexity. The 1930s, for example, invariably bear the label of the Great Depression decade; the 1940s, the time of total war. In the 1950s Americans attained a Cold War consensus on foreign policy and a sustained economic boom that made affluence synonymous with Americanism. The 1960s, however, are more difficult to define. Politicians, journalists, historians, and talk-show hosts continue to grapple with the legacy of the sixties. For conservatives, the decade marks a lamentable decline in respect for authority and tradition, lower moral standards (especially among the young), rampant social disorder, and a humiliating loss in Vietnam. For progressives, the ferment and disorder seem an inevitable consequence of the nation's encounter with problems deeply rooted in its past—racism, poverty, gender oppression, and a messianic foreign policy destined to lead the nation into a tragedy abroad.

The intervention of the United States in Vietnam alone might have divided the American people and defined the decade, but the escalation of the war and the protest against it both fueled and fed off of other divisive movements. It is no coincidence, for example, that student radicals and militant civil-rights workers formed an antiwar vanguard as early as 1966 and 1967. Moreover, women's experiences as civil-rights and antiwar activists revealed their own second-class status even within protest groups. They acquired the organizational skills and moral fervor needed to launch their own movement for full equality. The civil-rights agitation spawned an array of liberation struggles among other marginalized groups in American society as well.

The protesters' determination to change America was matched by an equal determination within established institutions and among their leaders to resist such change. Whether defending the racial status quo, Cold War policy, the prerogatives of gender, or the sanctity of entrenched institutions as varied as segregated schools, all-male clubs, or the military draft, defenders of the old order fought tenaciously to turn back the barbarians at the gates.

As controversies intensified, political discourse declined in logic and civility. Shrill and contemptuous toward opponents, both defenders and critics of the status quo frequently landed low blows against their antagonists. Whatever its legacy, the age was conspicuous for its hard-hitting, bare-knuckle politics. Not confined to Washington, D.C., or the state capitals, the politics of rancor engulfed much of the nation, including the sports world. No figure in sports took more punches in the melee than the heavyweight champion Muhammad Ali, known as Cassius Clay when he won a gold medal in the 1960 Olympics.

Clay's boxing career and personal odyssey often paralleled the developments of the 1960s and early 1970s, as he struggled to define his own identity as a young black man, his beliefs about civil-rights protests and goals, his position on the Vietnam War, his attitude toward women and their role, and his concept of the title he held. To understand Ali himself is difficult. To interpret him in the context of his time is a more daunting task. "The athlete of the decade has to be Cassius Clay, who is now Muhammad Ali," the sportswriter Jimmy Cannon asserted in 1970. "He is all that the Sixties were. It is as though he were created to represent them." A Joe Louis fan a generation earlier, Cannon liked neither Ali nor his time. "In him," Cannon suggested, "is the trouble and the wildness and the hysterical gladness and the nonsense and the rebellion and the conflicts of race and the yearning for bizarre religions and the cult of the put-on and the changed values that altered the world and the feeling about Vietnam in the generation that ridicules what their parents cherish." Cannon sided with the parents. "The Sixties were a bad time," he concluded, "but some of the years were wonderful."[1] A perceptive sports scribe, Cannon was less able as an historian. Perhaps Ali epitomized certain trends or traits of the sixties, but that role could be assigned to any number of people. Complex and confusing, the decade cannot be reduced to a single symbol. Ali was not "all that the Sixties were." Yet Ali's biography does provide a lens through which to view the incredible changes in America, from the advent of the modern civil-rights crusade in the mid-1950s to the resignation of Richard Nixon and the end of the Vietnam War twenty years later.

The first significant step of Ali's odyssey through this period began with a lynching in 1955. At that time thirteen-year-old Cassius Clay of Louisville, Kentucky, learned that two white men had maimed and murdered fourteen-year-old Emmett Till, a Chicago boy visiting relatives in the Mississippi Delta. Till carried a picture of his Chicago public-school class and claimed that a white girl in the photo was his girlfriend. In a local store in Money, Mississippi, he took a dare and said, "Bye, baby," to a white woman. Violating this taboo cost him his life. When authorities dragged his battered body from the Tallahatchie River, a heavy cotton-gin fan was tethered to his neck with barbed wire. The black press publicized his death; *Jet* magazine and the *Chicago Defender* printed pictures of Till's misshapen body. His mother dramatized the murder by allowing an open casket. The lynching shocked the nation. "I stood on the corner with a gang of boys, looking at pictures of him in the black newspapers and magazines," Muhammad Ali recollected. "In one, he was laughing and happy. In the other, his head was swollen and bashed in, his eyes bulging out of their sockets and his mouth twisted and broken." If the vivid photographs alone could not instill caution in the Clay boys, their father cited Till's fate to remind them that they lived in a society that produced and then pardoned white men who killed innocent black boys. "I felt a deep kinship to him when I learned he was born the same year and day I was," Ali noted of Till. "My father talked about it at night and dramatized the crime." For Clay and his peers, the slaying symbolized the white man's irrational hatred for blacks and the failure of established institutions to protect them.[2]

Acquittals in the Till case provoked new anger over the murder. That continuing rage and the success of the Montgomery bus boycott that began in late 1955 heralded the beginning of the modern civil-rights movement. Two years later, President Dwight Eisenhower dispatched federal troops to protect nine black students chosen to desegregate Central High School in Little Rock, Arkansas. The administration had decided that only force could compel compliance with the Supreme Court's 1954 desegregation ruling. While Cassius Clay trained for a berth on the Olympic boxing team in 1960, four students stood up for their rights by sitting down in defiance at a segregated lunch counter in Greensboro, North Carolina, on February 1. Other young blacks followed, and sit-ins swept across the South, reaching Louisville in April. In August, Clay won a gold medal in Rome by beating opponents from the communist bloc. He returned home to a celebration that might have initiated a new era of color-blind civic pride and interracial cooperation in Louisville. In Clarksville, Tennessee, whites and blacks joined together to honor their Olympic champion, the sprinter Wilma Rudolph, the first American woman to win three gold medals. "This particular parade had a social significance far beyond the welcoming of Wilma Rudolph back home," she observed. "Clarksville . . . was still a segregated city, and [the] parade actually was the first integrated event in the history of the town. So was the banquet . . . that night . . . the first time in Clarksville's history that blacks and whites had gathered under the same roof for the same event." If the diverse populations of these cities could take common pride in their black athletes, perhaps whites and blacks there and elsewhere could find common ground in addressing the nation's racial inequities.[3]

The *Louisville Defender* chronicled Clay's homecoming. His father, a sign painter and muralist, painted the front stairs of their old Kentucky home red, white, and blue and placed flags on the front porch. City officials provided Clay a motorcade escort from the airport to a reception; his former high school awarded him a letter jacket; Kentucky legislators named him an honorary page. But the romance did not last long, and the gold medal proved no shield against entrenched bigotry.

As recalled in Ali's autobiography, *The Greatest,* a gang of white motorcyclists, their leather jackets adorned with Confederate flags, bristled when Clay, gold medal around his neck, and his friend Ronnie King ordered sandwiches and shakes in a segregated downtown restaurant. The owner refused to serve them. One biker called Clay an "Olympic nigger" and told him to hand over his medal as ransom to the gang's leader. Purportedly pursued across the Ohio River by the gang, Clay escaped injury when his streetwise friend upended the leader's cycle with his own motorbike and held him at knifepoint until the other bikers turned tail and headed back to town. Sure of their safety, Clay and King prepared to return home on the remaining motorbike. Clay, however, first walked to the center of the bridge. "I held the medallion just far enough out so that it wouldn't tangle in the bridge structure," he remembered, "and threw it into the black water of the Ohio. I watched it drag the red, white and blue ribbon down to the bottom behind it."[4]

While inaccurate in detail, the story was metaphorically true. Clay had hoped that his Olympic triumph would guarantee him the basic rights and privileges of any American citizen. But in his disillusioning experiences after his return, he faced the cruel dilemma experienced by blacks since the first Africans arrived on the shores of the New World in 1619. Could individual character and achievement overcome the stigma of pigmentation? The American past offered scant hope that most whites could put character before color in dealing with blacks. During the restaurant confrontation with the gang, Clay had considered phoning a white Louisville policeman and former trainer for help. But he did not call. Social mores in Louisville in 1960 afforded higher status to a white motorcycle bum than a black gold medalist. "Other states keep apace with the changing times," the *Louisville Defender* complained, "while Kentucky clutches tightly to outmoded ideas and remains behind a veil of prejudice and bigotry." The city that smelled of bourbon and thoroughbreds also carried the unmistakable stench of racism and apartheid.[5]

Clay's encounter with this hometown "prejudice and bigotry" dampened his usual optimism. In Rome in 1960 he had flawlessly followed a script for a future American hero. By all accounts he was the model Olympian—gregarious, entertaining, adept with the foreign press, and impressive in his sport. A Soviet reporter asked him how he felt about competing for a nation that relegated him to second-class citizenship. "The USA is still the best country in the world, counting yours," he lectured the reporter. "I ain't fighting off alligators and living in a mud hut." Clay later regretted the remark when Louisville's mayor prodded him to repeat it before a delegation at city hall and when a young Nigerian chided him for perpetuating a stereotype of Africa. Whatever his second thoughts, Clay seemed to be following in the footsteps of former heavyweight champion Joe Louis. When Louis was training for a match against Germany's Max Schmeling in 1938, a Nazi publicist asked him how he could represent the United States when he and his people suffered such rank discrimination. "There's a lot wrong with America," Louis conceded, "but there ain't nothing Hitler can fix." Impressed by Clay's conduct in Rome, the *Louisville Defender*'s sports editor, Clarence Matthews, dubbed him "Ambassador Clay" and claimed that he had proved a "bigger asset" to his nation "as an ambassador of goodwill" than as a mere athlete.[6]

The reference to "Ambassador" Clay was apt, since the family name originated with Cassius Marcellus Clay, an abolitionist, slaveholder, lawmaker, minister to Russia, and a leader in the revision of the Kentucky state constitution in 1890. A month after returning to Louisville, Clay the boxer placed his newfound celebrity behind another movement for constitutional reform. "I have always been proud of my name," he told a member of the reform committee. "I'm even more proud after what you have told me about Ambassador Clay and the Constitution. Our teacher told us he was a great man with an open mind to see things so clearly in 1890."[7]

Hailed for his Olympic achievement, Clay, like the nation, faced the future hopeful that greater triumphs lay ahead. He wanted to be an agent of progress. Fifteen years later, however, in the mid-1970s, he and his fellow Americans looked back at events that had staggered the nation. Urban decay and black unrest had spawned bloody and destructive riots. Protest mounted as the Vietnam War claimed more lives and dragged on with neither victory nor disengagement in sight. Bitter debates over social change, federal programs, law and order, and the war polarized domestic politics. Economic problems and political scandals eroded faith in American institutions. Black protest, white backlash, and the controversy over the war in Vietnam touched virtually all Americans, including Cassius Clay. He converted to Islam and changed his "proud" name to Cassius X, then to Muhammad Ali—just as a street hustler named Malcolm Little had repudiated his "slave name" and the subordination it implied by adopting the name Malcolm X. Ali defied the draft during the height of the war, igniting a controversy that he could not have envisioned as he rode a limousine from the Louisville airport through the happy crowd that had welcomed him home.

During the tumultuous sixties the line blurred between the political and the personal, as Ali learned when his conversion and his name change provoked a heated debate. Ali was drawn into the maelstrom of civil-rights politics when he expounded a racial code that angered mainstream movement leaders. Raised a Baptist, in keeping with black custom in the South, Ali denounced Christianity as a "slave religion" when he embraced Islam. His religion also led him to reject the war in Vietnam. He outraged prowar Americans when he refused induction into the army in 1967. Boxing authorities rescinded his title and banned him from competition for forty-three months. In this increasingly politicized and polarized era, Ali came to symbolize many causes to many people. Extolled or excoriated, Ali the symbol lost the nuance and ambiguity of Ali the individual.

When John Kennedy, the youngest elected president, replaced Dwight Eisenhower, the oldest retiring president, the transition seemed to be one of generation as well as political party. During the 1960 campaign Kennedy had summoned the American people to take the offensive in the Cold War to reverse the Communists' recent gains. For Kennedy and other Cold War liberals, the red menace abroad appeared more threatening than racist oppression at home. In this context, athletics became a surrogate for war. If the Russians had more missiles, as Kennedy alleged, then perhaps the United States could partially compensate by winning more medals in Rome. If the Russians held a scientific edge because of Sputnik in 1957, then the United States might deploy a counterstrike with athletes who vanquished their Soviet rivals. Olympic victories might impress neutral peoples around the globe by demonstrating American supremacy in international competition. In such a struggle a gold medal, like a purple heart, signified great service to the country. Above all, excellence in athletics would serve as a metaphor for renewed national vigor.

The Kennedy administration lacked a civil-rights strategy when it took office in 1961. Yet it quickly conveyed an image of dynamism and purpose in foreign affairs, an energy that might eventually be applied to domestic problems. Kennedy vowed to win the space race and launched the program that landed an American on the moon in 1969. He also pledged to win the Cold War and initiated a military buildup unprecedented in peacetime. In addition, Kennedy expanded the American commitment to the frail government of Ngo Dinh Diem in South Vietnam. In his inaugural address he exhorted Americans to "pay any price, bear any burden, meet any hardship, support any friend, oppose any foe to assure the survival and the success of liberty." Drawing on the nation's heritage of pioneering and conquest, the administration adopted "The New Frontier" as its slogan. Early in Kennedy's term the competition with Communism shifted from the Olympic stadium in Rome to Cuba, Laos, Berlin, and Vietnam. After Kennedy raised the stakes in Southeast Asia, Johnson and Nixon waged a bloody ground and air war there. Caught up in the anticommunist crusade, these policy makers tended to view dissent as disloyalty, even treason. Though able to rally Americans around the flag in the short term, the presidents all pursued an overly ambitious agenda bound to bring eventual failure and frustration.

The lost crusade overseas coincided with unprecedented unrest at home, making the period from 1960 to 1975 among the most unsettling in American history. Change came quickly, often chaotically; the ferment produced a powerful backlash apparent by early 1968. In the thick of it all was Muhammad Ali.

Civil-rights agitation first challenged the Cold War consensus. In the 1950s and early 1960s, black leaders preached nonviolent, passive resistance to challenge bigotry, mainly in the South. The potential for violence, however, always lurked beneath the surface, as local activists sometimes split with national leaders over the right of self-defense and retaliation against white attacks. In the North and West, urban riots in the mid-1960s raised the specter of domestic armed conflict. Prejudice and discrimination were not confined to the South, but in the North they were, as James Farmer noted, "diffuse, scattered, and often concealed." In 1964 Malcolm X pointed out that racism was a national and international problem, not a regional one. Moreover, he doubted that the tactics then used could effect a remedy, since racism was ingrained in established institutions. "Dixie," Malcolm X concluded, "means all that territory south of the Canadian border."

Like white racists in the South, urban machine politicians resisted change in the North. Dorothy Tillman, a Southern Christian Leadership Conference (SLC) staffer, worked in Mayor Richard Daley's Chicago. "The blacks in this city was worse off than any plantation down south that we had to deal with," Tillman argued. "You know, down south you lived on the plantation, you worked it, and you had your food, clothing, and shelter. Up here they lived on a plantation with Boss Daley as slave master. Their jobs, their clothes, their shelter, food, that all depended on Boss Daley." When Martin Luther King led an open-housing march through Daley's suburban neighborhood in 1966, whites taunted the marchers by donning blackface and minstrel garb. According to the activist and comedian Dick Gregory, whites chanted their wishes to the tune of the Oscar Mayer wieners jingle:

> Oh, I'd love to be an Alabama trooper,
> That is what I'd truly like to be,
> 'Cuz if I was an Alabama trooper,
> I could shoot the niggers legally.

Black athletes in northern cities saw rampant bias. "Cleveland was a city divided, East Side and West Side, blacks and whites," the Browns fullback Jim Brown noted. "Blacks who went to Little Italy were often attacked." Bill Russell, the Celtics center, noticed similarities between Boston and Birmingham. "I'd tell newspaper reporters that I found Boston to be the most segregated city I'd seen," he explained. "I was always on defense, just like in basketball." In late 1964 the former heavyweight champion Floyd Patterson sold his lavish Scarsdale, New York, home at a loss. Suburban neighbors were unfriendly, and white children repeatedly harassed his daughters and called them "niggers."[8]

The most volatile stage of the civil-rights movement coincided with American escalation in Vietnam. Rising black militancy and increasingly shrill antiwar protests alarmed Americans. Student demonstrations heightened tensions and complicated the presidencies of Lyndon Johnson and Richard Nixon. At universities and colleges from Boston to Berkeley, students questioned the means and ends of higher education, sometimes waging battles of their own against campus administrators and state regents. Student activists advanced the antiwar movement by organizing teach-ins, leading local protests, mobilizing marches in Washington, and aiding draft resistance. Sometimes extremists resorted to sabotage and violence.

By early 1968 a continuing stalemate in Vietnam and more intense opposition to the war convinced President Johnson to announce a bombing halt and his decision not to seek reelection. "There were deep divisions in the country, perhaps deeper than any we had experienced since the Civil War," Johnson wrote in his memoirs. "They were divisions that could destroy us if they were not attended to and ultimately healed. But they were also divisions I felt powerless to correct." Johnson, according to an aide, Harry McPherson, avoided universities late in his term and traveled mainly to military bases, veterans' conventions, and farm conferences, "using these like stepping stones in a torrent." Persistent unrest over the war drove Johnson's successor, Richard Nixon, to distraction. His administration's obsession with its critics inspired a campaign of domestic surveillance, and revelations about black-bag methods undermined Nixon's legitimacy, eventually forcing him to resign. So the schisms at home destroyed two presidents, and as the bloodshed in Vietnam mounted, violence in America increased. Assassins took the lives of several leaders—Medgar Evers and President Kennedy in 1963, Malcolm X in 1965, Martin Luther King and presidential candidate Bobby Kennedy in 1968. Others—black and white—lost their lives in civil-rights murders, race riots, police raids on Black Panthers, extremists' bombings, and crackdowns on dissent at Jackson State and Kent State universities in 1970.[9]

Social upheaval prompted rapid cultural change. By the mid-1960s the nation had a "counterculture" as well as a culture, further splitting Americans along generational, ideological, and behavioral lines. On February 9, 1964—two weeks before Clay knocked out Sonny Liston to win the heavyweight title—the Beatles debuted on American television. So began the "British invasion," with long-haired musicians armed with guitars, amplifiers, and drums replacing the musket-bearing Redcoats of times past. The decibel level of the new music often matched that of the political disputes. Arguments over the volume of the stereo rocked countless homes. On the heels of the Beatles and the Rolling Stones came acid rock from San Francisco with its anthems to psychedelic drugs. Mainsteam Americans grew restive with the "hippies'" seemingly insatiable appetite for protest, sex, drugs, and rock 'n' roll. Radical prankster Abbie Hoffman in 1968 called for "the blending of pot and politics into a potlitical [sic] grass leaves movement." Accused of inciting insurrection, Hoffman countered, "What could we disrupt? America was falling apart at the seams." Whatever Hoffman's role, many voters resented the disorder and longed for tranquillity, creating a political base for Nixon, George Wallace, Spiro Agnew, Ronald Reagan, and other "law and order" candidates. This white backlash was not only antiblack but antiprotest as well.[10]

Even popular culture had its polarizations. Music fans could choose between Sergeant Barry Sadler's "Ballad of the Green Berets" and Barry McGuire's "Eve of Destruction" (Sadler sang of "silver wings upon their chests, these are men, America's best," while McGuire intoned, "You're old enough to kill, but not for votin,' you don't believe in war, so what's that gun you're totin'?"). Norman Lear's television series "All in the Family" featured frequent barbs traded by blue-collared Archie Bunker and his student son-in-law Mike "Meathead" Stivic. Split by gender, party, and generation, the family often had days that were not happy, nor did father know best. Each episode began with Archie and his wife, Edith, belting out the show's theme song, a nostalgic tribute to former times of softer music, shorter hair, well-defined sex roles, self-reliance, and everyone and everything in its place:

> Boy, the way Glenn Miller played,
> Songs that made the hit parade,
> Guys like us, we had it made,
> Those were the days.
> And you knew who you were then,
> Girls were girls and men were men,
> Brother, we could use a man like Herbert Hoover again.
> Didn't need no welfare state.
> Everybody pulled his weight.
> Gee, our old LaSalle ran great.
> Those were the days.[11]

Then as now, attitudes toward Muhammad Ali paralleled attitudes toward his time. "I loved the 1960s," Jim Brown, a friend and fan of Ali's, admitted; "America met Rebellion, got its pompous ass woken up." Sonia Sanchez, an activist with the Congress of Racial Equality (CORE), thought that Ali transcended boxing. "I don't like fights and fighters, but I love Muhammad Ali," she explained. "And I love Muhammad Ali because he was not just a fighter, he was a cultural resource for everyone in that time, black students, white students, green students, brown students, blue students. He cut across every race, every religion." The reporter Robert Lipsyte credited Ali with "providing a window on a lot of social, political, and religious things that were going on in America; a window into the black world that wouldn't have been available to most of his [white college] listeners any other way."[12]

Muhammad Ali faced hard choices in troubled times. The last bare-knuckle championship match occurred in 1889, but bare-knuckle politics entered its heyday as Ali gained prominence in the mid-sixties. Preferring candor over conciliation, Ali spoke his mind and often offended people. Some chided him gently; others doffed their gloves and swung with bare knuckles.

The angry politics of race and religion engulfed Ali. In the early 1960s respected civil-rights leaders were *Negroes,* Christians, and integrationists. When Clay won the title in early 1964, he announced that he was *Black,* a Muslim, a separatist, and would go by the name Cassius X until he received his Islamic name. The disputes over civil rights did not just divide blacks from whites; blacks argued among themselves, as did whites. Activists concurred on the goal of full equality, but rival leaders and factions often disagreed about methods and prospects. The NAACP, CORE, SCLC, the Urban League, and, initially, the Student Nonviolent Coordinating Committee (SNCC) endorsed legal remedies and passive resistance. In the field, however, local rebels often owned guns, convinced that their ability to retaliate deterred attacks. "I had a Winchester," confessed Ed Gardner, a Birmingham pastor, but he added that it was "a nonviolent Winchester." For trying to register to vote, Mississippi's Hartman Turnbow saw his house firebombed and sprayed with bullets in 1963 and 1964. He shot back. At the Democratic Convention in 1964, Turnbow argued with Martin Luther King about guns. "This nonviolent stuff ain't no good," Turnbow advised King. "It'll get ya killed." A black woman nearby asked Turnbow what he recommended. "It ain't but one thing that is good," he replied. "What[ever] the Mississippi white man pose with, he got to be met with. If he pose with a smile, meet him with a smile, and if he pose with a gun, meet him with a gun." In Bogalusa, Louisiana, Charles Sims, a World War II veteran, founded the Deacons for Defense and Justice in 1964. "You got yo' thing, I got mine," he explained to King. "It was necessary for us to pick up the gun in Bogalusa." Yet Sims defied categorization. Though he led a well-armed militia, he deplored the "black power" rhetoric of 1967 and regretted the resulting rift between blacks and supportive whites. The "militants," he complained, "didn't have a damn thing but face and ass . . . face for showin', ass for sittin' on. That's all they had."[13]

Elijah Muhammad's followers preferred separation from the "white devils" over integration with them. When Clay announced his affiliation with the Nation of Islam, a reporter asked if he was a "card-carrying member" of the sect. "I'm no troublemaker," he explained to the press. "I don't believe in forced integration. I know where I belong. . . . Stay with our own. Tigers stay with tigers, red ants stay with red ants. Cubans stay with Cubans." He doubted that protests worked. "I ain't no Christian," he added. "I can't be when I see all the colored people fighting for forced integration get blowed up. They get hit by stones and chewed by dogs and they blow up a Negro church and don't find the killers." He planned to avoid demonstrations and "all those white women who wink[ed]" at him. He defended Elijah and Malcolm. "The way people talk about them," he complained, "you'd think they had horns on their heads."

The press and boxing officials, not Ali, initially made a major issue of his religion. Critics grumbled that he had transformed the title into a pulpit of hate. "I pity Clay," Jimmy Cannon wrote, "and abhor what he represents." World Boxing Association commissioner Abe Green advised Clay to choose between "being the fighter who won the title or the fanatic leader of an extraneous force which has no place in the sports arena." Other observers, however, wondered what all the fuss was about. Angelo Dundee, Ali's trainer, who had changed his own name from Mirenda, liked and respected his fighter as a person. "What's in a name?" he mused. "To me, he was still the same individual, same guy. Actually, I didn't know what a Muslim was, really, because I thought it was a piece of cloth. . . . What the heck's the difference what a guy's religion is?" Robert Lipsyte sensed that "most of the writers, particularly the older ones, felt more comfortable with the mob figures around Liston than with the Muslims around Clay." Howard Cosell thought that older reporters refused to adapt to changing times. "They wanted him to be another Joe Louis," Cosell remarked, "a white man's black man." The Muslims' asceticism clashed with the traditional subculture of the fistic fraternity. Moreover, the Muslims' distaste, even disdain, for whites (and blacks who did not belong to the sect) made many writers uneasy.[14]

With the exception of the Muslims' own *Muhammad Speaks,* the black press generally regretted Clay's remarks on religion and race but defended his freedom of conscience. "Our difference is not with Clay's choice of a religious group although we do have our reservations about the motives of this particular sect," noted Frank Stanley of the *Louisville Defender.* "We are dismayed at the Louisville youth's disassociation with the desegregation movement. Negro youths all over the country have given too much to this freedom fight for it to be dismissed so lightly." Sports editor Cecil Blye questioned the champion's intelligence. "His most recent rantings on integration and the Black Muslims," Blye wrote, "cause us to wonder what gives in the mental area of Cassius' beefy frame." William "Sheep" Jackson of the *Cleveland Call and Post* defended the boxer's freedom of association. "We have no use for the Muslims," Jackson admitted, "but if Clay went to their meetings, it is his business. We have the Ku Klux [Klan] in the South and they hide behind a mask."[15]

Former black champions were asked about the controversy. "Clay is a good enough fighter," Joe Louis remarked, "but it's unfortunate that he's a member of the Black Muslims. A champion should represent all sects, not just one." Eager to regain the title, Floyd Patterson depicted his pursuit of Ali as a modern Christian crusade. "He's practically turned the title over to the Black Muslims," Patterson complained in late 1964. "They preach hate and separation instead of love and integration." If he defeated Clay, "maybe the Black Muslims would repudiate him," Patterson added. "It would be my small contribution to civil rights." A year later Patterson grew more shrill. "Clay must be beaten and the Black Muslims' scourge removed from boxing," he insisted. Though Clay had a right to his religion, Patterson in turn had "the right to call the Black Muslims a menace to the United States and a menace to the Negro race. . . . The Black Muslims stink."[16]

The choices that young people made in the 1960s often caused family conflict, and the Clays had their share. The Clay boys, Cassius and brother, Rudy, caused no major problems as children and adolescents in the 1940s and 1950s. "Both them boys . . . were good boys growing up," Cassius Clay, Sr., said of his sons. "They didn't give us any trouble. . . . I dressed them up as good as I could afford, kept them in pretty good clothes. And they didn't come out of no ghetto." The brothers' religious conversion, however, strained family ties.

Pat Putnam of the Miami *Herald* heard rumors of the rift and interviewed the elder Clay several days before the Liston fight. The Muslims, Clay complained, had estranged his sons from him and his wife, Odessa, and he feared a possible attack by the sect. Oscar Fraley uncovered other details of the feud. The challenger had asked his mother to leave his Miami quarters and return to Louisville; his father had also left the house. In a heated argument Clay senior had threatened to "whup" his two boys and Malcolm X besides. The Muslims had been proselytizing his son since the 1960 Olympics. "They have been hammering at him and brain-washing him ever since," he grumbled. "He's so confused now that he doesn't even know where he's at." Intent on getting the Clays' money, the Muslims had "ruined" the two sons. The elder Clay hoped the sect would be expelled from the United States.

Clay won the title from Liston, but the happy event did not reunite the family. The champion visited his parents in late 1965, his mother told Jack Olsen, but he stayed in a downtown hotel rather than with them. "He came out to visit us, but he only stayed 25 minutes, kept a cab waiting outside in the driveway," she noted. "He hasn't been back since. He's been told to stay away from his father because of the religious thing, and I imagine they've told him to stay away from me, too. Muslims don't like me because I'm too fair-complected." Howard Bingham, a photographer who became Ali's best friend, remembered the rift years later. "Ali's father wasn't the kind to hold back. He always spoke what was on his mind," Bingham recalled. "He'd say the Muslims were a racket and that Elijah Muhammad was just after Ali's money. And Ali would go crazy because he was really into the religion, and no one could say anything bad to him about Elijah Muhammad. There was some pushing here and there."[17]

The Muslim tie also alienated Ali from his wife, Sonji Roi, a former *Tan* model. She chafed under the onerous restrictions placed on women by the Muslim faith, and the marriage lasted less than a year. "He told me if I stopped smoking, drinking, and changed my diet and wore long dresses to the Temple it would be all right," she explained after Ali filed for divorce. But she could not reconcile the Muslims' expectations with her own desire for some autonomy and control. "They've stolen my man's mind," she complained in late 1965. She suspected that Elijah had ordered Ali to choose between her and his religion. She acquiesced to the split. "I wasn't going to take on all the Muslims," she explained later. "If I had, I'd probably have ended up dead."[18]

Odessa Clay's suspicion that the Muslims rejected her because she was "too fair-complected" represented another strain in race politics at the time. A sense of black pride infused the entire movement, but Muslims particularly stressed consciousness and identity of color and urged closer ties between African Americans and Africa. Not long after winning the title Ali and Malcolm X met with African delegates at the United Nations. (Malcolm X had been urging American blacks to support independence and development in Africa while imploring Africans to use the UN to press for full human rights for American blacks.) Then Ali, his brother (who had taken the Muslim name Rahaman), Bingham, Osman Karriem, and Elijah's son, Herbert Muhammad, ventured to Africa.[19]

Like other Americans, black and white, Ali had formed images of Africa that had originated with movies about "the dark continent." Attempting to reclaim their roots, American blacks in the 1960s challenged the stereotypes that denigrated both Africans and African Americans. "Africa was the continent of my heritage, but I only knew it from the Tarzan movies," Dick Gregory confessed. "Having been born and raised in America, I identified more with the white man as I watched those movies." After challenging the lily-white Mississippi delegation at the 1964 Democratic Convention, activist Fannie Lou Hamer and a group of SNCC workers funded by the singer Harry Belafonte toured Africa. "I was treated much better in Africa than I was treated in America," Hamer observed. "I saw how the government was run there and I saw where black people were running the banks. I saw . . . a black stewardess walking through a plane and that was quite an inspiration for me. It shows what black people can do if we only get the chance in America." In Nairobi, John Lewis and other SNCC members met Malcolm X. "For the first time," Lewis reflected, "you saw a group of black men and women in charge." On Malcolm's flight to Mecca, black pilots invited him into the cockpit. "I can't tell you the feeling it gave me," he told Alex Haley. "I had never seen a black man flying a jet." After several trips to Africa, Ali reversed his images of Africans and Americans. In Zaire to fight George Foreman in 1974, Ali stated:

I wish all black people in America could see this. In America, we've been led to believe that we can't do without the white man, and all we know about Africa is jungles. All we see of Africa is a bunch of natives leading white men on a safari, and maybe one of the white men is trapped by a gorilla and the natives save him. We never get shown African cars and African boats and African jet planes. They never tell us about the African TV stations. And everything here is black. The soldiers, the president, the faces on the money. It doesn't seem possible, but twenty-eight million people run this country, and not one white man is involved. I used to think Africans were savages. But now that I'm here, I've learned that many Africans are wiser than we are. They speak English and two or three more languages. Ain't that something? We in America are the savages.

Though Ali sided with Elijah in the leader's break with Malcolm X, he pursued the vision of Pan-Africanism that had marked the last two years of Malcolm's life. More than any predecessor, Ali reigned as heavyweight champion of the *world*.[20]

The exposure to Africa reinforced Ali's racial pride, but his awareness of racist imagery and its impact stemmed from his own experience and his instruction by several Muslim ministers. "I used to say a Negro woman can't do nothing for me but show me which way the white woman went," Ali admitted to Jack Olsen. "I'm showing you how I was brainwashed and thought that white was prettier than my kind." He explained his childhood confusion to Isaac Sutton, an *Ebony* photographer who befriended him. "When I was a little kid, I always knew something was wrong," he remarked. "Everything good was supposed to be white. And I'd ask my mama, why is Santa Claus white? Why is Jesus white? . . . Miss America was white. The good cowboy always rode a white horse. Angel food cake is white and devil's food cake black. . . . even the President lived in a *white* house." Ali, however, countered that *black* was beautiful. He criticized opponents who fled black neighborhoods to live among whites. Before the first Liston fight, Ali promised to punish the champion for moving to a Denver suburb.

> He's not doing as he should,
> Because he lives in a white neighborhood.
> And because he doesn't like black,
> I'm going to put him on his back!

For Patterson the refrain was much the same: "I'm going to put him on his back / So that he will start acting black."

Ali paid dearly for his racial pride. "I turned down an offer to play in a movie in England," he told a Harlem reporter, "because they wanted me to appear with a white woman." His joining the Nation of Islam cost him "some $500,000 in possible commercial contracts," he told an *Ebony* writer in 1965. "I have turned down another $500,000 from several concerns," he added, "because they wanted me to do something I think is dead wrong—chase white women in films." Critical of mixed dating and intermarriage, Ali refused a Hollywood offer to play the part of Jack Johnson, the first black champion, who had riled the nation before World War I with his marriages and affairs with white women. "Black women," Ali stated, "are the prettiest women on earth." Ali lavished attention on black children. "I just love my own kind," he told Charles Sanders. "There is nothing more beautiful than the so-called American Negro child. Black people are gentle by nature, and when you see a little black child you see in it all the sweetness and gentleness of the black race."

To many observers, however—including those linked to mainstream civil-rights groups and the black press—the line between fierce racial pride and black prejudice was a fine one. Muslim leaders condemned whites for centuries of oppression and called for a separate state because they doubted the races could ever live together in harmony. Malcolm X insisted that an integrated coffee shop was no recompense for over three hundred years of slavery and subordination. In addition, he advised blacks to acquire guns to defend themselves against wanton attacks. In the charged atmosphere of the 1960s, strident criticism of whites and advocacy of retaliation against them earned the Muslims the label "hate group."

Like Malcolm X, Ali often found himself under siege, condemned by whites who resented the Muslims' rancor and by blacks who remained committed to integration. Jack Olsen, a writer, experienced the Muslims' animus toward whites. At Ali's bungalow in black Miami, he recalled, "I got the cold shoulder from everybody. If I wasn't overtly treated rudely, I was spoken down to, or more often not spoken to at all." Certain Muslims in the entourage seemed to loathe whites, and Ali often seemed to concur. "Cassius Clay's attitude on race," Olsen noted, "is a tortured confusion of truth, half truth and untruth based on hatred and distrust of the oppressing whites and pity and compassion for the victimized Negroes." The sportswriter Jerry Izenberg noticed a change in Ali at this time. "He'd be talking with you about something, and one of the Muslims would come into the room and the conversation would change completely," he recalled. "My feeling was, he wanted to please them." Ali had the zeal typical of a new convert. But his theology and his personality clashed. Muslim preaching stressed the evil of whites and urged avoidance of them, but Ali found it hard to demonize whites and his profession made it hard to exclude them, at least white men.[21]

The preaching of Elijah Muhammad and his ministers also disturbed blacks. During spring training in the early 1960s Curt Flood and his black St. Louis Cardinal teammates stayed with Clay in "the same segregated motel" in Miami. Flood, Bob Gibson, and Clay became friends, and Clay invited them to a Muslim meeting. "The speeches—or sermons," Flood noted, "were rampantly, savagely racist." But he doubted that Clay held such views. Floyd Patterson labeled the sect "a colored Ku Klux Klan." Jackie Robinson, who broke the color barrier in major league baseball in 1947, held a post with Chock Full O' Nuts, a white company that employed many blacks, and wrote a weekly column for the black press in the early 1960s. Malcolm X chided Robinson for his longtime reliance on powerful white patrons such as Dodger owner Branch Rickey, Governor Nelson Rockefeller, and executive William Black. He also complained that Robinson maligned the Muslims and neglected the ghetto. Robinson struck back. "I reject your racist views. I reject your dream of a separate state. . . . You mouth a big and bitter battle, Malcolm, but it is noticeable that your militancy is mainly expressed in Harlem where it is safe." (Robinson and Patterson had traveled to Mississippi and Alabama to support civil-rights projects there.)[22]

The furor baffled Ali. "Everyone is worried about my religious beliefs," he told reporters in Harlem in early 1964. "People are no longer curious about my fighting ability." He wondered why everybody was "so shook up" about him. "I don't wanta marry no white woman, don't wanta break down no school doors where I'm not wanted," he explained. In 1966, the *Life* magazine photographer Gordon Parks spent time with Ali in Miami while the boxer trained to fight Henry Cooper in England. (Ali was so unpopular at home that promoters staged four of his five fights abroad that year.) Parks asked Ali about his reputation among Americans. "What do they want?"

Ali snapped. "I ain't promoting alcohol and sex, hugging on some white woman's head. So what if I am the first black athlete to stand up and say what I feel!" He denied that he hated whites. "Hate! Hate! Hate! Who's got time to go around hatin' whites all day!" Ali retorted. "I don't hate lions either—but I know they'll bite! What does the white man care if I hate him anyhow? He's got everything going for him." What Parks saw convinced him of Ali's sincerity. "I never witnessed the hate he was supposed to have for whites," Parks noted.[23]

The religion issue might have faded had the media not harped upon it. After his second triumph over Sonny Liston in 1965, Ali told Robert Lipsyte, "I would never talk about my religion if people didn't keep asking me." The private, however, could become intensely public when conscience clashed with orthodoxy or the dictates of the state.

As the Vietnam War escalated in the mid-sixties, religion and race largely determined Ali's response. Historically, other boxing champions reacted more predictably to such events. In 1942, with considerable fanfare and praise from the media, Joe Louis joined the army. But while Louis entertained troops during World War II, Elijah Muhammad served a prison term for refusing induction. Sugar Ray Robinson also joined the army, but Malcolm X had registered as a Muslim and conscientious objector during the Korean War. Officials asked him if he knew what that meant. "I told them," Malcolm explained, "that when the white man asked me to go off somewhere and fight and maybe die to preserve the way the white man treated the black man in America, then my conscience made me object." Ali's resistance to the draft and to war thrust him into the increasingly acrimonious debate over Vietnam. To the various factions contesting American policy, he became an important symbol—reviled by some but revered by others. His stand aroused the enmity of millions, cost him his crown and a fortune, and proved even more controversial than his Muslim affiliation.[24]

The story of Ali and the selective service is a complicated one. The military had initially rejected him because of his poor marks on aptitude tests. When informed he had failed to achieve a minimum score, Ali retorted, "I said I was the greatest, not the smartest." Despite the witty response, he was bothered by publicity about his failure. "For two years the army told everybody I was a nut," Ali groused to Gordon Parks. "I was ashamed! My mother and father was ashamed!" Desperate for replacements as casualties mounted in Vietnam, the army lowered its standards, making Ali eligible for service. He sought a religious deferment in 1966 and hired legal counsel. In the spring of 1967, the selective service drafted him. He refused induction. The government then indicted him. An all-white jury took only twenty-one minutes to convict him of draft evasion. A federal judge imposed the maximum sentence—five years in prison and a $10,000 fine.

Like the schism over religion, the draft question divided the Clay family and Ali's friends and colleagues. "The controversy with the army worried me," Odessa Clay admitted. "I wanted him to join." She phoned her son and urged him to accept induction. Friends such as Sugar Ray Robinson advised him to obey the law rather than Elijah Muhammad. Jackie Robinson criticized Ali for his course: "I can't help wondering how he can expect to make millions of dollars in this country," Robinson, a World War II veteran, noted, "and then refuse to fight for it." Joe Louis took his shot: "He's a guy with a million dollars worth of confidence," Louis said of Ali, "and a dime's worth of courage. I could have whipped him." In the summer of 1966 Floyd Patterson argued that Ali was "trapped" by the Muslims and that his desire for deferment was "working against the civil-rights movement and the best interests of the nation." He added that he, however, "would fight willingly in Vietnam." When Ali refused induction Patterson ducked questions about the decision but placed himself in the opposite corner by promising to travel to Vietnam to entertain troops. A month later Patterson called on marines at Khe Sanh. At Herbert Muhammad's request, a group of prominent black athletes led by Jim Brown met with Ali in Cleveland to discuss his options. But unlike Robinson, Louis, and Patterson, they simply advised Ali to make his own decision. The varied reactions to Ali's course showed how extensively both black and white Americans were divided over the war.[25]

Ali's tie to the antiwar movement was initially tenuous. After the 1-A reclassification, reporters hounded him with questions about his plans. To the Muslims around him, the government's move proved that whites would do anything to silence a proud black man. At Ali's Miami home, Robert Lipsyte heard the Muslims' taunts: "Oh, they're gonna get your ass. They're gonna send you to Vietnam. Some cracker sergeant is gonna kill you. They're gonna frag you with a grenade." In this atmosphere yet another reporter phoned Ali and asked him about the war and the enemy. "Man, I ain't got no quarrel with them Viet Cong," Ali objected. "And bang. There it was," Lipsyte recalled. "That was the headline. That was what the media wanted."

Ali did not understand fully the intricacies of foreign policy but he was not entirely ignorant. His mentors Elijah and Malcolm had devised an extensive critique of white imperialism, exploitation, and intervention. Just as the pictures of Emmett Till had sickened Ali a decade earlier, television news and photographs of the carnage in Vietnam disturbed him now. "I had seen a series of pictures in a magazine showing mangled bodies of dead Viet Cong laid out along a highway like a row of logs," he recollected, "and a white American officer walking down the aisle of the dead taking the 'body count.'" In the photo a "little naked girl" with "her eyes wide, frightened" searched for loved ones among the bodies. He clipped the picture and remembered the haunting image.

Protest against the war increased among others all around him, yet his stance seemed to draw inordinate attention from the press and politicians. "I see signs saying 'LBJ, how many kids did you kill today?'" he told Gordon Parks. "Well, I ain't said nothing half that bad! I don't know nothing about Vietnam. Where is it, anyway? Near China? Elijah Muhammad teaches us to fight only when we are attacked. My life is in his hands." Reporters from the *Louisville Defender* talked with Ali when he visited his hometown prior to his induction date. "I fear Allah more than the government," he explained. "Whatever happens to me, I have got to stick by my religious beliefs 100 percent." Besides his religious reasons for resistance, he doubted the war would help his people. "If I thought goin' to war would bring freedom, justice and equality to 22 million Negroes," Ali pointed out, "they wouldn't have to draft me, I'd join tomorrow."[26]

Early in his career Ali's bragging and self-promotion had annoyed many sportswriters. Then his embrace of the Muslims in 1964 angered more. But as the war in Vietnam escalated and American casualties increased after 1966, Ali's refusal to enter the army expanded and intensified sentiment against him. Though some writers and commentators defended him, an army of scribes and politicians denounced him. With domestic support for the war still strong in 1966 and early 1967, there was little tolerance for draft resistance. Boxing authorities stripped Ali of his title and barred him from competition. The government lifted his passport. But with mounting losses and no victory in Vietnam in late 1967, 1968, and 1969, more Americans grew pessimistic and turned against the war, though most did not join demonstrations against it. By late 1970 Ali could return to the ring. But for three years he had been a prime target in the widening war at home.

The debate over Vietnam rankled black journalists because it posed several unappealing alternatives for them. The same president who sent American troops to fight and die in Vietnam had also championed the most significant civil-rights legislation in a century. To denounce the war was to denounce Lyndon Johnson, and older editors and leaders hesitated to take that step. The first black dissenters were young SNCC leaders—John Lewis, Julian Bond, and Stokely Carmichael. Clubbed and teargassed by state troopers in 1965, a shaken Lewis told a crowd, "I don't understand why President Johnson can send troops to Vietnam, troops to Africa, and to the Dominican Republic, and cannot send troops to protect people in Selma, Alabama, who just want to vote." Others also preferred a war for rights at home over the intervention abroad. "We ain't going to Vietnam!" Carmichael vowed in 1966. "Ain't no Vietcong ever called me nigger. . . . I will not fight in Vietnam and run in Georgia!" Black women picketed a Harlem recruiting station with placards reading, "are the viet cong our enemy? our enemy is right here!" In the spring of 1967, Martin Luther King labeled the United States government "the greatest purveyor of violence in the world today." American war policy, he argued, victimized the weakest and poorest in both the United States and Vietnam.

The resistance to the war and the draft alarmed many black leaders and commentators. "We are bringing up a breed of 'womanish men' who are draft card burners and draft dodgers and cowards at heart," columnist Gordon Hancock complained in early 1966. Resorting to crude redbaiting, he blamed King and Bond for "appeasement and surrender" and labeled King and Carmichael "mouthpieces for communism." *Louisville Defender* editor Frank Stanley rejected the argument that the war diverted scarce resources from domestic needs. "Our nation, the world's richest and most powerful," he wrote, "is big enough to support both a war in Vietnam and a successful war on poverty here at home." The *New York Amsterdam News* editor agreed: "Johnson's approach to the war abroad and the war at home is humane and aimed at bringing about the greatest good to the greatest number of people on both war fronts." Jackie Robinson also defended Johnson. "I believe the President deserves the support and confidence of the American people on the Viet Nam issue," he wrote in late 1967.

Some writers specifically targeted Ali. A. S. "Doc" Young dubbed him "the eminent mouth organist . . . Ali Blah Blah" and suggested that "regardless of whether LBJ is right or wrong . . . it just isn't kosher to flee from military duty like a frightened gazelle." James Hicks questioned the government's motives for drafting Ali but recommended that he comply. "Clay should serve his time in the Army just like any other young, healthy, all-American boy," Hicks advised. "[But] what better vehicle to use to put an uppity Negro back in his place than the United States Army!" Ali received no sympathy from his hometown paper. Sports editor Cecil Blye welcomed his demise and anticipated a prison term. "Cassius Clay had a responsibility to himself and the boxing game that had given him so much," Blye argued, "but Clay is a slick opportunist who clowned his way to the top. . . . Hail to Cassius Clay, the best fighter pound for pound that Leavenworth Prison will ever receive." At Howard University a man heckled Ali and volunteered to serve in his place for a thousand dollars. "Your life," Ali replied, "is worth more than a thousand dollars, brother."[27]

If prominent blacks poked at Ali with light jabs, many whites resorted to uppercuts and crosses. "Cassius," Red Smith complained, "makes himself as sorry a spectacle as those unwashed punks who picket and demonstrate against the war." Upset by Ali's comment that he had no quarrel with the Viet Cong, former marine and champion Gene Tunney chastised him by telegram: "You have disgraced your title and the American flag and the principles for which it stands. Apologize for your unpatriotic remark or you'll be barred from the ring." After refusing induction, Ali and his lawyers tried to evade reporters by rushing to a cab. An old white woman waving a small flag shouted at him, "You headin' straight for jail. You ain't no champ no more. You ain't never gonna be champ no more. You get down on your knees and beg forgiveness from God! My son's in Viet Nam, and you no better'n he is. He's there fightin' and you here safe. I hope you rot in jail. I hope they throw away the key."

Politicians jumped on the bandwagon. Congressman Frank Clark of Pennsylvania, a World War II pilot, denied that Ali or anybody else had the right to resist military duty because of doubt about the nation's role in Vietnam. "To welch or back off from that commitment," Clark told House colleagues in early 1966, "is as unthinkable as surrendering to Adolf Hitler or Mussolini would have been in my days of military service." In time of need, Clark declared, "each man, if he really is a man," owed the country his service. "From this standpoint," he continued, "the heavyweight champion has been a complete and total disgrace to the land that has provided him with the opportunities to make millions of dollars." Clark praised veterans' groups for their plans to picket any theater that carried Ali's fights and urged all Americans to boycott him. After reading an article outlining Ali's preparations to return to the ring in 1970, Congressman Robert Michel opposed any fight for the "infamous draft dodger" and exhorted the Justice Department to obtain "a speedy trial and sentence" for Ali. "The article said that Mr. Clay was out of shape, overweight, and winded," Michel gibed. "No doubt this comes from his desperate and concerted efforts to stay out of the military service while thousands of patriotic young men are fighting and dying in Vietnam." Illinois governor Otto Kerner and Mayor Richard Daley, backed by the *Chicago Tribune,* denounced Ali and blocked him from fighting in the state. House Armed Services Committee chair L. Mendel Rivers assured veterans that his committee would seek to get Ali into the military even if selective service exempted him. In California, the state boxing commission had enough votes to grant Ali a license, but Governor Ronald Reagan intruded. "That draft dodger will never fight in my state, period," he vowed.[28]

Not only Ali but those who sympathized with him grew embattled. Hate mail inundated Howard Cosell when he began using the boxer's Muslim name. When Cosell faulted officials for revoking Ali's title before he was convicted of any crime, the volume and vehemence of the complaints increased—"tens of thousands of letters," Cosell recalled, "directed to me, beginning with the general refrain, 'You nigger-loving Jew bastard.'" Walking by a Manhattan construction site in 1971, Cosell was confronted by several hardhats. "Here he is, the Jew who loves Clay," one of them taunted. "We know you, Cosell. What is with you and that traitor, that black son of a bitch? The guy should never be allowed to fight again." George Plimpton called on Cosell in the ABC building in New York and encouraged him to demand Ali's reinstatement. Cosell, according to Plimpton, said he supported Ali but feared that a sniper might shoot him through his office window if he took such a course. "I can't tell you what I went through for defending him," the columnist Jerry Izenberg, a Korean War veteran, told Thomas Hauser. "All the cancellations of my newspaper column, the smashed car windows, the bomb threats; the thousands of letters from Army war veterans talking about Jews like me and concentration camps."[29]

The year 1967 was not auspicious for a black man to defy the draft. "I knew we'd win at trial," recalled Carl Walker, the federal lawyer who prosecuted the case. "At that time, any jury in the United States would have convicted him." Recurring protest, civil disobedience, and violent crime had spurred cries for law and order and reassertion of authority. Already fragmented over domestic issues, the nation now faced a widening schism over foreign policy. Moreover, fringe groups seemed ready to step up sabotage and terrorism. "We fight a civil war abroad while one grows at home," the journalist I. F. Stone warned in late 1966. "A new kind of secession is in the air." When Shirley Chisholm entered Congress in early 1969 she noticed that politicians went about business as usual, largely oblivious to the national crisis. "What I saw was this country at war with itself," she noted, "and no one in a position of power paying any attention, our lives deteriorating around us and scarcely anyone trying to find out why and stop it."

At this troubled time, invective and caricature often marked political discourse. One draft resister, Raymond Mungo, informed his board in 1968 that the United States was "the greatest force for evil, the worst hater of mankind, unscrupulous murderer, alive today." The country, he said, tottered "on the verge of civil war," and he was "glad of it." Mungo compared American leaders to the Nazis. "And," he scoffed, "I don't intend to play Jew for any of you." A 1967 editorial in the *Berkeley Barb* pointed out that many young people found their society "corrupt, vile, and heinous" and refused "to obey any of its dictates" in order to avoid "a living death, killing others as we died." The far left saw exploitation and oppression everywhere. "Tolerance of rational dissent has become an insidious form of repression," Paul Krassner maintained in 1968. "The goal now is to disrupt an insane society."

Those in power often responded in kind. In early 1964, FBI agents informed Director Hoover that Martin Luther King would probably avoid indiscretions with women in Milwaukee because city police had reserved a hotel room adjacent to his. "I don't share the conjecture," Hoover sneered. "King is a 'tom cat' with obsessive degenerate sexual urges." Hoover and the FBI waged a prolonged vendetta against King, harassed other black leaders, and even placed Ali under surveillance. Hoover's bosses in the White House often reacted similarly to their critics. A woman reporter angered President Johnson with stories he deemed unflattering. "What that woman needs is you," he told his aide, Harry McPherson. "Take her out. Give her a good dinner and a good fuck." Johnson instructed one assistant to arise before dawn daily to read the *Congressional Record* and mark all comments about him. Johnson read the material over breakfast, then instructed staff to call any legislator critical of him. The president, his adviser Lawrence O'Brien realized, tended "to equate criticism with disloyalty." Incensed by Senator J. William Fulbright's opposition to the war, Johnson mimicked the Arkansas lawmaker, attributed his dissent to racism and resentment, and mocked him as Senator "*Half*bright." The venomous mood took its toll on McPherson. "By the end of 1968 I was (like most of the country, I think) tired of political issues," he admitted. "I was tired of seeing every dispute turned into an apocalyptic struggle between good and evil, tired of looking at life though a political lens." Muhammad Ali marveled at "the pent-up hatred and bitterness" he had unleashed in the country. But rather than shrink from it, he sought to confront it. "I want to go in a ring," he stated, "and wave my cape before the bulls—the Maddoxes, the White Citizens Councils, the Believers in the War."[30]

Nixon and his advisers tried to build a new Republican majority through a strategy of "planned polarization." No administration in American history went further to reward friends and punish foes. On the presidential yacht, Nixon confided his feelings about his critics to his aide, Charles Colson: "One day we will get them—we'll get them on the ground where we want them. And we'll stick our heels in, step on them hard and twist—right, Chuck, right?" The press, antiwar protesters, black dissidents, and liberal Democrats infuriated the president and his advisers, prompting them to compile an "enemies list." The type of retaliation against these enemies varied: denying interviews and invitations to the White House; planting negative (and usually false) stories with pliant journalists; snooping for political dirt through illegal wiretaps, breaking and entering, and theft; fabricating documents and bogus public opinion; sabotaging campaigns; directing the FBI and IRS to harass critics. "Within the iron gates of the White House, quite unknowingly, a siege mentality was setting in," Colson reflected in his memoirs. "It was now 'us' against 'them.' Gradually as we drew the circle closer around us, the ranks of 'them' began to swell."

The president and his aides saw no legitimacy in their opponents and caricatured their beliefs and values. Nixon in mid-1972 urged Pat Buchanan to write "a good quotable piece" that could be "broadly circulated," showing that the broadcast media, the chief news magazines, and the *Times* and *Post* had an "editorial bias [that] comes down on the side of amnesty, pot, abortion, confiscation of wealth (unless it is theirs), massive increases in welfare, unilateral disarmament, reduction of . . . defenses, and surrender in Vietnam." Defined in such terms, the administration's critics could be dismissed as hedonists, hypocrites, and turncoats. White House shredders undoubtedly destroyed much evidence about domestic operations, but surviving information reveals the administration's willingness to achieve partisan ends by almost any means. Defeat of opponents such as McGovern was not enough; they had to be destroyed. "This arrogant son of a bitch, in my opinion, is a traitor," Colson wrote in 1972. "Instead of running for President, he should be running from the gallows." Four years and a prison term later, former presidential counsel John Dean looked back in shame. "Slowly, steadily, I would climb toward the moral abyss of the President's inner circle," Dean lamented, "until I finally fell into it, thinking I had made it to the top just as I began to realize I had actually touched bottom."[31]

In this fractious age Muhammad Ali seemed at times to be in the very center of controversy, at other times beyond or above it. Though his actions had political ramifications, he largely avoided partisan politics. Ali spoke often about black pride and advancement, yet he distanced himself from public protest and demonstrations. In an age of declining church attendance and increasing speculation about "the death of God," Ali found in Islam his sail and anchor. His faith gave him resolve to do what he thought was right and the strength to withstand the reaction. In a culture preoccupied with consumption and status, Ali seemed unconcerned with material things after he found Allah. Generous with his time and money, he occasionally impressed even those who disdained him. In a somber age, he amused millions with his poetic predictions ("You think the world was shocked when Nixon resigned? / Wait till I whup George Foreman's behind."); his hyperbole (he claimed to be "so mean" that he could "make medicine sick"); his pranks and magic tricks. One of the most widely recognized people on earth, Ali—like black champions before him—struggled to reconcile a very public life with his private self. Judged harshly by his critics, Ali remained remarkably even-tempered and tolerant. "God, he was special," Angelo Dundee concluded. "You know, the whole time he wasn't allowed to fight, I never heard him complain or show animosity toward anybody. He's not bitter about the years he lost, and that amazes me."[32]

Prominent at a particularly contentious time, the champion who could "float like a butterfly" could not evade the entangling nets of race politics and foreign policy. His views on racial matters annoyed integrationists, yet his advocacy of voluntary separation merely recognized an enduring reality: the nation had long been deeply divided physically and psychologically by race. His knowledge of Vietnam was limited, but so was that of Kennedy, Johnson, Nixon, and their advisors, who floundered in attempts to devise a winning strategy in Southeast Asia. When victory eluded them and critics assailed their policies, they tried to conceal American losses and quell domestic dissent. When South Vietnam collapsed, nullifying the American sacrifice, they scrambled for scapegoats. Ali instinctively felt that the conflict was too distant and too ambiguous to justify American intervention. Events proved him right.

The period from 1960 to 1975 claimed many lives and reputations. Ali was one of few prominent Americans who emerged with greater stature at the close of the era than at its beginning. A generation, perhaps more, will be needed for historians to reach a consensus on this period. It seems clear, however, that Ali's reputation will reside on the opposite side of the balance sheet from the reputations of Johnson, Nixon, Hoover, and Wallace.

After protracted wrangling, fight promoters finally cleared Ali's return to the ring by matching him against Jerry Quarry in Atlanta, Georgia, on October 26, 1970. With passions still high across the country, Ali's reemergence provoked widely disparate reactions. The night before his departure for Atlanta, Ali received a gift-wrapped package. Blue Lewis, a sparring partner, opened it, shrieked, then dropped it on the floor. The box contained a black chihuahua, its head severed from its bloody body, with an accompanying message: "We know how to handle black draft-dodging dogs in Georgia. Stay out of Atlanta!" A small Confederate flag served as a signature. Housed at the cabin of state senator Leroy Johnson, Ali witnessed more dangerous signs of hostility. One night gunshots flashed out of the darkness. Later the phone rang. "Nigger," a voice warned, "if you don't leave Atlanta tomorrow, you gonna die. You Viet Cong bastard! You draft-dodging bastard! We won't miss you next time!"

By 1970, however, blacks had learned to pursue their goals despite white threats and terror. Intimidation had not halted the civil-rights crusade, even after the assassinations of Evers, King, and others. To Jesse Jackson, Ali's return to the ring in Atlanta seemed a fitting climax to the decade's struggle for social justice. "I'm glad to see it happening in Martin Luther King's hometown," Jackson told members of Ali's entourage before the fight. "He would have loved it this way."[33]

Ali and his handlers pondered the meaning of fighting Quarry, a white boxer, in the Deep South. They cast Quarry in the role of "the great white hope." Ali drew upon Western movies—perhaps the most influential purveyor of melodramatic images of good against evil—to clarify the metaphysics of the match. Quarry, Ali suggested, would emerge a hero if he won, like the lone gunman who made the West safe for women and children. "Lose this one and Quarry'll be a movie star," Ali predicted. "By beatin' me, he'll be so valuable. He'll be in big cinemas, probably playin' in a top Western, the man who defeated Muhammad Ali. Like the man who shot Liberty Valance. He'll be a great man." Similar to other showdowns in politics and foreign affairs, the bout took on aspects of a Manichean struggle.[34]

Hollywood, however, had to find another hero. Despite the long exile, Ali beat Quarry and began his ascent back to the top. The outcome disappointed those who longed for the days when champions Jack Dempsey and Rocky Marciano had symbolized white supremacy by holding the most coveted crown in sports. Blacks' gains in sports during the 1960s complemented advances in other fields and contributed to their growing determination to attain full equality. No longer did blacks move to the back of the bus or say what whites wanted to hear. No longer did they accept picking cotton, scrubbing floors, toting baggage, and washing clothes as their natural lot in life. Subordinated to white power for centuries, the nation's African Americans sought "black power" by 1970, even if many avoided that loaded phrase. Ali had become a symbol of black pride and defiance of white authority. Like black activists, student radicals, antiwar protesters, and feminists, Ali represented still another threat to a fragile status quo. "As the present now will later be past, the order is rapidly fadin'," wailed Bob Dylan. "And the first one now will later be last, for the times they are a-changin'."[35]

As Ali entered the ring in Atlanta, his cornerman, Bundini Brown, shouted above the crowd, "Ghost in the house, ghost in the house!" He meant that the spirit of Jack Johnson hovered over the ring, awaiting a proud black man's triumph over another white hope. Ali's handlers compared the Quarry fight to the legendary 1910 battle between black champion Jack Johnson and the white former title holder Jim Jeffries. "I grew to love the Jack Johnson image," Ali remarked after his triumph. "I wanted to be rough, tough, arrogant, the nigger the white folks didn't like." When he spoke with James Earl Jones, the actor who played Johnson in the play and the movie *The Great White Hope*, Ali compared his ordeal to Johnson's exile after conviction on a White Slave Traffic Act charge. "History all over again," Ali told Jones.

But to characterize Ali as another Jack Johnson distorts the lives of both champions. Ali gained celebrity at a troubled time, but the time did not define him, nor did he symbolize his time. He first gained recognition because of his superb boxing skills. He acquired celebrity and international stature because he transformed his title into an entity that transcended sport. He risked fame, fortune, and even freedom to follow his conscience in a period of brutal bare-knuckle politics. His story, then, reveals a complicated symbiosis between character and context, not "history all over again" but history unique in time and place.[36]

Notes

1. Jack and Tom Cannon, eds., *Nobody Asked Me, But . . . The World of Jimmy Cannon* (New York: Holt, Rinehart and Winston, 1978), 149–50, 151.

2. Interview with Curtis Jones, in Henry Hampton and Steve Fayer,

with Sarah Flynn, *Voices of Freedom: An Oral History of the Civil Rights Movement from the 1950s through the 1980s* (New York: Bantam, 1990), 3; Muhammad Ali, with Richard Durham, *The Greatest: My Own Story* (New York: Random House, 1975), 34–35; Thomas Hauser, *Muhammad Ali: His Life and Times* (New York: Simon and Schuster, 1991), 89. For a useful study of the Till case, see Stephen J. Whitfield, *A Death in the Delta: The Story of Emmett Till* (New York: Free Press, 1988).

3. Wilma Rudolph, with Martin Ralbovsky, *Wilma: The Story of Wilma Rudolph* (New York: New American Library, 1977), 143–45.

4. *Louisville Defender* (hereafter abbreviated as *LD*), September 15, 22, October 20, 1960; Ali, *The Greatest*, 59–60, 64–77.

5. *LD*, April 2, 1959. In early 1960 the editor Frank Stanley grumbled that "Louisville has virtually stood still since the desegregation of public schools, pools, parks and public buildings." *LD*, February 25, 1960.

6. *LD*, September 1, 1960; Ali, *The Greatest*, 62–63; Huston Horn, "Who Made Me—Is Me!" *Sports Illustrated* (hereafter abbreviated as *SI*), September 25, 1961, 42; *Time*, March 22, 1963, 79; "The Ten Biggest Lies About Joe Louis," *Ebony*, August 1953, 55; *LD*, September 8, 15, 1960. Robert Lipsyte of the *New York Times* thought that Clay's retort to the Soviet reporter seemed "at the time like a press agent's quote." Lipsyte, *Sportsworld: An American Dreamland* (New York: Quadrangle, 1975), 79.

7. *LD*, October 6, 1960.

8. James Farmer, *Lay Bare the Heart: An Autobiography of the Civil Rights Movement* (New York: Arbor House, 1985), 258; Malcolm X, "Liberation by Any Means Necessary," in *Afro-American History: Primary Sources,* ed. Thomas R. Frazier, 2d ed. (Chicago: Dorsey, 1988), 394–95; Hampton et al., *Voices of Freedom*, 300; Dick Gregory, with James McGraw, *Up from Nigger* (New York: Stein and Day, 1976), 106; Jim Brown, with Steve Delsohn, *Out of Bounds* (New York: Kensington, 1989), 66; Bill Russell and Taylor Branch, *Second Wind: The Memoirs of an Opinionated Man* (New York: Ballantine, 1979), 206; *Norfolk Journal and Guide* (hereafter *NJG*), April 11, 1964; *New York Amsterdam News* (hereafter *NYAN*), September 26, 1964; *LD*, October 15, 1964; Malcolm X, with Alex Haley, *The Autobiography of Malcolm X* (New York: Grove, 1965), 308.

9. Lyndon Baines Johnson, *The Vantage Point: Perspectives of the Presidency 1963–1969* (New York: Holt, Rinehart and Winston, 1971), 427, 553; Harry McPherson, *A Political Education* (Boston: Little, Brown, 1972), 264. For material on Ali's lectures at colleges during his exile, see Tex Maule, "For Ali, a Time to Preach," *SI*, February 19, 1968, 26–28, 31; Hans J. Massaquoi, "The Unconquerable Muhammad Ali," *Ebony*, April 1969, 169–78; interviews with Muhammad Ali, Julian Bond, Belinda Ali, and Robert Lipsyte, in Hauser, *Muhammad Ali*, 185–90; Ali, *The Greatest*, 177, 250.

10. Abbie Hoffman, "Revolution for the Hell of It," in Judith Clavir

Albert and Stewart Edward Albert, *The Sixties Papers: Documents of a Rebellious Decade* (New York: Praeger, 1984); Abbie Hoffman, *Soon to Be a Major Motion Picture* (New York: Grosset and Dunlap, 1980). A fine study that analyzes both cultural and political developments is William L. O'Neill, *Coming Apart: An Informal History of America in the 1960s* (Chicago: Quadrangle, 1971).

11. Barry Sadler and Robin Moore, "The Ballad of the Green Berets," Music Music Music Inc., ©1963, 1964; P. F. Sloan, "Eve of Destruction," Trousdale Music, ©1965; Lee Adams and Charles Strouse, "Those Were the Days," New Tandem Music, ©1971.

12. Brown, *Out of Bounds,* 125; interview with Sanchez, in Hampton et al., *Voices of Freedom,* 328; interview with Lipsyte, in Hauser, *Muhammad Ali,* 190.

13. Interviews with Gardner, Turnbow, and Sims, in Howell Raines, *My Soul Is Rested: Movement Days in the Deep South Remembered* (New York: Putnam, 1977), 140–41, 262–66, 416–23. See also the interview with Cleveland Sellers of SNCC, in Hampton et al., *Voices of Freedom,* 284–86. For affidavits describing the harsh and often deadly actions by white law-enforcement figures and citizens in Mississippi, see *Mississippi Black Paper* (New York: Random House, 1965), a collection of affidavits and statements compiled by the Council of Federated Organizations.

14. Washington *Star,* February 27, 1964; *New York Times,* February 28, 1964; Hauser, *Muhammad Ali,* 81–84; Huston Horn, "The First Days in the New Life of the Champion of the World," *SI,* March 9, 1964, 27, 57; Angelo Dundee, with Mike Winters, *I Only Talk Winning* (Chicago: Contemporary Books, 1985), 192–93; interview with Dundee, in Hampton et al., *Voices of Freedom,* 328–29; Lipsyte, *Sportsworld,* 88–90; Howard Cosell, *Cosell* (Chicago: Playboy Press, 1973), 175–77.

15. *LD,* February 6, March 5, 1964; *Cleveland Call and Post* (hereafter abbreviated as *CCP*), March 7, 1964.

16. *NJG,* May 23, 1964; Floyd Patterson, with Milton Gross, "I Want to Destroy Clay," *SI,* October 19, 1964, 43–44; Floyd Patterson, "Cassius Clay Must Be Beaten," *SI,* October 11, 1965, 98. When Patterson repeatedly used *Clay* instead of *Ali,* Howard Cosell noted, it seemed like "a deliberate attempt by Floyd to cast himself in the role of the good guy." *Cosell,* 163; Budd Schulberg, *Loser and Still Champion: Muhammad Ali* (Garden City, N.Y.: Doubleday, 1972), 47. For Patterson's story, see Floyd Patterson, with Milton Gross, *Victory over Myself* (New York: Bernard Geis Associates, 1962).

17. Interviews with Pat Putnam and Harold Conrad, in Hauser, *Muhammad Ali,* 15, 64–67; Miami *Herald,* February 7, 1964; *NJG,* February 15, 1964; *St. Louis Argus* (hereafter abbreviated as *SLA*), March 6, 1964;

Jack Olsen, "Growing Up Scared in Louisville," *SI*, 101; Jack Olsen, "Learning Elijah's Advanced Lesson in Hate," *SI*, May 2, 1966, 37–38, 43; interview with Bingham, in Hauser, *Muhammad Ali*, 119.

18. *SLA*, July 9, 1965; *LD*, July 1, 1965; *NJG*, June 12, July 3, 1965; *NYAN*, July 17, 1965, January 22, 1966; Gil Rogin, "Not a Great Fight, But It Was a Real One," *SI*, December 6, 1965, 108; Ali, *The Greatest*, 120–21, 189–201; interview with Sonji Clay, in Hauser, *Muhammad Ali*, 130–31.

19. *CCP*, March 14, 1964; *NYAN*, March 7, 14, 1964; interview with Alex Haley, in Hauser, *Muhammad Ali*, 101–2; Malcolm X, *The Autobiography of Malcolm X*, 354–57; "Muhammad Ali in Africa," *SI*, June 1, 1964, 20–24; interview with Osman Karriem, in Hauser, *Muhammad Ali*, 109.

20. Gregory, *Up from Nigger*, 210; J. H. O'Dell interview with Hamer, in Frazier, ed., *Afro-American History: Primary Sources*, 365–66; interviews with Harry Belafonte and John Lewis, in Hampton et al., *Voices of Freedom*, 204–6; Hauser, *Muhammad Ali*, 265–66.

21. Olsen, "Learning Elijah's Advanced Lesson," 38; Isaac Sutton, "Intimate Look at the Champ," *Ebony*, November 1966, 154; *NYAN*, January 25, 1964; Rogin, "Not a Great Fight," 45; *NYAN*, January 16, 1965; Robert G. Hunter, "Big Muddle among the Big Ones," *Ebony*, May 1965, 114; Charles L. Sanders, "Muhammad Ali's Challenge to Black Men," *Ebony*, January 1975, 132; Edwin Shrake, "Taps for the Champ," *SI*, May 8, 1967, 22; Ali, *The Greatest*, 320; interview with Olsen, in Hauser, *Muhammad Ali*, 121; Olsen, "Learning Elijah's Advanced Lesson," 37–38; interview with Izenberg, in Hauser, *Muhammad Ali*, 122–23.

22. Curt Flood, with Richard Carter, *The Way It Is* (New York: Trident, 1970), 28–29; *SI*, August 5, 1963, 27; *NJG*, December 14, 1963.

23. *NYAN*, March 7, 1964; *Newsweek*, March 9, 1964, 51; Gordon Parks, *Voices in the Mirror: An Autobiography* (New York: Doubleday, 1990), 248, 250; Gordon Parks, *To Smile in Autumn: A Memoir* (New York: W. W. Norton, 1979), 160–61. Ali's racial views are also discussed in Brown, *Out of Bounds*, 186; Dundee, *I Only Talk Winning*, 199; Cosell, *Cosell*, 187; interview with Plimpton, in Hauser, *Muhammad Ali*, 282–83; *SI*, January 21, 1974, 24. See also Sugar Ray Robinson, with Dave Anderson, *Sugar Ray* (New York: Viking, 1970), 347; Wilfred Sheed, *Muhammad Ali: A Portrait in Words and Photographs* (New York: Thomas Y. Crowell, 1975), 181, 226; and José Torres, "Notes on the Champion," *Black Sports*, February 1978, 12.

24. Lipsyte, *Sportsworld*, 91; *Muhammad Speaks*, April 7, May 12, 1967; Malcolm X, *The Autobiography of Malcolm X*, 203.

25. *LD*, March 26, 1964; *NJG*, March 28, 1964; Ali, *The Greatest*, 125–28, 136–38, 155–71; Sheed, *Muhammad Ali*, 109; Hauser, *Muhammad Ali*, 16, 142–47, 166–70; Parks, *Voices in the Mirror*, 250; Robinson, *Sugar Ray*,

348–50; *NYAN,* May 13, 1967; *NJG,* May 13, June 10, July 15, 1967; Floyd Patterson, "In Defense of Cassius Clay," *Esquire,* August 1966, 57–58; Bill Russell, with Tex Maule, "I Am Not Worried About Ali," *SI,* June 19, 1967, 19–21; Brown, *Out of Bounds,* 191–92; interviews with Brown, Kareem Abdul-Jabbar, and Bill Russell, in Hauser, *Muhammad Ali,* 177–79; interview with Abdul-Jabbar, in Hampton et al., *Voices of Freedom,* 330–31.

26. Interview with Lipsyte, in Hauser, *Muhammad Ali,* 144–45; interview with Bingham, ibid., 47; Ali, *The Greatest,* 134; Parks, *Voices in the Mirror,* 250; Parks, *To Smile in Autumn,* 161–62; *LD,* April 6, 20, 1967; Robert H. Boyle, "Champ in the Jug?" *SI,* April 10, 1967, 30.

27. "SNCC Statement on Vietnam," January 1966, in *The New Radicals: A Report with Documents,* ed. Paul Jacobs and Saul Landau (New York: Random House, 1966), 250–52; Ralph David Abernathy, *And the Walls Came Tumbling Down* (New York: Harper and Row, 1989), 333; interview with John Lewis, in Raines, *My Soul Is Rested,* 212; Gordon Parks, *Born Black* (Philadelphia: J. B. Lippincott, 1971), 93–94; Parks, *Voices in the Mirror,* 239; *NYAN,* July 30, 1966; Martin Luther King, Jr., "A Time to Break Silence," April 4, 1967, in *A Testament of Hope: The Essential Writings of Martin Luther King, Jr.,* ed. James Melvin Washington (San Francisco: Harper, 1991), 231–44; Martin Luther King, Jr., *The Trumpet of Conscience* (New York: Harper and Row, 1967); *NJG,* January 15, 1966, April 8, 9, 1967; *LD,* January 6, 1966; *NYAN,* January 22, 1966, October 21, 1967, February 26, March 26, 1966; *LD,* November 22, 1967; *Muhammad Speaks,* May 5, 1967.

28. New York *Herald-Tribune,* February 23, 1966; Ali, *The Greatest,* 127–28, 138, 142–44, 174–75; *Congressional Record,* 89th Congress, 2d Session, vol. 112, pt. 5, 5880 (March 15, 1966); *Congressional Record,* 91st Congress, 2d Session, vol. 116, pt. 23, 31210–31211 (September 10, 1970); *LD,* February 24, 1966; William Barry Furlong, "The Wind that Blew in Chicago," *SI,* March 7, 1966, 26; interview with Harold Conrad, in Hauser, *Muhammad Ali,* 208–9. In March 1973, Ali *did* fight in California, meeting ex-Marine Ken Norton in San Diego, a navy town and a stronghold of Golden State conservatives. Norton won.

29. Cosell, *Cosell,* 360–61; Bill Rhoden, "Howard Cosell Tells It Like It Is," *Ebony,* December 1976, 76–77; Myron Cope, "Would You Let This Man Interview You?" *SI,* March 13, 1967, 82; George Plimpton, *Shadow Box* (New York: Putnam, 1977), 136–37. Seldom had Mark Twain's insight proved more apt: "It is by the goodness of God that in our country we have those three unspeakably precious things: freedom of speech, freedom of conscience, and the prudence never to practice either of them." Mark Twain, *Following the Equator* (Hartford: American Publishing Co., 1897), 195.

30. Interview with Carl Walker, in Hauser, *Muhammad Ali,* 180–81; I. F. Stone, *In a Time of Torment* (New York: Random House, 1967), 366–67; Shirley Chisholm, *Unbought and Unbossed* (Boston: Houghton Mifflin, 1970), 99; Massimo Teodori, ed., *The New Left: A Documentary History* (Indianapolis: Bobbs-Merrill, 1969), 350–51, 363–64; Albert and Albert, *The Sixties Papers,* 416; Athan Theoharis, ed., *From the Secret Files of J. Edgar Hoover* (Chicago: Ivan Dee, 1991), 100; Joseph A. Califano, Jr., *The Triumph and Tragedy of Lyndon Johnson: The White House Years* (New York: Simon and Schuster, 1991), 169, 336–37; Lawrence O'Brien, *No Final Victories: A Life in Politics—from John F. Kennedy to Watergate* (Garden City, N.Y.: Doubleday, 1974), 192, 225; McPherson, *A Political Education,* 455; Ali, *The Greatest,* 144, 276.

31. Charles W. Colson, *Born Again* (Old Tappan, N.J.: Chosen Books, 1976), 41, 45, 61; Nixon to Pat Buchanan, June 10, 1972, Colson to Jay Lovestone, "personal," April 29, 1972, in *From: The President—Richard Nixon's Secret Files,* ed. Bruce Oudes (New York: Harper and Row, 1989), 475, 431; John W. Dean III, *Blind Ambition: The White House Years* (New York: Simon and Schuster, 1976), 31. See also William Safire, *Before the Fall: An Inside View of the Pre-Watergate White House* (Garden City, N.Y.: Doubleday, 1975), 307–15, 341–65, 690; Elizabeth Drew, *Washington Journal: The Events of 1973–1974* (New York: Macmillan, 1975), and J. Anthony Lukas, *Nightmare: The Underside of the Nixon Years* (New York: Penguin, 1988 [1976]).

32. Ali, *The Greatest,* 320–21, 106–7; Hauser, *Muhammad Ali,* 269; Plimpton, *Shadow Box,* 302; interview with Dundee, in Hauser, *Muhammad Ali,* 460–61; Dundee, *I Only Talk Winning,* 254.

33. For an overview of the politics of promoting Ali's return to boxing, see Harold Conrad's remarks in Hauser, *Muhammad Ali,* 208–9; Schulberg, *Loser and Still Champion,* 58–66; and Ali, *The Greatest,* 267–75. For accounts of the buildup to the bout with Quarry, see: Ali, *The Greatest,* 302, 311–18; Mark Kram, "Smashing Return of the Old Ali," *SI,* November 2, 1970, 18–19; George Plimpton, "Watching the Man in the Mirror," *SI,* November 23, 1970, 88; Plimpton, *Shadow Box,* 138–64; Schulberg, *Loser and Still Champion,* 74–81.

34. *SI,* October 26, 1970, 19; Ali, *The Greatest,* 330.

35. Bob Dylan, "The Times They Are A-Changin'," M. Whitmark and Sons, ©1963.

36. Ali, *The Greatest,* 319–20, 324; Plimpton, *Shadow Box,* 152, 164; Lacy Banks, "The Biggest Fight in History," *Ebony,* March 1971, 135; Mark Kram, "He Moves Like Silk, Hits Like a Ton," *SI,* October 26, 1970; Hans J. Massaquoi, "The Private World of Muhammad Ali," *Ebony,* September 1972, 148; interview with Jones, in Hauser, *Muhammad Ali,* 197–98;

James Earl Jones, with Penelope Niven, *Voices and Silences* (New York: Scribners, 1993), 210–11; Sheed, *Muhammad Ali,* 30; Plimpton, "Watching the Man in the Mirror," 88; Mark Kram, "Manila—For Blood and Money," *SI,* September 29, 1975, 35; Schulberg, *Loser and Still Champion,* 153. I explore the idea of a dynastic succession among black heavyweights and detail the continuities and contrasts among Johnson, Louis, and Ali in a book I am writing about twentieth-century race relations and black champions.

7

Rebel with a Cause: Muhammad Ali as Sixties Protest Symbol

Jeffrey T. Sammons

This essay does not measure Muhammad Ali by standards of moral or political correctness. It is self-evident that he, like any human, is flawed. My previous work on the boxer treats some of those defects. Other contributors to this book have done the same. Here I choose not to "know" him as he "truly" was, but to discuss the ways he moved me and so many others, especially people of my generation, to pride, self-respect, and defiance. No blemishes of character, personality, words, or actions can invalidate his impact. After all, "truth," like "beauty," is subjectively derived.[1]

My objective is to place a movement, a people, a sport, and, ultimately, a person in the center of historical events and scholarship. For many, the 1960s were a time of hedonism, of a senseless destruction of values, of the trashing of institutions. Many remember the era for its flower children, Jimi Hendrix, Janis Joplin, free love, LSD, and communal living—people and phenomena that can be considered subversive. Nonetheless, cultural opposition has not received its due from historians of the period. Nor have blacks and the civil-rights movement—I prefer to call it the "freedom struggle," because "civil rights" is subject to narrow definitions and time frames—been treated as central to that opposition. As the historian Bret Eynon has astutely observed, scholars of the era tend to focus on a single movement and remain "indifferent to relationships between its constituent" parts. The New Left and civil-rights movements, for example, are rarely linked. When the latter is recognized as a motivating factor in the rise of white student activism, little attention is paid to the mechanisms of influence and their centrality.[2]

Unfortunately, blacks find themselves compartmentalized in the history of this critical juncture in the American experience. Thus, it is not surprising that Ali—as a boxer, a black, and a member of the Nation of Islam—is even farther removed from the discussion. If culture is devalued in these analyses, boxing is dismissed. If blacks in the civil-rights mainstream are marginalized by scholars, then the Nation of Islam resides on the outer fringe. Nonetheless, a close inspection of this remarkable man and boxer will place him—a black hero of popular culture—in the center of the sixties, while locating him within the context of his people, nation, and sport.

According to Howard Zinn, "blacks and whites have always been morally intertwined in American history, even when physically separated, even when playing out the roles of subordinate and superordinate."[3] Thus the black freedom struggles and the heightened black consciousness of the late fifties, with their activism, militancy, and radicalism, touched the sensibilities of whites, many of whom were moved to question old attitudes and behaviors. None was affected more than white students, as blacks pricked their consciences, gave them their cues, and even trained them in the tactics of direct confrontation and opposition in the Congress of Racial Equality (CORE) and the Student Nonviolent Coordinating Committee (SNCC).[4] Few remember that, following speeches by Stokely Carmichael, protesting black students died in gun battles with police at Texas Southern and South Carolina State universities, before the highly publicized and widely condemned fatal shooting of white students at Kent State. Shortly thereafter, police killed students at Jackson State University in Mississippi, but that tragedy too got relatively little press attention and remains a mere footnote to history.[5] These tragic incidents on black southern campuses reflected African American students' continued activism and heightened militance directed against the injustices of a racist American society. White students' rejection of racism, militarism, and materialism derived in part from black actions against a social order dominated by elder white Anglo-Saxon males.[6]

Perhaps no single person embodied the ethic of protest and intersected with so many lives, ordinary and extraordinary, as did Muhammad Ali. His very name can evoke the turbulent decade of Black Muslims, Malcolm X, Angela Davis, H. Rap Brown, "The Great Society," Vietnam, Ella Baker, General Hershey, dashikis, Afros, "Black Power," MLK, JFK, RFK, and LBJ.[7] Sometimes referred to as the Fifth

Beatle, Ali fit in with those Liverpudlians, a deracinated group of foreign invaders with broad appeal, "weird" clothes, long hair, and "revolutionary" music.[8]

But we need not look that far for Ali's counterpart as rebel. Although few have made the connection, we could see another southern boy and solo performer as a closer relative of Ali in spirit and form—Elvis Presley. Both men, one as "The King" and the other as "The Greatest," reached a level of fame in which the mere mention of a single name triggers immediate recognition and vivid memories. On the surface, the link might seem tenuous, considering Elvis's silence on political matters, his celebrated military service, and the rumors that circulated about his views on race.[9] Yet, what Elvis was to the concert stage, Ali was to the ring. If Elvis was, according to Joe Klein, "the baby boomers' first, naughty declaration of independence from the unhip, bourgeois values of their parents," then Ali was its exemplification.[10] While Elvis chose to keep his views on the Vietnam War to himself, he did not publicly oppose other entertainers who expressed theirs. Although Elvis met President Richard M. Nixon, became a symbol of his "silent majority," and allegedly volunteered to inform for the FBI, the bureau's director reportedly dismissed him as unsuitable for its image.[11] The rejection suggests that Elvis might have been more threatening than he himself imagined or that J. Edgar Hoover was more delusional than anyone had thought possible. Certainly Elvis embraced Ali before he became safe and acceptable. Later, in 1972, Elvis gave Ali a robe with the rhinestone inscription "People's Choice" for his second bout against "Great White Hope" Jerry Quarry. The gesture demonstrated a recognition of Ali's status and a transcending of race, which countless others seemed unable to duplicate.[12]

Social critics often fail to recognize the influence of entertainers and athletes beyond their circumscribed realms. Boxers especially, even great heavyweight champions, have been viewed, in Ishmael Reed's words, as mere "grand hunk[s] of flesh, capable of devastating physical destruction." As Reed observed about Muhammad Ali, "He may be brilliant, but even his brilliance is used to praise his flesh."[13] But Reed detected something more: "Ali represented the New Black of the 1960s, who was the successor to the New Negro of the 1920s, glamorous, sophisticated, intelligent, international, and militant."[14] Sometimes in spite of himself, Ali challenged the stereotype in ways no other boxer had ever done. He set out to do more than box and carry "the bucket while the white men count the money."[15] In the process, he took prizefighting where it had never ventured before—not even in the days of Jack Johnson or Joe Louis—and showed us the centrality of sport, particularly boxing, to the larger society.

Boxing is a male ritual that evokes a lost warrior tradition while conditioning the masses to conventionalized and depersonalized violence. Roman leaders understood that metropolitan control involved "bread and circuses." Free wheat and public shows represented the forces holding the empire together. One must see boxing as serving a function similar to that of the gladiatorial spectacle. Though such ancient confrontations were overtly political in nature and purpose, conventional histories tend to ignore them as such because they have relegated mass spectator sports to the realm of leisure.[16]

Few academics have accorded boxing much respect. Yet, as Gerald Early has observed, "each boxing contest is a morality play, dialectical encounter, and universe-of-force display on canvas." Ultimately, it, like a gladiatorial spectacle, is an activity in which ideas of order are contested, and usually reaffirmed.[17]

Ali must be treated in this context. Certainly he and many of his followers believed that he fought for a way of life. For Ali to score victories in the ring, a circumscribed arena with its own rules, seemed tolerable, but when he took his fight beyond that arena, as his gladiatorial "ancestor" Spartacus had done, the forces of an ordered white-dominated society responded to the perceived threat.

Even as Cassius Clay, Ali represented the disillusionment of many blacks with generations of unfulfilled dreams and broken promises. Patience lost virtue as the NAACP's legalistic war against racial inequality stalled after the much-heralded victory in the *Brown* decision of 1954, which declared school segregation unconstitutional.[18] Emboldened by that Supreme Court ruling but disappointed with its implementation, many African Americans became more militant, combining legal tactics with boycotts and civil disobedience. Rosa Parks's courageous refusal to yield her bus seat to a white person sparked a long-planned attack on the Montgomery, Alabama, city government in the form of a bus boycott by hundreds of workers who risked jobs, livelihoods, and even their lives by refusing to ride in second-class conditions.[19]

With Martin Luther King, Jr., as their spiritual leader, and bolstered by women and children on the front lines, blacks marched down the road of activism. Yet, by the early sixties, many believed that the pace of the march that King led had slowed to a crawl. A new black militancy emerged, producing insightful people who found sources of oppression wherever they existed, including the world of sport. Some observers concluded that black athletes often served as pawns, covering up the system's transgressions against their own people. These "New Blacks" no longer accepted the premise that the athletic accomplishments of African Americans confirmed that the present system worked for all citizens; that if the masses of blacks were competitive, disciplined, hardworking, patriotic, and Godfearing, they too could realize the American dream.[20]

Newly sensitized blacks jettisoned athletic heroes they believed guilty of perpetuating these dangerous myths. Floyd Patterson, described by LeRoi Jones (now Amiri Baraka) as a "fruit of the missionary ethic, the tardy Horatio Alger, and the glad hand of integration," soon found himself out of place and time among the more militant African Americans. Patterson, a black man partially anglicized by his values, stood for white, "Liberal/Missionary America" and his fights would, according to Jones, defend the existing neocolonialist system.[21]

Malcolm X watched such developments with intense interest and purpose. As chief spokesperson for the Nation of Islam, his fiery oratory and uncompromising challenges to authority made him one of the most feared men in America. He was described by Budd Schulberg as a black intellectual with a burning scorn for "the collective white man and the so-called American Negro."[22] Reminiscent of Frederick Douglass, Malcolm considered prizefights exploitive affairs, in which whites gleefully permitted blacks to act like animals. But Malcolm went a step further than the brilliant abolitionist and human-rights leader, reasoning that mechanisms of social control worked both ways, that power flowed in many directions. Malcolm sensed that the time was right to exploit the obvious link between sport and society.[23]

Though earlier black leaders, such as James Weldon Johnson and Walter White of the NAACP, already saw such a connection in the thirties and forties and employed athletes and athletics in the cause of "civil rights," they could not use sport as an oppositional strategy in ways that Malcolm X would. The Nation of Islam's nationalist objectives were not rooted in the basic ideals of American society but instead challenged the value, validity, and very existence of those ideals.[24] Concluding that those who controlled boxing champions wielded real and symbolic power, Malcolm X set out to stage-manage Ali's career. Malcolm's own views and deeply held religious and political convictions would be transmitted and amplified through his mouthpiece—the young, brash Cassius Marcellus Clay, already, secretly, Cassius X, and soon to be Muhammad Ali. Ali represented a weapon of enormous potential, who, under Malcolm's direction and influence, could spread the message of Allah and "convert" thousands. The throne of the heavyweight king would be a power base for the Nation of Islam.[25]

As a black fighter, Clay represented a distinct break from the past.[26] He was, according to Maurice Berube, destined to become "a folk hero, one of the first truly black men to challenge America in black terms." He was neither "the humble Negro champion like Joe Louis" nor "the 'non-white' champion, Jack Johnson, who terrified whites by seeking white prerogatives."[27]

At first, Clay appeared to be a Madison Avenue product created as a foil for the bestial new champion, Sonny Liston, a boxer closely linked to organized crime and representing what LeRoi Jones called "the huge Negro, the bad nigger, a heavy-faced replica of every whipped up woogie in the world." In a way that only Jones could articulate, Liston "was the underdeveloped, have-not (politically naive), backward country, the subject people, finally here to collect his pound of flesh."[28] But Clay turned out to be more than most bargained for, as his blustery ranting and playground poetry hid an inner racial anxiety.[29]

In the end, Ali proved difficult for anyone—even Malcolm X—to control. Often scorned for poisoning the young boxer's mind, Malcolm soon learned that the anger he thought he had harnessed was turned against him, as Ali chose Elijah Muhammad over his mentor.[30] The choice, according to Jones, proved that Ali was still "a homeboy, embracing this folksy vector straight out of hard spiritualism of poor Negro aspiration."[31] Nonetheless, Ali kept enough of Malcolm and his own independence to threaten powerful institutions, sportive and otherwise, while contributing to the radicalization of millions of Americans, especially the young.

Forever linked in peoples' minds with Malcolm, and with a "foreign" religion, Ali became a dangerous alien in his own land and among some African Americans. Class and generational differences led many to refuse to call him by his new name. Few, however, could deny his courage in insisting on his right to define himself and his identity, even if they failed to see how his acts empowered them. His victory over Liston for the heavyweight championship led to predictions that, henceforth, Ali would fight with weapons never before carried into an American ring: his faith in a nonwestern religion (though the Nation of Islam, like black Christianity, was infused with African American culture) and his belief that he was part of a global family of nonwhites that would eventually defeat a Caucasian minority.[32] This characterization of his potential reflected Malcolm's views more than Ali's, but it revealed that power could emanate from perception and become real in the process.

The boxing world reacted harshly to the young champion's religious conversion. The World Boxing Association quickly suspended Ali's title for conduct detrimental to the best interests of boxing and eventually stripped him of it for arranging a rematch with Liston. For reasons that are not entirely clear, the three most important state boxing commissions—New York, California, and Pennsylvania—refused to go along with the association's decision, thereby creating a disputed title. Interestingly, one of Ali's staunchest defenders was Senator Richard Russell, a diehard segregationist from Georgia, who maintained that Ali was being unfairly persecuted for holding separatist beliefs in a totalitarian-integrationist climate. Russell's strategy continued a tradition that linked segregationists to black separatists—from the colonizationists to Booker T. Washington, from Marcus Garvey to the Nation of Islam (the latter two even had dealings with the Ku Klux Klan).[33]

For Ali, the boxing ring had provided a unique opportunity—and a highly visible, prestigious, and powerful arena—for his remarkable talent to distinguish itself. His extraordinary skills as a boxer, combined with his wit, good looks, flamboyance, courage, and independence, carried him not only to the top of his profession but beyond the ring as a transcendent and transformative figure. Perhaps adding to Ali's elevation as symbol were the seeming contradictions he embodied. While there was so much of Ali that gave validity to descriptions of prizefighting as the "sweet science" and "manly art," he was also an iconoclast. It was the simultaneous attraction and repulsion of those within his sport that made Ali so fascinating. And though hostility to the obvious political side of Ali gets most of the scholarly and lay attention, the cultural component of Ali's oppositional role might be his most meaningful and enduring legacy. As Michael Eric Dyson argues, it is no accident that Ali's eldest daughter, May May (Maryum), is a rapper, imitating, transforming, and "sampling" her father's prose and poetry.[34]

Ali's actions in the ring offended, even threatened, many officials, fans, and casual observers. They believed he was corrupting the standards of athletic behavior with his blatant displays of black cultural styles in body and mouth. His "wolfing" or "trash talking," his self-promotional poetry, and the "Ali Shuffle" seemed to run contrary to the pattern set by the humble, unassuming, no-frills demeanor and style of Joe Louis. If Louis stood for quiet dignity then Ali represented loud arrogance. If Louis was blue-collar then Ali was somewhere between zoot suit and dinner jacket. Combined with his other departures from the norm, Ali represented what Robin D. G. Kelley might call a multiple signifier of opposition—rejecting "American patriotism," integrationism, athletic codes of behavior, and obligatory black humility.[35] Neither Ali's words nor his movements seemed appropriate for athletic heroes.

A return to Elvis shows the force of oppositional culture. Elvis's black-inspired gyrations led to waist-down television censorship in the late 1950s as many people decried the damage the singer inflicted on American and Christian values.[36] While Ali could not sing, he was a musical artist in the ring. Boxing, according to Larry Neal, is "just another kind of rhythmic activity," from jumping rope (dancing) to punching the speed bag (drumming). "Fighters must understand the principles of rhythmic modality," Neal maintains. The boxer who understands them best is most likely to win.[37] No one manipulated space and motion in a rhythmic fashion better than Ali. At the same time, he verbally taunted opponents, mocked them with his dazzling shuffle, and feigned injury to lull them into a false sense of security. In doing so, he revolutionized boxing style and further removed the sport from white control—in a cultural and symbolic sense, not fiscally or organizationally.

In addition to all of this was what we might call Ali's "re-gendering" of the sport. While not widely noted by his opponents in and out of the ring, Ali's "dandification" of boxing contributed to both his appeal and his repulsiveness. A keen student of Gorgeous George, a bleached blond, foppish "champion" wrestler, Ali mastered the techniques of oppositional villainy by adopting qualities men like to associate with women.[38] He harped on his good looks, referring to his face as pretty, not handsome. He acted emotional, even hysterical, in contrast to the stoic calm or menacing gaze expected of warriors about to enter combat. In the ring Ali more closely resembled a ballet dancer than a boxer, with smooth, glistening skin almost devoid of body hair. To "float like a butterfly and sting like a bee" was hardly in the Jack Dempsey or Joe Louis tradition of masculinity.[39]

More disturbing to his detractors, and even to some of those who supported him, was the spread of his cultural impositions beyond the ring. Just as Nazi officials saw jazz—"nigger/Jew music"—as a threat to the order, not lending itself to a martial beat or social conformity, some observers recognized in Ali, as Neal put it, "the urbanized philosopher . . . having a tendency to sound down mammy-loving country boys who lack causes, and who are grateful for any desperate break they can get."[40]

From the end-zone dance of Elmo Wright to the adoption of Islamic names by black athletic heroes such as basketball great Lew Alcindor (Kareem Abdul-Jabbar) and football star Bobby Moore (Ahmad Rashaad), Ali's oppositional style interlaced itself into the social fabric.[41] Worse, countercultural gestures and names were quickly surpassed by acts of resistance, such as the Olympic boycott in 1968. Jabbar was one of the few world-class athletes who boycotted the games and spoke out about his decision in spite of enormous pressure to participate. Yet, staying home proved less costly than competing and defying. Tommie Smith and John Carlos protested alone— or so it seemed at the time, since few realized that Peter Norman of Australia, thought to be erect in "polite attention" for the medal ceremony, wore a badge in a show of solidarity with the protesters. Smith and Carlos stood with heads down and fists raised in a black-power salute, though they shared one pair of black gloves, at once dramatizing the gesture and revealing the lack of organization behind it. The imprecision of their gesture, however, did not blur the message. Hypersensitive Olympic officials, sensationalists in the media, and posturing politicians condemned the "spoilsports" for defiling the "sacred" occasion, with all its nationalistic overtones.[42] Nonetheless, the revolt against authority spread to college campuses as black athletes assumed the unfamiliar role of student-protest leaders. Even more alarming to authorities, the blight infected white athletes, as football players sported shoulder-length hair and drooping mustaches in contempt of military dress and grooming codes. Some of them even cited connections between sport, militarism, and a repressive Nixon administration.[43]

Not surprisingly, a person of Ali's complexity carried out actions equally complex in their effect. His attacks against other blacks have been attributed to everything from religious zealotry to self-hatred to class bias. Ali's uncritical acceptance of the teachings of Elijah Muhammad led him on occasion to advocate death for celebrities whose lifestyles he considered unacceptable. Although extreme and rare, his position, Ishmael Reed believed, "reminds one that blacks who are freedom fighters to whites are often slavers and bully boys to Afro-Americans."[44] More characteristic was Ali's demeaning treatment of black opponents, often associating them with other forms of animal life. Reed suspected that Ali's description of Liston as a "big black ugly bear" and Frazier as "King Kong" might be an invoking of "the skin privileges of his caste," just as his references to his own beauty might have paid unwitting homage to Caucasian features.[45] However, the evidence does not seem to support Reed's analysis of Ali's use of such epithets as color-based self-hatred. Rather it seems a class-related test in which Ali saw himself as respectable and the others as "lower orders." Interestingly, Gerald Early combined the two perspectives by concluding that Ali abhorred "blacks who traditionally made things 'hard for the race.'" To Early, Ali, in part, "was as much of a striver as a hard-working, light-skinned hero from a Charles Chesnutt or Jessie Fauset novel."[46] Larry Neal also saw in Ali's attitude an elitist element that drove him to condemn the legacies of slave culture, manifested in the change of his name, rejection of a slave diet, and suppression of a "gospel impulse."[47] Still, most of Ali's actions and his language revealed no shame in being black and no desire to seek privilege in "white blood." The Nation of Islam taught that whites were inferiors created by a mad scientist. As a believer, therefore, Ali was part of a movement defining a new standard of blackness. In the process, both the movement and Ali defamed a black past that had much to praise as well as condemn—one to which many blacks still clung.

Nonetheless, Ali did not totally divorce himself from a slave culture and its contemporary offspring. A case can be made that Ali was the consummate trickster of black folklore, the fast and clever rabbit evading dogs, bears, and gorillas—the signifying monkey outwitting no less than "the man."[48] Moreover, tricksters often denounced one another. Ali once publicly referred to Leon Spinks as a "nigger," then realized his indiscretion and tried to recover by explaining that only "niggers" could use the dreaded epithet, making clear that, to him, source and context were everything. The practice continues today as rappers use the term with unprecedented frequency in the public arena, claiming that through their voices the word becomes antivenin, that the poison is in the user rather than the term. Richard Pryor, a public pioneer in this matter, once thought similarly but had a change of heart, as revealed in classic encounters with Dick Cavett and Chevy Chase, concerning the inappropriateness of the use of the term by anyone.[49]

Of course, some of this behavior was about the selling of Muhammad Ali. Rarely missing a promotional opportunity, Ali realized his mouth attracted press attention, which in turn sold fight tickets and "psyched out" opponents. But, to understand this side of Ali we must consider something analysts have missed. Ali seems to have viewed his rivals as extensions or front men for others, thus he attacked whites through them, employing words in a semantic war before, during, and after the symbolic one in the ring. In this sense Ali was probably less a loose cannon than a smart bomb. His words had clear targets, although they inflicted some "collateral damage." It seemed to Ali a small price to pay for making the point that "every brother ain't your brother."[50] The motives behind Ali's words and actions, along with their consequences, might be questioned, but there is no doubt that Ali as trickster represented the extent of black political impotence, traditionally defined.

Ali defeated Sonny Liston in a controversial rematch, which ended in a mysterious first-round knockout from a phantom punch. The Ali victory eliminated the "invincible" former champion as a contender. With Liston out of the way, a new strategy for defeating Ali, the undesirable alien champion, became necessary. No capable white opponents existed, but a more subtle campaign was needed to bring down Ali and what he represented. Thus, Floyd Patterson "rose" from boxing's grave—after two humiliating and devastating losses to Liston—as the redeeming Christian, a savior of moderate-liberal, integrationist American values.[51]

The matchup, a promoter's dream, symbolized a Holy War, or so it seemed. Patterson insisted on calling Ali "Clay." In further disrespect for Ali's new faith, he compared the Nation of Islam to the Ku Klux Klan, hitting closer to home than he could have imagined, as Malcolm X would reveal. Yet, in reality religion mattered less than racial ideology, patriotism, and society's standards for proper athletic behavior.[52] Patterson failed miserably in his "crusade." Ali punished him brutally throughout the fight.[53]

The more Ali fought, won, and boasted, the more he personified discontent and unrest. And his influence continued to extend beyond blacks, making him the ultimate "crossover" artist long before the term found wide usage in popular culture. His "cross-racial" bonding with the antiwar generation made Ali the most visible victim of the Vietnam War psychosis that was captured in the phrase "Love it or leave it." In 1963, when many still considered Ali charmingly obnoxious, the selective service classified him 1-Y—mentally incompetent to serve in the armed forces. Only a few hostile congressmen reacted, railing against the classification as an insult to "every mother's son" serving in Vietnam. But once Ali became champion and a Muslim, a chorus of vengeful voices called out for his reclassification.[54]

The objective on the part of some seemed to be "co-optation," making Ali a part of the establishment. The government plan required Ali to replay the role Joe Louis had performed in World War II as morale builder and role model for blacks. In exchange Ali would be guaranteed no combat duty.[55] Although Louis and Ali sought justice for their people, the gulf between them is measured in the tone, form, and message of their responses. In a voice of moderation and cooperation just as conservative and economical as his fighting style, Louis said that although there was "a lot wrong with America," there was nothing "Hitler could fix."[56] Ali responded to the pressure to support the war in Vietnam in characteristically radical, irreverent, and defiant rhyme:

> Keep asking me, no matter how long.
> On the war in Vietnam,
> I sing this song
> I ain't got no quarrel with the Vietcong.[57]

Ali's first reaction to reclassification revealed more shock and bewilderment than willful defiance or even clever poetry. Even the oft-quoted "Man, I ain't got no quarrel with them Vietcong" came only after persistent and continuous questioning from the press on the day of his reclassification, according to an eyewitness, Robert Lipsyte. Nonetheless, Ali's subsequent statements and actions lived up to the poetic objection as Ali signaled the pointlessness of the war and the racism of America when he thoughtfully offered, "I'm expected to go overseas to help free people in South Vietnam, and at the same time my people here are brutalized and mistreated."[58] So many whites were scandalized because, in a few words, Ali affirmed that America's enemy was not his, that American racism itself was his real foe. Ali's defiance proved all the more galling because of his status as a sports hero who refused to play by the rules. It unleashed an angry and vengeful reaction from the highest levels of American government, for the nation's greatest symbolic warrior had rejected his nation's imperialistic adventures and militaristic values. He was a living contradiction, and a threat to the existing order. The oft-quoted comment of the sportswriter Jimmy Cannon bears repeating, for it captures so well the anger against the young, the fear of their cultural rebellion:

> Clay is part of the Beatle movement. He fits with the famous singers no one can hear and the punks riding motorcycles with iron crosses pinned to their leather jackets and Batman and the boys with their long dirty hair and the girls with the unwashed look and the college kids dancing naked at secret proms held in apartments and the revolt of students who get a check from dad every first of the month and the painters who copy the labels off soup cans and the surf bums who refuse to work and the whole pampered style-making cult of the bored young.[59]

Ali's draft notice quickly followed Cannon's February 22, 1966, editorial.[60]

What few people accepted was that Ali's objection to this increasingly unpopular war emanated from a higher source than politics. So great was his faith, Ali vowed to face a firing squad before denouncing Elijah Muhammad and the religion of Islam.[61] Among black public figures, Ali's stance was unequivocal and uncompromising. As for the mainstream civil-rights organizations, only SNCC had preceded Ali in officially opposing the war. On January 6, 1966, three days after the killing of a SNCC organizer in Tuskegee, Alabama, a spokesperson publicly denounced the undeclared conflict as a racist assault upon peoples of color here and abroad. Not only did the statement widen the gap between SNCC and old-line civil-rights organizations such as the NAACP and the Urban League, it also earned the group the enmity of the Johnson administration.[62] Martin Luther King, Jr., deeply troubled by the war, refused to condemn SNCC, and on April 4, 1967, in an event sponsored by Clergy and Laymen Concerned About Vietnam, King came out against the war. Andrew Young compared the reaction following the speech to "a torrent of hate and venom."[63] King had expected responsible and reasonable people to support him but was shocked to find the *New York Times* and *Washington Post* joining the assault, painting him as unpatriotic. According to Harry Belafonte, the attacks on King helped to create "a climate of hate and distortion" that led to his death.[64]

Ali made his decision with a clear understanding of what awaited him and he never wavered in the storm. His reading of the Qu'ran instructed him to reject all wars unless they were just, meaning a religious war against nonbelievers. Justice William O. Douglas declared that Ali's refusal was "a matter of belief, of conscience, of religious principle." But few others agreed, certainly not Douglas's Supreme Court colleagues, who ultimately would determine Ali's fate.[65]

Despite the ambivalence of his Muslim manager, Herbert Muhammad, who saw the loss of a cash cow for the Nation of Islam, and a plea for caution from a group of prominent African American athletes, Ali continued to refuse induction into the armed forces. As he later told college audiences: "The wealth of America and the friendship of all the people who support the war would be nothing if I'm not content internally and if I'm not in accord with the will of Almighty Allah."[66]

Ordered to report for induction on April 28, 1967, Ali found enthusiastic young people outside the federal courthouse in Houston, urging him to refuse the draft. They carried signs reading: "Ali, your fight is in the ring" and "Hep, Hep Don't take that step" (the latter referred to the customary step forward signifying acceptance of the draft order). Ali probably appreciated the moral support, but he had already made up his mind to stay put as the others stepped forward.[67]

Within hours of his action, boxing commissions stripped Ali of his license. Without due process, his ability and right to earn a living had been denied. The sporting press fueled the opposition, ranting that

"Clay seems to have gone past the borders of faith. He has reached the boundaries of fanaticism."[68]

Government officials shared the view and took extraordinary steps to make an example of Ali. In the process they created a living martyr. Despite the fact that the Justice Department's own hearing examiner recommended conscientious objector status for Ali, the department advised the draft board to reject his claim based on its conclusion that Ali failed "to satisfy each of the three basic tests for qualification as a conscientious objector."[69] The conscientious objector must exhibit opposition to war in any form, opposition based on religious training and belief, and sincerity of opposition. In a categorical denial of his claims, the Justice Department's letter to the Draft Appeal Board stated that Ali's beliefs did not "preclude military service in any form, but rather are limited to military service in the Armed Forces of the United States." As for the second test, it also maintained that the teachings of the Nation of Islam were primarily racial and political and not religious. Last, the Justice Department concluded that Ali had failed to meet the third test because his claims were not consistently manifested but only surfaced when military service became imminent. Thus, the board had little recourse but to reject Ali's appeal for reclassification. It did so but without citing these reasons in its decision, an omission that proved critical in the final outcome of the case.[70]

The prosecution of Ali demonstrated the government's zealous pursuit of the war effort and its unbridled hostility to those in opposition. Moreover, it revealed the power of bureaucratic institutions, which, although composed of individuals, seem to have a mentality of their own that often overwhelms individual beliefs and actions. Indeed, the quest for power often involves an articulation of positions that move the actor(s) as close to the seat of power as possible.[71] The cast of characters involved in the prosecution and the handling of the case demonstrate how personal conscience and even the rule of law suffer in organizations designed to protect the *status quo*. The breakdown becomes even more serious when government and its citizens have a siege mentality and justify the flouting of civil liberties in the name of national security.[72]

The roles and actions of several officials illustrate the dynamics of bureaucratic institutions and individual action within them. First, Ramsey Clark, considered the most liberal Attorney General in the history of the nation, approved Ali's prosecution. He defended his actions on the grounds that Ali had violated the law and that his own avoidance of television left him out of touch with events. Second, Thurgood Marshall—once the nation's leading civil-rights attorney— was, as Solicitor General, technically in charge of the prosecution. His earlier involvement necessitated his recusal when the case reached the High Court, where he then sat. Third, Carl Walker, a black man, was the assistant U.S. attorney in Houston who largely conducted the prosecution. Despite a fondness for Ali, Walker maintained that he was only doing his job. In a telling interview with Thomas Hauser, Walker admitted that politics played a large role in the case. Many feared that if Ali were allowed to escape the draft, others would be encouraged to join the despised Nation of Islam, making it much bigger, and the U.S. military considerably smaller, in the process. Walker's additional observation about the rare rejection of the hearing examiner's recommendation lent support to his assessment of the primacy of politics over law.[73] Last, some evidence used to build the government's case came from a wiretapped conversation between Ali and Martin Luther King, Jr. The tap was on King's phone, authorized by Robert F. Kennedy.[74]

On June 20, 1967, an all-white jury found Ali guilty of draft evasion. Despite a prosecution request for leniency, Judge Joe Ingraham imposed the maximum sentence allowable—five years' imprisonment and a fine of ten thousand dollars. Moreover, the judge ordered the confiscation of Ali's passport, which precluded his earning a living in the ring. The fact that Ali's record had only one blemish, a speeding ticket, and that he had agreed to ask followers of the Nation of Islam to stay away from Houston and call off all demonstrations, made no difference. The champ had to pay for what authorities considered threatening actions. Persecution followed Ali everywhere. During his release on appeal, law officers in Florida arrested and jailed him for a traffic violation. The episode showed Ali the horrors of incarceration, the pervasiveness of the hostility toward him, and the distinct possibility of his serving a full sentence for draft evasion. Yet, he announced upon his release that he was prepared to stick to his principles and face the consequences.[75]

From that moment on, Ali became the undisputed champion of the antiestablishment crowd. The college campus, a refuge of free expression, gave him a place to find his voice. There he elaborated on his defiance in terms that resonated with his antiwar audience, who saw him as the representative of their own generation's distrust of institutional authority. Despite considerable disagreement with his younger, largely white audiences, Ali became their hero because of his stand on the war. Students seemed willing to overlook his positions on integration, intermarriage, drugs, and the counterculture, all of which flowed from his Islamic faith. Ali's differences with other black Americans also receded to the extent that he assumed the status of victim and martyr and that his message became serious, sober, and purposeful: "I could make millions if I led my people the wrong way, to something I know is wrong. . . . Damn the money. Damn the heavyweight championship. I will die before I sell out my people for the white man's money."[76]

Now Ali's fate was in the hands of his lawyers, the courts, and public opinion. Although the mood of the country had changed since Ali first refused induction, many wanted him punished. Yet, the Supreme Court could not ignore all that was going on around it. Riots had shaken some of the nation's largest cities and threatened countless others. Assassins had killed Martin Luther King, Jr., and Robert F. Kennedy. Many Vietnam veterans now protested the war, massive numbers of students mobilized around the country, a Pentagon official revealed a secret war against Cambodia, and large numbers of well-established lawyers marched on the nation's capital in opposition to the war.[77]

Consensus builders on the Supreme Court had to find grounds for compromise between those who wanted Ali's conviction—with its explosive consequences—to stand and those who wanted conscientious objector status for him, with its revolutionary potential. The Justice Department gave the High Court a way out. In conceding that two of its findings were in error, the Justice Department could only conclude that Ali was not in opposition to all wars. Since the Draft Appeal Board had never cited the specific basis for rejection of his claim, Justice Potter Stewart argued that in theory the denial could have been based on the other grounds, which the Justice Department no longer considered valid.[78] The Court found appropriate precedent in *Sicurella v. United States,* in which the Court had been "asked to hold that an error in an advice letter prepared by the Department of Justice did not require reversal of a criminal conviction because there was a ground on which the Appeal

Board might properly have denied a conscientious objector classification." The Court ruled that the department's error made the entire proceedings faulty, thereby having the possible effect of undermining the integrity of the Selective Service System, which "demands . . . that the Government not recommend illegal grounds." The long-established rule of law embodied in *Sicurella* and other settled precedents required that the conviction be overturned.[79]

On June 28, 1971, the Court announced its decision. Although "hardly a ringing declaration of religious freedom," according to Thomas Hauser, one might argue that Ali's supporters and other opponents of the war did not care. What mattered was that the decision set Ali free on the terms he had chosen.[80] It was a victory for all who opposed the war and who believed that legitimate conscientious objection need not demand "religious" conviction as much as a moral one. No boxing victory that Ali ever won could surpass his victory in the U.S. Supreme Court. Had he never won another fight in the ring his status as a legend was secure, his identification with the rebellious youth never greater. Muhammad Ali was the ultimate symbol of the sixties.

His place in history notwithstanding, Ali, the *non pareil,* was not satisfied. He wanted his title back and in heroic fashion would regain it, even after a defeat at the hands of Ken Norton seemed likely to end his career. On the way, Ali benefited from a change in the American social and political climate. Many, now tired of the war and aware of its suspect purpose and conduct, viewed him as a courageous man who suffered for adherence to principles.[81] Thus when he met George Foreman for the undisputed heavyweight championship on October 30, 1974, the underdog Ali had become the sentimental favorite. In typical Ali fashion, he outwitted his opponent with a "rope-a-dope" tactic and scored a shocking eighth-round knockout over the much larger and younger Foreman.[82]

With that win, dissidents lost exclusive rights to their living martyr. His fistic and popular resurrection led to his acceptance, appropriation, and sometimes cooptation as an American hero, symbolized by the extension of an invitation by President Gerald Ford to Ali for a White House visit, which the champ made on December 10, 1974.[83] With delusions of being the "black Kissinger," Ali soon found himself doing some unpopular bidding, among Third World nations, for Jimmy Carter's Olympic boycott against the Soviet Union and, in a move less popular with liberals, campaigning for Ronald Reagan. Yet, these acts do not diminish Ali's stature or devalue his contribution, for they came after a period of enormous sacrifice and suffering, such as no athlete before him or after has ever endured. Through a unique combination of athletic talent, charisma, wit, and courage that placed him in the vortex of an incredibly turbulent and dynamic historic period, he truly earned the self-proclaimed title of "The Greatest."

Postscript

After the conference at which I presented a version of this essay, I began to reassess what I had said. Muhammad Ali's attendance at the conference perhaps influenced my tone and treatment, but my insensitivity to gender questions also played a part. Reflection and subsequent events convinced me to express my new feelings and understanding.

Of all his human flaws, none troubles me more than Ali's sexism. Its most overt manifestations came in the seventies, after the period I am considering here. Nonetheless, his treatment of and attitude toward women in the sixties formed the foundation of his misogyny since then. While his courage and sacrifice on so many fronts compensated for most other defects, his sexism was not a mere blemish but a profound failure. Ali did not transcend the sexism of his times, his profession, or his chosen faith.

Ali's attitudes passed as normal and natural in many quarters at the time. Even though I had serious reservations about his open and outrageous affair with Veronica Porche in the Philippines, I still idolized him. In that respect I am in very good company, for even Sonia Sanchez said without qualification that despite a dislike for boxers and boxing she loves Muhammad Ali because he transcended his sport and became a cultural resource.[84] Yet Ali's sexist behavior cannot be ignored or excused, even if Sanchez and others would describe him as a "gentle man," and even if Ali's behavior was relatively mild compared to that of Eldridge Cleaver, Huey Newton, and Stokely Carmichael, among others in the public eye.

As a symbol and role model, Ali influenced millions, but this influence could have a negative impact. His open disrespect for an apparently loving and loyal wife, Belinda, the mother of his children, caused untold pain to her and, by extension, to countless thousands of black women. Yet, even Belinda, now his ex-wife, chooses to lay the blame at the feet of others, convinced that the sexual culture of the Nation of Islam changed an innocent Ali into the insatiable womanizer he became during their marriage.[85] There is no doubt that some if not many within the religious organization oppressed the female members and exploited other women. Moreover, masculinist assumptions dominated the thinking of Malcolm X and consequently weakened his vision of black nationalism, for, among other things, he did not speak to the oppression of women.[86]

Boxing culture—intensely masculinist—has to accept considerable responsibility for Ali's behavior. Yet, in the end the man must be held accountable for his actions and responsible for correcting them. Nothing has changed my view on this issue more than the black, especially male, reaction to Mike Tyson's rape of Desiree Washington. The "man and woman in the street" response—to support Tyson and view the rape charges with skepticism and/or derision—was predictable, albeit lamentable; the ministerial reaction, however, was shocking and deplorable, from the rallying of more than fifty preachers on Tyson's behalf to the disgusting remarks Louis Farrakhan made at the Black Expo in Indianapolis a year after the tragedy.[87] At least one minister invited Tyson into the pulpit and made *him* appear to be the victim, a fact made even more reprehensible when we consider that many churches ban women from the pulpit because they are said to desecrate it. These reactions and others like them show the institutionalization of a perverse, deeply rooted mysogyny. Scholars and others can no longer ignore or devalue this issue on the grounds that to confront it will split the black community apart. The destructive consequences of sexism for African Americans are clear; its perpetrators must be exposed, held accountable, and shown that it is unacceptable. To overlook this problem in an Ali helps to create a climate for a Tyson, and ignoring the sexism of celebrities legitimates it in the larger culture. Any history of American society, the sixties, civil rights—or any other subject—that refuses to address this critical issue is fundamentally flawed.[88]

Notes

Completion of this essay was made possible in part by a Jesse Ball duPont Fellowship through the Virginia Foundation of Independent Colleges, awarded to the author as a Jesse Ball duPont Distinguished Black Scholar in residence at Hollins College, spring 1993.

1. See Jeffrey T. Sammons, *Beyond the Ring: The Role of Boxing in American Society* (Urbana: University of Illinois Press, 1988), 193–233.

2. Bret Eynon, "Community in Motion: The Free Speech Movement, Civil Rights, and the Roots of the New Left," *Oral History Review* (Spring 1989): 42–45.

3. Howard Zinn, *Postwar America: 1945–1971* (New York: Bobbs-Merrill, 1973), 210–12.

4. Ibid.; Eynon, "Community," 60–64.

5. Henry Hampton and Steve Fayer, with Sarah Flynn, *Voices of Freedom: An Oral History of the Civil Rights Movement from the 1950s through the 1980s* (New York: Bantam, 1990), 437–38; Harvard Sitkoff, *The Struggle for Black Equality: 1954–1980* (New York: Hill and Wang, 1981), 217; *Facts on File 1992,* 216, 299, 349, and 580.

6. Zinn, *Postwar America,* 210–16. A lack of concern for sexism revealed a blind spot that plagued the male-dominated movements of blacks and the New Left. Women coming out of the civil rights and other reform movements had to force their own issues onto the national agenda.

7. Ishmael Reed, "The Fourth Ali," in *God Made Alaska for the Indians* (New York: Garland, 1982), 61–62. Reed did not include women in his icons of the era. I have included the women to reflect the historic reality.

8. Budd Schulberg, "Chinese Boxes of Muhammad Ali," *Saturday Review,* February 26, 1972, 23–24.

9. Many blacks resented Elvis for having gained fame and fortune at the expense of black entertainers; his music and performance style "borrowed" heavily from African Americans. Despite his use of black backup singers and even the recording of a song about children in the ghetto, Elvis was judged and defined by many blacks for an alleged statement circulating in school yards that "all they could do for him was shine his shoes." No doubt, his poor southern roots contributed to the perception and alienation.

10. *New York Magazine,* March 30, 1992, 33

11. Albert Goldman, *Elvis* (New York: McGraw-Hill, 1981), 203; "Elvis: The Great Performances," CBS-TV, April 24, 1992.

12. Gary Smith, "A Celebration of Muhammad Ali: No Other Athlete Has So Commanded our Attention," *Sports Illustrated,* Nov. 15, 1989, 217. After I presented my paper, Ali produced from his briefcase a photo of Elvis and himself together, taken in the mid- to late-sixties.

13. Reed, "Fourth Ali," 39, 62.

14. Ibid.

15. Ibid., 63.

16. Keith Hopkins, "Murderous Games," *History Today,* June 1983, 21–22.

17. Gerald Early, "The White Intellectual, The Black Intellectual, Prize-fighting and the Racial Symbols of American Culture," paper presented at the American Studies Association, Miami, Fla., October 1990.

18. Lerone Bennett, Jr., "When the Man and the Hour Are Met," in *Martin Luther King, Jr.: A Profile,* ed. C. Eric Lincoln (New York: Hill and Wang, 1970), 12–13.

19. Jo Ann Gibson Robinson, *The Montgomery Bus Boycott and the Women Who Started It* (Knoxville: University of Tennessee Press, 1987), 43–45; Paula Giddings, *When and Where I Enter: The Impact of Black Women on Race and Sex in America* (New York: William Morrow, 1984), 261–65.

20. Jack Scott, *The Athletic Revolution* (New York: Free Press, 1971), 80–81.

21. LeRoi Jones, *Home: Social Essays* (New York: William Morrow, 1966), 156.

22. Schulberg, "Chinese Boxes," 23–24.

23. Douglass seems to have been the first to articulate clearly the view that sport was employed by slaveholders as an oppressive instrument and a diversionary device to occupy the minds and energies of slaves, thus preventing them from pursuing more useful activities and fully appreciating their plight. Even more, Douglass believed that the "sports and merriments" sanctioned by the slavemasters were among the most effective ways of "keeping down the spirit of insurrection." Although one might disagree with Douglass's conclusions that the power of sport flowed in one direction, he deserves praise for recognizing that sports were far more than games people play. Douglass's message of sobriety and industry seemed to resonate in the turn-of-the-century black community, despite the fact that it might have been a product of alienation from black culture. Booker T. Washington's teachings echoed Douglass's, for worship, education, and work left little time for sport or leisure in Washington's Calvinistic worldview. Nonetheless Washington did express regret in *Up from Slavery* that he did not give time to sport. It should come as little surprise, then, that Tuskegeeans would use tennis and golf as examples of their fitness for polite society. Washington's chief rival for the attention and allegiance of African Americans, W. E. B. Du Bois, saw the need to engage more directly and at length the problems associated with amusements among blacks. Writing on the subject in 1897, Du Bois noted blacks' tendency to "depreciate and belittle and sneer at means of recreation, to consider amusement (including sport) as the peculiar property of the devil, and to look upon even its legitimate pursuit as time wasted and energy misspent." Du Bois urged moderate participation but also analysis, for "proper amusement must always be a matter of careful reasoning and ceaseless investi-

gation, of nice adjustment between repression and excess." See W. E. B. Du Bois, "The Problem of Amusement," *Southern Workman* 27 (September, 1897), reprinted in *W. E. B. Du Bois on Sociology and the Black Community,* ed. Dan S. Green and Edwin D. Driver (Chicago: University of Chicago Press, 1978), 226–37.

24. Francis Broderick and August Meier, eds., *Negro Protest Thought in the Twentieth Century* (New York: Bobbs-Merrill, 1965), xiv–xv. Du Bois did seem to have some influence on two NAACP colleagues in this regard, for James Weldon Johnson's *Black Manhattan* places black athletes in the Harlem Renaissance and Walter White zealously protected the image of Joe Louis and valued his symbolic and real power in the fight against racism.

25. Schulberg, "Chinese Boxes," 23.

26. Jones, *Home,* 160.

27. Maurice Berube, "Defeat of the Great Black Hope," *Commonweal,* March 26, 1971, 54.

28. Jones, *Home,* 156.

29. Ibid., 159.

30. Schulberg, "Chinese Boxes," 23.

31. Jones, *Home,* 159–60. It is important to remember that Ali had joined the Nation of Islam in 1961. He did not meet Malcolm until 1962 in the Detroit Mosque. Before that time he had been sneaking into services and keeping his secret from the press. Malcolm appealed to Ali because of his frankness in publicly revealing the evils perpetrated by whites on blacks. See Hampton et al., *Voices of Freedom,* 324–25.

32. Schulberg, "Chinese Boxes," 23.

33. Judith Stein, *The World of Marcus Garvey: Race and Class in Modern Society* (Baton Rouge: Louisiana State University Press, 1986), 155–58. Malcolm X repeatedly charged that he had been ordered by Elijah Muhammad to negotiate a "non-aggression" pact with the KKK. The deal required the NOI to continue supporting separation in return for peaceful coexistence. According to Peter Goldman, Malcolm never provided hard evidence to support his allegations. See Peter Goldman, *The Death and Life of Malcolm X,* 2d ed. (Urbana: University of Illinois Press, 1979), 253.

34. Michael Eric Dyson, "Athletes and Warriors," paper delivered at symposium on Muhammad Ali and American Culture, Miami University, April 11, 1992. Sampling is a complex technique used by rap artists in which they add, overlay, and otherwise manipulate lyrics, sounds, and other elements from other sources when making their own recordings. Culture scholar Tricia Rose sees it as part of a transformation from an oral tradition in that it is a product of postliterate expression.

35. Robin D. G. Kelley, "The Riddle of the Zoot: Malcolm Little and

Black Cultural Politics during World War II," in *Malcolm X: In Our Own Image,* ed. Joe Wood (New York: St. Martin's, 1992), 160. Kelley maintains that when Malcolm donned a zoot suit his "body became a dual signifier of opposition—a rejection of both black petit-bourgeois respectability and American patriotism." In joining the Muslims, however, Malcolm found kindred spirits on the antipatriotic front, to a degree. But I am convinced that his problems with the Muslims had causal basis in the intensely bourgeois outlook of Elijah Muhammad, who created and directed a "state controlled" Washingtonian empire built on the blindly loyal efforts of folks sold on salvation, pride, and a sense of their own superiority. In that way the Nation of Islam was supremely elitist and intolerant. It made a few people very rich.

36. A. Goldman, *Elvis,* 203. Goldman believes that Ed Sullivan made a business decision and not a moral one in censoring Elvis, for he sensed that not showing "the King" from the waist down would make people think that more was going on than there was. Thus, Elvis would titillate a repressed audience, while assaulting the "uptight" fifties morality.

37. Larry Neal, "Uncle Rufus Raps on the Squared Circle," *Partisan Review,* Spring/Summer 1972, 48–51.

38. Ishmael Reed, "The Greatest: My Own Story," review in *Shrovetide in Old New Orleans* (New York: Doubleday, 1978), 122.

39. Ali's light footwork distinguished him from other heavyweights. His mother recalled that, unlike other boys, he walked on his toes as a child. See Thomas Hauser, *Muhammad Ali: His Life and Times* (New York: Simon and Schuster, 1991), 15.

40. Neal, "Uncle Rufus," 51. Neal's account of the first Ali-Frazier fight is absolutely brilliant on subjects ranging from boxing's internal dynamics to the variations in black culture. The assessment of what the "conversion" to the Nation of Islam required in regard to distance from certain culinary, religious, and social traditions is insightful. Nonetheless the analysis is seriously flawed in its discussion of women. There, it not only glosses over Ali's failings but also shifts blame from him to his opponents by associating Joe Frazier with "less respectable" types. Thus, Neal has revealed his own class bias by glorifying Ali and his ways while condemning the style of living represented by Joe Frazier. The relevant passage reads: "Boys like Frazier envision purple suits, full length Russian sable, beige El Dorados, the perfumed cluster of female flesh and triumphant kisses from the Sepia Queen. Ali . . . dreams of kissing the black stone of Mecca. No loose perfumed ladies there. The Muslim women wear long dresses; they pursue long periods of silence as they sidestep sin, murmuring polite Koranic knowledge" (50–51).

41. Sammons, *Beyond the Ring,* 205.

42. Lewis H. Carlson and John J. Fogarty, *Tales of Gold: An Oral History of the Summer Olympic Games Told by America's Gold Medal Winners* (Chicago: Contemporary Books, 1987), 383; William J. Baker, *Jesse Owens: An American Life* (New York: Free Press, 1986), 211–13; Charles Korr, "When Protest Made a Clean Sweep," *New York Times,* June 28, 1992, S 11.

43. Sammons, *Beyond the Ring,* 205. Arthur Ashe said about Ali's impact: "I can tell you that Ali was very definitely, sometimes unspokenly, admired by a lot of the leaders of the civil rights movement, who were sometimes even a little bit jealous of the following he had and the efficacy of what he did. There were a lot of people in the movement who wished that they held that sort of sway over African-Americans, but did not." As for Ali's influence on athletes, Ashe maintained: "Harry Edwards wouldn't have gotten a fraction of the support he got in 1968 to boycott the Mexico Olympics. Tommie Smith and John Carlos wouldn't have raised their fists. He was largely responsible for it becoming an expected part of a black athlete's responsibility to get involved." See Hauser, *Muhammad Ali,* 204–5.

44. Reed, review in *Shrovetide,* 123–24.

45. Ibid., 124.

46. Gerald Early, "Hot Spicks versus Cool Spades: Three Notes toward a Cultural Definition of Prizefighting," *Hudson Review* 34, no. 1 (Spring 1981): 44.

47. Neal, "Uncle Rufus," 50.

48. Lawrence Levine, *Black Culture, Black Consciousness: Afro-American Folk Thought from Slavery to Freedom* (New York: Oxford University Press, 1977), 102–24.

49. Reed, "Fourth Ali," 44.

50. This was a famous expression of the sixties among blacks, signifying that blackness demanded a radical race consciousness and activist spirit. It complemented the more overtly revolutionary adage, "If you're not part of the solution, you're a part of the problem."

51. Sammons, *Beyond the Ring,* 197–98.

52. Ibid.

53. Ibid.

54. Ibid.

55. Ibid.

56. Ulysses Lee, *United States Army in World War II, Special Studies: The Employment of Negro Troops* (Washington, D.C.: Office of the Chief of Military History, U.S. Army, 1965), 327.

57. *Revolutionary Worker,* Nov. 30, 1984, 8.

58. Many people, including the author, have assumed that Ali authored the famous line, "No Vietcong ever called me Nigger." Yet, Tho-

mas Hauser maintains that Ali denies ever making the statement but that it has found its way into the Ali legend because it fits his style and reflects what people want to believe about him. Even the writer Ishmael Reed contributes to the myth when he contextualizes Ali's opposition to the Vietnam War in contrast to Joe Louis's stance on World War II. Reed hypothesizes: "Can you imagine the uproar which would have happened if Louis came up with 'No Nazi Ever Called Me Nigger'?" Reed, "Fourth Ali," 44. For the full Lipsyte version of events, see Hauser, *Muhammad Ali,* 144–45, 187.

59. *New York Journal American,* February 22, 1966, cited in Hauser, *Muhammad Ali,* 145–46, 186–87.

60. Hauser, *Muhammad Ali,* 145–46.

61. *Clay, aka Ali v. United States,* 403 U.S., 698 October Term 1970, 707; Hauser, *Muhammad Ali,* 187.

62. Hampton et al., *Voices of Freedom,* 282. One individual who preceded Ali as an antiwar activist was Julian Bond. Nonetheless, Bond would become much better known for having his name placed in nomination for Democratic vice president, although he was ineligible because of age. A SNCC activist, Bond had just been elected to the Georgia House of Representatives. He spoke out against the war in 1966 and the House voted not to seat him because his statements allegedly violated the Selective Service Act and "tend[ed] to bring discredit to the House." The Supreme Court restored Bond to his seat, recognizing his right to free expression under the First Amendment. See Howard Zinn, *A People's History of the United States* (New York: Harper and Row, 1980), 475.

63. Hampton et al., *Voices of Freedom,* 344.

64. Ibid., 470.

65. *Clay v. United States,* 709–10.

66. Hauser, *Muhammad Ali,* 177–88.

67. Ibid., 168–69; Sammons, *Beyond the Ring,* 203.

68. Hauser, *Muhammad Ali,* 177, from Milton Gross, *New York Post,* June 22, 1967.

69. Hauser, *Muhammad Ali,* 239; *Clay v. United States,* 699–701.

70. *Clay v. United States,* 699–701.

71. Ole R. Holsti, "International Relations Models," 75, and J. Garry Clifford, "Bureaucratic Politics," 141–43, in *Explaining the History of American Foreign Relations,* ed. Michael Hogan and Thomas G. Patterson (New York: Cambridge University Press, 1991).

72. Clifford, "Bureaucratic Politics," 141–43

73. Hauser, *Muhammad Ali,* 174–81.

74. Bob Woodward and Scott Armstrong, *The Brethren* (New York: Avon Books, 1979), 156–60.

75. Hauser, *Muhammad Ali,* 179–81.

76. Ibid., 189.

77. Sammons, *Beyond the Ring,* 217.

78. Hauser, *Muhammad Ali,* 239.

79. *Clay v. United States,* 704–5.

80. Hauser, *Muhammad Ali,* 239.

81. Ibid., 280–81.

82. Sammons, *Beyond the Ring,* 226.

83. Hauser, *Muhammad Ali,* 281.

84. Hampton et al., *Voices of Freedom,* 328.

85. Hauser, *Muhammad Ali,* 307–20.

86. Patricia Hill Collins, "Learning to Think for Ourselves: Malcolm X's Black Nationalism Reconsidered," in Wood, ed., *Malcolm X,* 74.

87. Barbara Kopple, "Fallen Champ," a television documentary, CBS-TV, February 12, 1993.

88. Even as I come to this rather harsh conclusion, I must admit some discomfort. Heroes and accepted patterns of masculine behavior are not easily condemned by men, no matter what they say. Moreover, Ali, as I hope to have made clear, is not easily accommodated. Nothing demonstrates the problem more than a 1974 photograph of Ali with Belinda, then his wife; Veronica Porche, his lover and next wife; and Lonnie Williams, a longtime friend and his present wife. See Howard Bingham, *Muhammad Ali: A Thirty-Year Journey* (New York: Simon and Schuster, 1993), 134.

Narrative: Ali
(A Poem in Twelve Rounds)

Elizabeth Alexander

1.
My head so big
they had to pry
me out. I'm sorry
Bird (is what I call
my mother). Cassius
Marcellus Clay,
Muhammad Ali;
you can say
my name in any
language, any
continent: Ali.

2.
Two photographs
of Emmett Till,
born my year,
on my birthday.
One, he's smiling,
happy, and the other one
is after. His mother
did the bold thing,
kept the casket open,
made the thousands look upon
his bulging eyes,
his twisted neck,

her lynched black boy.
I couldn't sleep
for thinking,
Emmett Till.

One day I went
down to the train tracks,
found some iron
shoe-shine rests
and planted them
between the ties
and waited
for a train to come
and watched the train
derail, and ran,
and after that
I slept at night.

3.
I need to train
around people,
hear them talk,
talk back. I need
to hear the traffic,
see people in
the barbershop,
people getting
shoeshines, talking,
hear them talk,
talk back.

4.
Bottom line: Olympic gold
can't buy a black man
a Louisville hamburger
in nineteen-sixty.

Wasn't even real gold.
I watched the river
drag the ribbon down,
red, white, and blue.

5.
Laying on the bed,
praying for a wife,
in walk Sonji Roi.

Pretty little shape.
Do you like
chop suey?

Can I wash your hair
underneath
that wig?

Lay on the bed,
Girl. Lie
with me.

Shake to the east,
to the north,
south, west—

but remember,
remember, I need
a Muslim wife. So

Quit using lipstick.
Quit your boogaloo.
Cover up your knees

like a Muslim
wife, religion,
religion, a Muslim

wife. Eleven
months with Sonji,
first woman I loved.

6.

There's not
too many days
that pass that I
don't think
of how it started,
but I know
no Great White Hope
can beat
a true black champ.
Jerry Quarry
could have been
a movie star,
a millionaire,
a Senator,
a President—
he only had
to do one thing,
is whip me,
but he can't.

7. **Dressing Room Visitor**

He opened
up his shirt:
"KKK" cut
in his chest.
He dropped
his trousers:
latticed scars
where testicles
should be. His face
bewildered, frozen,
in the Alabama woods
that night in 1966

when they left him
for dead, his testicles
in a Dixie cup.
You a warning,
they told him,
to smart-mouth,
sassy-acting niggers,
meaning niggers
still alive,
meaning any nigger,
meaning niggers
like me.

8. Training

Unsweetened grapefruit juice
will melt my stomach down.
Don't drive if you can walk,
don't walk if you can run.
I add a mile each day
and run in eight-pound boots.

My knuckles sometimes burst
the glove. I let dead skin
build up, and then I peel it,
let it scar, so I don't bleed
as much. My bones
absorb the shock.

I train in three-minute
spurts, like rounds: three
rounds big bag, three speed
bag, three jump rope, one
minute breaks,
no more, no less.

Am I too old? Eat only
kosher meat. Eat cabbage,
carrots, beets, and watch

the weight come down:
two-thirty, two-twenty,
two-ten, two-oh-nine.

9.

Will I go
like Kid Paret,
a fractured
skull, a ten-day
sleep, dreaming
alligators, pork-
chops, saxophones,
slow grinds, funk,
fishbowls, lightbulbs,
bats, typewriters,
tuning forks, funk,
clocks, red rubber
ball, what you see
in that lifetime
knockout minute
on the cusp?
You could be
let go,
you could be
snatched back.

10. **Rumble in the Jungle**

Ali boma ye,
Ali boma ye,
means kill him, Ali,
which is different
from a whupping
which is what I give,
but I lead them chanting
anyway, *Ali*
boma ye, because
here in Africa

black people fly
planes and run countries.

I'm still making up
for the foolishness
I said when I was
Clay from Louisville,
where I learned Africans
lived naked in straw
huts eating tiger meat,
grunting and grinning,
swinging from vines,
pounding their chests—

I pound my chest but of my own accord.

11.
I said to Joe Frazier,
first thing, get a good house
in case you get crippled
so you and your family
can sleep somewhere. Always
keep one good Cadillac.
And watch how you dress
with that cowboy hat,
pink suits, white shoes—
that's how pimps dress,
or kids, and you a champ,
or wish you were, 'cause
I can whip you in the ring
or whip you in the street.
Now back to clothes,
wear dark clothes, suits,
black suits, like you the best
at what you do, like you
President of the World.
Dress like that.

Put them yellow pants away.
We dinosaurs gotta
look good, gotta sound
good, gotta be good,
the greatest, that's what
I told Joe Frazier,
and he said to me,
we both bad niggers.
We don't do no crawlin'.

12.

They called me "the fistic pariah."

They said I didn't love my country,
called me a race-hater, called me out
of my name, waited for me
to come out on a stretcher, shot at me,
hexed me, cursed me, wished me
all manner of ill-will,
told me I was finished.

Here I am,
like the song says,
come and take me,

"The People's Champ,"

myself,
Muhammad.

CONTRIBUTORS

ELIZABETH ALEXANDER teaches in the English department at the University of Chicago. She is author of *The Venus Hottentot* and has completed a new poetry manuscript, "Body of Life." Her essays on black literature and popular culture have appeared in *The Village Voice, Signs,* and *American Literary History,* and her book *On Black Masculinity* is forthcoming from Oxford University Press. She is currently working on a play, "Diva Studies."

GERALD EARLY, Professor of English at Washington University in St. Louis, is the author of *Tuxedo Junction: Essays on American Culture; The Culture of Bruising: Essays on Prizefighting, Literature, and Modern American Culture;* and *Daughters: On Family and Fatherhood.* He is currently working on a book about Fisk University.

ELLIOTT J. GORN is Professor of History and American Studies at Miami University (Ohio). He is the author of *The Manly Art: Bare-Knuckle Prize Fighting in America;* coauthor, with Warren Goldstein, of *A Brief History of American Sports;* and coeditor of *The Encyclopedia of American Social History.* His essays have appeared in *The American Historical Review,* the *Journal of American History,* and *American Quarterly.* Gorn is currently writing a biography of Mary Harris "Mother" Jones.

OTHELLO HARRIS is Associate Professor of Physical Education, Health and Sport Studies and Faculty Affiliate in Black World Studies at Miami University. His research interests include stratification, race relations, and sport participation. His work has been published in journals such as *The Black Scholar, Sociology of Sport Journal,* and *The Journal of Social and Behavioral Sciences.* In addition, he has authored chapters in numerous books.

THOMAS R. HIETALA, Associate Professor of History at Grinnell College, earned his advanced degrees at Yale University. His first book, *Manifest Design* (1985), reexamined the origins of American expansion in the 1840s. He is now completing a decade-long project on twentieth-century race relations based on the lives and times of black heavyweight champions Jack Johnson, Joe Louis, and Muhammad Ali.

ROBERT LIPSYTE is sports and city columnist for the *New York Times.* He is the author of sixteen books, including *Sportsworld: An American Dreamland* and, with Peter Levine, *Idols of the Game.*

MICHAEL ORIARD is a professor of English at Oregon State University. His books on the relations of sport to American culture include *Dreaming of Heroes: American Sports Fiction, 1868–1980; The End of Autumn: Reflections on My Life in Football; Sporting with the Gods: The Rhetoric of Play and Game in American Culture;* and *Reading Football: How the Popular Press Created an American Spectacle.*

RANDY ROBERTS is Professor of History at Purdue University. He is the author of *Jack Dempsey: The Manassa Mauler* and *Papa Jack: Jack Johnson and the Era of White Hopes* and the coauthor, with James Olson, of *Winning Is the Only Thing: Sports in America since 1945.* Roberts is also the author of numerous textbooks and edited collections. His most recent books are *Heavy Justice: The State of Indiana v. Michael G. Tyson,* cowritten with J. Gregory Garrison, and *John Wayne—American.*

JEFFREY T. SAMMONS teaches history at New York University. He has published extensively in sport history and African American history, including *Beyond the Ring: The Role of Boxing in American Society.* He is currently at work on a social and cultural history of American golf.

DAVID K. WIGGINS is Professor of Physical Education at George Mason University. He is the coeditor of the *Journal of Sport History;* has published numerous articles dealing with the history of black athletes in American sport; and has edited *Sport in America: From Wicked Amusement to National Obsession* and coedited, with George Eisen, *Ethnicity and Sport in North American History and Culture.*

INDEX

Books in the Series Sport and Society

Stagg's University: The Rise, Decline, and Fall of Big-Time Football at Chicago   *Robin Lester*

Muhammad Ali, the People's Champ   *Edited by Elliott J. Gorn*

REPRINT EDITIONS

The Nazi Olympics   *Richard D. Mandell*

Sports in the Western World
Second Edition   *William J. Baker*